Introduction to MANAGEMENT ACCOUNTING

Introduction to
MANAGEMENT ACCOUNTING

Dr. Anil Tandon

ANMOL PUBLICATIONS PVT. LTD.
NEW DELHI-110 002 (INDIA)

ANMOL PUBLICATIONS PVT. LTD.

Regd. Office: 4360/4, Ansari Road, Daryaganj,
New Delhi-110002 (India)
Tel.: 23278000, 23261597, 23286875, 23255577
Fax: 91-11-23280289
Email: anmolpub@gmail.com
Visit us at: www.anmolpublications.com

Branch Office: No. 1015, Ist Main Road, BSK IIIrd Stage
IIIrd Phase, IIIrd Block, Bangalore-560 085 (India)
Tel.: 080-41723429 • Fax: 080-26723604
Email: anmolpublicationsbangalore@gmail.com

Introduction to Management Accounting

First Edition, 2010

ISBN 978-81-261-4480-8

PRINTED IN INDIA

Printed at Mehra Offset Press, Delhi.

Contents

Preface

Introduction to Management Accounting is designed to supply information to internal decision makers of a given organization, to facilitate their decision making, to motivate their actions and behavior in a desirable direction, and to promote the efficiency of the organization. It is accounting based and individual, organization, strategy, problem, and decision-centered. An understanding of each of these foundations may allow the management accountant to design a management accounting system more responsive to the diverse needs and demands emanating from within and without the organization. A recurrent theme of each of these chapters is that a failure to grasp any of these conceptual foundations of management accounting may result in deficiencies in the management accounting systems and inadequacies in the provision of the diverse services required by both the small and the complex organizations of today.

This textbook should be of interest to a variety of reader groups, including researchers in the management accounting area and accounting practitioners interested in the careful design of a management accounting system. The book can also be useful as additional material for a typical graduate or postgraduate course in management accounting. The student in management accounting should be aware not only of the new multidimensional scope of the field but also of the conceptual foundations that justify this extended scope.

Author

Chapter 1

Introduction

MANAGERIAL ACCOUNTING

The set of techniques and thought to which devoted is usually referred to as *managerial accounting*. Managerial accounting is that branch of accounting thought and practice concerned with providing information that is useful to decision makers within the enterprise in making decisions related to the deployment of resources and exploitation of enterprise opportunities. It should be emphasized that the boundaries of managerial accounting are not rigid. Managerial accounting has in common with financial accounting a focus on the enterprise and its activities.

It differs in the sense that it serves a class of decision makers whose decision interests are generally different from those of the decision makers served by financial accounting. In addition, many of the decision models that have evolved for management use and for which accountants supply the necessary information inputs have been developed within the disciplines of managerial economics and managerial finance. These decision models are often described as part of managerial accounting because it is necessary to understand management decision models in order to supply decision-relevant information. It is becoming more and more widely recognized that business organizations operate through the coordinated efforts of human beings. Hence, success of most management decisions hinges on motivating the individuals involved to conduct their activities in a manner most consistent with the objective of the decision.

The study of the interactions of individuals within organizations has for some time been important to the design of management accounting systems. Since the tools for such study have been developed in the behavioural sciences, the accounting discipline has increasingly embraced the behavioural sciences as a source for improved research and practice.

Role of Accountant in Business

In a functional sense, the accountant's role in supplying information for internal decision makers is much like the accountant's role in providing information to external parties. He does not engage in the decision choice itself. Instead, he participates in the earlier stages of the decision-making process, usually by providing information about alternatives for the consideration of decision makers.

To the extent possible, the accountant maintains a detached attitude so as to avoid biasing the information provided in favour of any particular alternative. Otherwise he preempts the decision maker's role to some extent. But this does not mean that the accountant cannot perform part of the evaluation stage of the decision process in addition to supplying basic information or alternatives.

When he participates in the internal decision-making process, the accountant enjoys a closer relationship with the decision maker than is the case in financial accounting. Hence, the decision maker and the accountant can engage in a two-way "give-and-take" process until the accountant has a better understanding of the decision maker's decision model and information wants. As a result, the information provided in managerial accounting is often in fairly adequate final form for making choices between alternatives. This is less feasible in financial accounting.

MANAGEMENT DECISIONS

Management Objectives and Constraints

The value of this approach is that, in general, different classes of management decisions can be identified with specific types of objectives and constraints. The key to differences in types of objectives and constraints characterizing particular decision situations is, in turn, often explainable in relation to the time span of enterprise activities that will be influenced by the decision choice.

One usually finds it helpful to separate management activities and decisions into long-run and short-run categories. Long-run decisions: Long-run decisions are defined as those decisions whose outcomes commit the enterprise or directly influence its activities for many future periods. The long run is thought of as a span of time sufficiently long that a significant project or programme of the enterprise can be planned, implemented, and run its course. Short-run Short-run decisions are defined as decisions whose outcomes commit the enterprise or directly influence its actions for perhaps only one year at most. The latitude available in selecting alternatives in the short run is restricted considerably by the commitments made by the enterprise in past long-run decisions.

Long-run Objectives

Usually, the enterprise starts with an endowment of cash, its money capital, constituting a claim against resources, products, and services available in the economy. The enterprise expends a portion of that cash to acquire resources and uses those resources in the production of products or services. The products or services, in turn, are sold to other economic units that at some point remit cash to the enterprise in exchange. The new cash flows renew the enterprise's ability to acquire the same or different resources for employment in further production of products and services.

In this process there is usually a division of the enabling economic function, the enterprise function. Owners and creditors supply the necessary capital. Management identifies the most promising opportunities to provide products and services; it acquires, organizes, and directs the necessary resources to exploit identified opportunities. The contribution of suppliers of capital and the contribution of management complement each other. Each group identified presumably provides a unique opportunity for the other through the organizational unit, the business enterprise. Each group will presumably wish to withdraw its resources from the relationship if other opportunities appear more attractive. The implication of this possibility for management is significant.

Profit Maximization.

If the enterprise consistently fails to produce products and services whose values exceed the costs of resources used, it will actually dissipate its money capital and jeopardize its ability to survive.

In either case, the opportunity for management to use its talents to the fullest is dimished by the faltering supply of money capital at the disposal of the enterprise. The best insurance against such a situation is for management to pursue a long-run objective of maximizing the value of the excess of the cash flows received for products and services provided to customers over the cash expended for resources used. Only in this way can management ensure that sufficient money capital will be available to maximize its own opportunities to employ its talents. This basic goal of management is often referred to as the profit maximization goal.

Goals.

Long-run profit maximization is the preeminent goal of business enterprises in a market economy. But note the emphasis on "long-run." The statement would be shortsighted without that emphasis and would be contrary to the current stated policies of most significant business organizations.

Those policies often include such goals as:

- Betterment of employee morale,
- Employee education and training,
- Protection of the environment,
- Improved product quality,
- Community service, or
- Contribution to basic research in a particular field.

In the short run, one would expect such goals to conflict frequently with the pursuit of maximum profits. But clearly all are related, or rather *necessary,* to achieve maximum profits in the long run. So, if a very broad view of long-run profitability is taken, then the single goal of long-run profit maximization generally embraces all so-called *other* goals.

Constraints

A distinguishing feature of long-run decisions is that they are relatively free from internally imposed constraints. Nevertheless, because long-run decisions (commitments) must be made as of a point in time, certain externally imposed constraints apply-at least in part.

Among the largely externally imposed constraints on long-run decisions are the laws and customs of society, the state of technology, the size of the population and labour force, worldwide and local supplies of natural resources, and so forth, which exist at the time of decision.

Of course, some of these constraints can be influenced to some degree by an individual enterprise; for example, the passage of a new law may be the result of lobbying efforts on the part of business, or changes in the customs of society may be influenced by advertising campaigns. But in general, as of the time of any given long-run decision, external constraints impose some limitation on the enterprise.

Although externally imposed constraints affect each enterprise to varying degrees, there are two specific constraints on long-run decisions that are usually unique to each individual enterprise. First, at a given point in time, each enterprise faces a limited number of long-run opportunities that it can effectively exploit because of its location, its prior activities, and the composition of its management. Second, each enterprise faces a limited supply of money capital with which to embark on alternative long-run courses of action.

Although, as with the constraints mentioned above, management can alter these two restrictions in the long run, the alterations themselves may require the immediate commitment of scarce money capital and take some time to effect. Hence, at any given decision point, long-run alternatives are restricted by these two limitations.

Management Decisions and Accounting Information

The first requisite to success is active seeking of opportunities, either to provide new and better products or services or to develop new and better means of production.

The former requires involvement, at least at some minimal level, in research into present markets and consumer (or industrial) preferences, plus product development research.

The latter requires at least some involvement with industrial engineering as well as organizational, institutional, and behavioural research.

All of these are essentially information-seeking activities contributed by specialists other than accountants. The contribution of accountants comes into play in another important requisite to long-run success of the enterprise-the selection of the most promising set from among the identified alternatives.

Capital and Budgeting

The essential feature of long-run opportunities (alternatives) is that they usually require considerable initial outlays of the enterprise's limited money capital for implementation. Initial outlays include expenditures for such things as long-lived assets to be employed in the programme, legal fees, and further costs of developmental and organizational research.

Over many future periods, related additional outlays are required to produce benefits in the form of cash inflows or lower total outlays than the programmes they replace. Since long-run programmes generally require outlays of scarce money capital, the process of selecting the best set of alternatives is usually referred to as *capital budgeting*.

Capital budgeting

Capital budgeting is the process of choosing the best set from among the available long-run opportunities requiring significant outlays of money capital.

Role of Accounting in Capital Budgeting

We have already noted that the objective of management in the long run is to maximize the excess of cash receipts for products and services over cash outlays for resources used in production. We have also noted, however, that most long-run programmes involve initial outlays of cash to get started, followed by many periods of additional outflows and inflows.

The attractiveness to management of a long-run programme, project, or product line ultimately hinges on its real economic features, that is, the physical capabilities, quality, and demand for a product; the kinds and quantities of resources required to carry out a programme; and the kind of organization structure and production techniques required for implementation. Such information, as noted earlier, comes from nonaccounting sources such as marketing personnel, industrial engineers, and organization development specialists. The role of the accountant in bringing these relevant economic attributes of an alternative into focus for management *is to translate them into the cash inflows and outflows that they imply for present and future periods.*

Example: The Company has manufactured a well-known line of quality fiberglass skis for the last ten years. The company was one of the first to experiment with fiberglass skis and as a result of early technical gains has become very successful. Of late, however, the company faces a threat to its long-run success. Many competitors have entered the market, and the competition has reduced Shoosh's prospects for continued increases in its sales of skis.

The president of the company has been very unhappy with the prospect of a declining share of the market. In searching for alternatives, she has concluded that whereas many competitors make finished skis, few suppliers can produce high-quality metal edges used in making skis. Shoosh Company, however, has the know-how to do the job. But to make the edges for sale to other ski manufacturers, Shoosh Company will need an immediate factory and equipment expansion that will have a ten-year life, costing $120,000, with no salvage value in the end.

The first step in determining the net present value of the factory expansion is estimation of the future cash inflows and outflows associated with the project. Unfortunately, in practice no one is going to tell the accountant directly what these amounts are going to be, except for the initial outlay of $120,000. Instead he has to work with the sales manager, production engineer, plant manager, and others who will plan and control the new manufacturing operation in order to determine what new cash inflows and outflows to expect from the operation.

First he approaches the sales manager and requests estimates of how many pairs of edges will be sold and at what price in each of the next ten years. The sales manager estimates that $30 would be a competitive price for the edges (per pair). At that price he estimates that on the average 5,000 pairs of edges can be sold each year for the next ten years.

Meanwhile the production engineer has determined the quantities of material, labour, and miscellaneous other resources required for production in addition to the new factory facilities.

Requirement of Resource

Materials: Each pair of edges requires a 10' × 1/8" × 3/16" bar of cold rolled steel alloy.

Manufacturing labour: Two hours of skilled labour will be required in total to complete each pair of edges.

Other costs-annual: Supervisor's salary Cleanup, repairs, and maintenance Insurance, taxes, etc.

With the information based on physical production plans, the accountant turns to the personnel manager and the purchasing agent to determine the cash costs of the production requirements for the edges. He estimates the *annual* net cash inflow from production and sales of the edges. The accountant then presents the company president with decisionready information relevant to the factory expansion. Assuming that the president has confidence in the accountant's ability to gather the necessary information and make the necessarily uncertain projections of cash flows as well or better than anyone else in the organization, she will undertake the plant expansion, since it has a positive net present value of $15,080.

Example: brings into focus two important aspects of all managerial activity. First, it illustrates an important feature of the accountant's role in the business enterprise, alluded to earlier. Notice that the accountant has actually prepared a ready-made decision value for the decision maker, that is, the net present value of the decision alternative. Recall that we noted earlier that there usually is (or should be) a close working relationship between the accountant and an internal decision maker. As a result, the decision maker can communicate to the accountant features of his specific decision model, including such things as the time preference rate that he feels is appropriate for discounting the expected cash flows from a particular project, to which the accountant does not have access in the case of external parties. Hence, at the discretion of the decision maker, the managerial accountant may perform not only the information-gathering step in the decision process but parts of the problem definition and evaluation steps as well. It is important to note, however, that as more of the decision process is assumed by the accountant, the risk increases that the accountant will intentionally or unintentionally introduce his own biases into the decision. The accountant should of course maintain a detached attitude insofar as possible. But the decision maker should nevertheless be aware of this risk in determining the degree to which decision responsibility is delegated to the accountant.

The second important aspect of managerial accounting (also alluded to earlier) is the managerial accountant's responsibility as a translator. Since the management of the enterprise is almost always interested in the effects of the decisions on cash flows, an important part of the managerial accounting function is the translation of the resource flows connected with a product, project, or programme into financial or money flow implications. One of the most general sets of skills or tools employed by managerial accountants to execute their role as translators is *cost behaviour analysis,* a set of techniques described in the following section.

ANALYSIS OF COST BEHAVIOUR

The discovery and application of cost and revenue behaviour patterns are relevant in producing information for all types of management decisions. Hence it is appropriate that we turn next to some discussion of this important topic. The introduction to long-run management decisions and the related accounting contribution provides the context in which to examine the application of cost behaviour patterns.

A Flexible Tool

As noted earlier, an important task in managerial accounting is the association of financial (money) flows with the resource flows that are expected from various decision alternatives. One very general concept employed in performing this task is the *concept of cost* (the "cost principle" in conventional financial accounting is a special application of the concept of cost):

Cost: A cost is a resource sacrifice, usually measured in money terms, *associated* with a particular decision alternative, for example, conduct of an activity, production of a product, acquisition of a resource, or operation of an organization.

Costs measured in money terms are associated with various kinds of management decision alternatives in order to evaluate the alternatives in the context of the long-run goal of the enterprise, that is, profit maximization. The basis of association of costs with particular decision alternatives is usually *cost behaviour patterns* derived through *cost behaviour analysis*.

Cost behaviour pattern: A cost behaviour pattern is a functional relationship between various activities or events that represent a decision alternative and the cost that is expected to be incurred in connection with that alternative.

Cost behaviour analysis: Cost behaviour analysis is the process of discerning and describing forms of cost behaviour patterns.

Basic Types of Cost Behaviour Patterns: Experience in discerning cost behaviour patterns in practice has led accountants to expect certain recurring patterns. The simplest, most frequently encountered, and most easily recognized patterns of cost behaviour are the patterns we refer to as *fixed* and *variable* costs.

Fixed costs: Fixed costs are costs whose amounts do not change regardless of the level of enterprise activity (within certain limits called the relevant range).

Relevant range: The relevant range is that *range of activity* within which the *level of actual activity* is expected to occur in the normal course of events.

Spectrum Sales Company is planning a new sales territory. It is considering opening a new branch sales office. Activities will start with one salesman; additional sales staff will be added when monthly sales exceed $20,000 per salesman. But the territory will not grow beyond a staff of five salesmen, since it is company policy to split off a new territory at that point.

If the new territory is opened, office space sufficient to accommodate a secretary and from one to five salesmen will be rented. The monthly rent for the office will be $500 regardless of how many people use it. Thus, within the relevant range of activity for the new sales territory, the monthly cost of rent is a fixed cost.

The pattern inherent in fixed costs. On the horizontal axis is measured the level of activity in terms of monthly sales dollars (in thousands) for the territory. (The maximum of $100,000 is determined by a maximum of five salesmen at $20,000 each before a new territory is split off.) On the vertical axis is the level of monthly rent cost. The horizontal line at a level of $500 above the horizontal axis shows that within the relevant range of $0 to $100,000 sales, rent cost is invariant (fixed) with respect to activity.

Fixed-Cost Pattern

Variable costs can exhibit a variety of patterns but they all have a common definitional characteristic:

Variable costs: Variable costs are costs whose amounts increase as activity increases and decrease as activity decreases—though not necessarily proportionately.

If Spectrum Sales Company opens its new territory, it intends to compensate its sales staff with salaries plus commissions of 5 per cent of sales dollars. Monthly commission costs therefore vary proportionately with the level of sales dollars. If sales are $20,000 per month, sales commissions will be $1,000 (.05 × $20,000). If sales double to $40,000, sales commissions also double to $2,000 (.05 × $40,000).

Although many kinds of variable costs actually vary proportionately, not all variable costs behave in this way. For example, if an activity doubles but the related variable cost increases less than double, we say it varies with the activity at a decreasing rate. If a cost more than doubles as activity doubles, we say it varies with activity at an increasing rate. The three patterns. Many variations in cost behaviour lie between the simple extremes of strictly variable and strictly fixed costs. Although it is not our intention to be exhaustive, it might interest the reader to see some additional patterns that have been suggested to describe other frequently encountered types of cost behaviour.

Discerning Cost Behaviour Patterns

One of the great challenges of managerial accounting is to discover the behaviour of various costs with respect to activities that are of concern in managerial decisions. Although many cost behaviour patterns are rather obvious, others are not clear or intuitively obvious at all.

Example: In manufacturing its product, Stunning Beauty Company uses one pound of material at $2 per pound for every unit of product produced. Thus material costs vary proportionately with total activity measured in units of product produced. Maintenance costs, on the other hand, do not seem to obey any such strict rule.

Some kinds of maintenance requirements are necessary from time to time regardless of the level of activity, but they do not seem to occur at regular intervals. Other kinds of maintenance requirements occur regularly and increase with activity but not proportionately. All in all, specification of the expected behaviour of maintenance costs with respect to activity is considerably more difficult than specifying the expected behaviour.

In discerning patterns of cost behaviour, particularly nonobvious patterns, accountants typically use one (or all) of the following techniques:

- Construction of cost behaviour schedules from engineering or production specifications of a product or process
- Analysis of past cost data to discern evident patterns
- Experience with cost behaviour of similar products or processes in the past, plus judgment and intuition

Within the limits of time and other resources available for cost analysis, accountants generally prefer more objective and scientific approaches (number 1 and some techniques embraced by number 2) rather than resorting strictly to experience, judgment, or intuition.

Cost Behaviour Patterns

How are cost behaviour patterns used in managerial decision making? First the cost behaviour implications of various activities and events are used to construct an overall cost function for a decision alternative or decision variable. Then the cost function (usually together with a revenue function) is manipulated to generate decision-relevant information about the alternative or variable.

Since managerial decision making often focuses on the production and sales of products and services, accountants are frequently concerned with using cost behaviour patterns to supply information for production-sales decisions. This type of application has the special label of *cost-volume-profit analysis* (sometimes called *break-even analysis*). Cost-volume-profit analysis is so frequently used in practice that it is a most appropriate context for acquainting the reader with the application of cost behaviour patterns.

Constructing Cost and Revenue Functions:

The accountant's role in a long-run capital-budgeting decision (new product line) with Example Shoosh Ski

Company). That capital-budgeting decision involved determination of the net present value of the set of future cash flows associated with production and sale of the proposed product over a ten-year period. Most of the accountant's task involved estimation of the annual costs and benefits (cash outflows and inflows) from production and sales of the product.

Then, since the president of the company had already specified the appropriate time preference rate for the risk involved, the stream of annual net cash inflows was discounted and compared with the initial outlay.

Though highly simplified, the example served to illustrate how the accountant constructed from various physical production, sales, and price data the annual net cash inflow to be expected from the product. But many potential benefits of that construction were ignored at the time. By returning to the basic situation described in Example, we can elaborate the further potential that recognition and use of cost behaviour patterns offer.

Example: Suppose that after the accountant prepared the net present value of the new product line (edges) for Shoosh Ski Company, the president changed her mind about the appropriateness of the 10 per cent discount rate. The president had some misgivings about her original assessment of risk associated with the new product line and asked a number of questions about the annual net cash to be expected for the coming ten years.

Some of her questions were as follows:

- Suppose a presently unknown competitor enters the market at the same time we do, and we end up splitting annual sales right down the middle, that is, 2,500 pairs of edges per year each?
- How low can our annual sales be without cash outflows exceeding cash inflows from sales in any given year?
- By how much can we lower selling price to sustain sales at 5,000 pairs of edges in any given year and still not experience losses (net cash outflows) in that year?

The accountant for Shoosh is chagrined by all these questions. He thought he had done a good job of satisfying the president's original request, but now he feels he has to retrace all of his steps to answer this barrage of questions. How could the accountant have avoided his chagrin? These types of questions are very common. Therefore, it is usually worthwhile to be prepared for them by making certain assumptions and constructing (or specifying) revenue, cost, and profit (net cash flow) functions in advance and stating them in terms (variables) of interest to management. To do this in the case of production-sales-type situations, accountants make certain simplifying assumptions on which they often base uncomplicated but useful revenue, cost, and profit functions.

Typical simplifying assumptions include the following:

- Within the relevant range virtually all costs can be classified into the two simple behaviour categories of *fixed* and *variable.*
- Variable costs vary (approximately) proportionately with activity.
- A short-run analysis (typically no more than one year) is sufficient to encompass all significant consequences of decisions to be made.
- All sales are for cash (or there is no net buildup of accounts receivable during the period), meaning that revenue and cash inflow from sales are approximately equal.
- All products produced are sold (or no net buildup of inventory takes place), so that production activity (in units of product) approximately equals sales activity.
- All units sold, within the relevant range, in any given period will be sold at the same price.

Simplified Cost-Volume-Profit Model:

On the basis of assumptions such as the foregoing, the accountant can formulate simplified revenue, cost, and profit functions. For instance, based on assumption number 6 above, the total revenue (*TR*) for a period will equal the number of units sold (*q*) times the price per unit (*p*).

Similarly, based on assumptions 1 and 2, total cost (*TC*) will equal the sum of a fixed component (*f*) and a proportionate variable component equal to the number of units produced and sold (*q*) times the per-unit variable cost (*v*). Profit or net cash flow represented by p will equal total revenue minus total cost. These simple relationships can be represented symbolically.

Basic Cost-Volume-Profit Relationships,

$TR = pq$

$TC = vq + f$

$\pi = TR - TC$

substituting Equation for *TR* and Equation for *TC* in Equation, we get

$\pi = pq - (vq + f)$

$\pi = pq - vq - f$

Cost-Volume-Profit Analysis. The advantage of the cost-volume-profit model, provided the six assumptions are approximately applicable to the individual situation, the accountant can answer a wide variety of management questions.The value of any one of the model variables in a given situation can be found by solving Equation after determining the values of the other variables for that situation.

Example: Suppose, for instance, that the Shoosh Company accountant had been alert to cost behaviour patterns when he estimated the annual net cash inflow from production and sales of the new product line. He found that the material and labour costs per pair of edges were $4 and $16, respectively. Suppose that he had then checked with the production engineer and found that those per-unit costs would apply for production levels from 2,000 to 6,000 pairs of edges per year. The other production costs, including the $10,000 supervisory salary, $15,000 cleanup and maintenance, and $3,000 insurance, taxes, and so forth, would remain the same as long as actual production activity fell within that range.

Similarly, suppose the sales manager, upon inquiry, had confirmed that all sales in any given year would be made at the same price, that is, no preferential prices would be quoted to any customer.

He had estimated earlier that \$30 would be a competitive price for a pair of edges. If the accountant had thus been alert to the general expected patterns of behaviour of costs and revenues associated with the new product line, he could have readily answered the president's three questions as follows:

- If a competitor enters the market for edges at the same time Shoosh enters and halves Shoosh sales to 2,500 pairs per year, Shoosh will experience an annual net cash outflow of \$3,000, calculated as follows:

  $p = \$30;\ v = \$20;\ q = 2{,}500;\ f = \$28{,}000$

  Solve for,

  π

  $\pi = pq - vq - f$

  $\pi = (\$30 - 2{,}500) - (\$20\ 2{,}500) - \$28{,}000\ \ \pi = \$75{,}000 - \$50{,}000 - \$28{,}000$

  $\pi = \$75{,}000 - \$78{,}000$

  $\pi = -\$3{,}000$

- Sales have to reach a level of at least 2,800 pairs in order for cash inflows to equal cash outflows in any given year, that is, for profit to equal zero (this is often referred to as the break-even point in sales volume):

  $p = \$30;\ v = \$20;\ f = \$28{,}000;\ \mathrm{p} = 0$

  Solve for q

  $0 = (\$30 \times q) - (\$20 \times q) - \$28{,}000$

  $0 = (\$30 - \$20) \times q - \$28{,}000$

  $0 = \$10 \times q - \$28{,}000$

  $\$10 \times q = \$28{,}000$

  $q = 2{,}800$ pairs of edges

- Selling price could be lowered by \$4.40 to \$25.60, and the company would still break even if it sustained sales of 5,000 pairs of edges per year:

  $\mathrm{p} = 0;\ v = \$20;\ q = 5{,}000;\ f = \$28{,}000$

  Solve for p,

  $0 = (\mathrm{p} \times 5{,}000) - (\$20 \times 5{,}000) - \$28{,}000\ (p - \$20) \times 5{,}000$

= $28,000

p = $28,000 ——— + $20 5,000

p = $25.60

Clearly, the plausible variations on the kinds of questions asked by the company president in the example are virtually unlimited.

The great advantage of cost-volume-profit analysis is that by summarizing cost behaviour patterns into simple functional forms, many of the answers can be supplied with the same set of basic cost data through relatively simple algebraic manipulation. It should be recognized, however, that cost-volume-profit analysis and the several other applications of cost behaviour patterns are subject to two important limitations.

First, the simplifying assumptions limit the applicability of information generated by manipulations of *simplified* cost functions to the extent that the assumptions are not descriptive of reality in a given situation.

Second, although manipulation of cost data within the simplified cost-volume-profit framework is relatively easy once the data are available, it is often difficult to discern actual cost behaviour patterns and to secure the necessary data. Nevertheless, these two limitations are overcome in practice sufficiently often to make cost-volume-profit analysis a most important management accounting tool.

Since the advent and proliferation of computing machinery, the problems associated with manipulating more complex cost functions have lessened consider-ably.

Managements can therefore be provided with more accurate information from more realistic revenue, cost, and profit models, provided they acquire or rent the expensive computers to perform the manipulations.

Even though the functions used in such cases will be more complex, the process of constructing and utilizing them to provide information for management is the same as for the simple model. Thus our illustration of the simplified model is sufficient to highlight the analysis and use of cost behaviour patterns and functions for management decisions.

DIFFERENTIAL COST ANALYSIS

We can make a similar observation about costs (and revenues). Even though a cost presumably always represents a resource sacrifice, one can usefully distinguish between *differential* and *nondifferential* costs (revenues) for any given decision situation.

Differential cost (revenue): A cost (revenue) whose level differs between decision alternatives, that is, different courses of action.

Nondifferential cost (revenue): A cost (revenue) that does not differ between decision alternatives.

This distinction is significant because decisions are based on the expected consequences of choosing one alternative versus another. Nondifferential costs (revenues) are consequences that do not differ between alternatives and therefore should not affect the decision maker's preference for one alternative over another. Differential costs (revenues), on the other hand, are expected consequences that differ between the alternatives and therefore ought to influence the decision maker's choice. In general, then, differential costs (revenues) are relevant to the given decision, and non-differential costs (revenues) are irrelevant. The important thing, therefore, is to be able to distinguish between differential and non-differential costs and revenues in providing information for all kinds of management decisions. What makes this most challenging is that a given cost item may be differential for one decision purpose and non-differential for others.

Example: Assuming that the Shoosh Ski Company actually invested in the new ski edge production facility, recall the estimates of variable costs of $20 per pair of edges and fixed costs of $28,000—for volumes up to an annual production level of 6,000 pairs of edges. Further assume that the company sells 5,000 pairs of edges as planned during each of the first three years of ski edge production.

Early in year four the president of Shoosh Company receives an urgent telephone call from a well-known Swiss ski manufacturer. His company's edge-making facility has just been destroyed by fire and he is offering to buy 1,000 pairs of quality Shoosh edges for $24 a pair on a "one-time-only" basis. Should the president accept this offer?

For purposes of this decision, the Shoosh Company fixed costs of $28,000 are non-differential—that is, they do *not* vary whether the Swiss offer is accepted or not. The only differential costs are the variable costs of $20 per pair of edges. If the sale to Switzerland takes place, Shoosh Company will have a net additional cash inflow of $4,000 in the year of the sale. Thus the Swiss offer should be accepted.

But suppose now that before the Swiss manufacturer's offer, Shoosh was already producing and selling 6,000 pairs of edges per year and was thus operating at the top of the range of production at which the $28,000 fixed costs could be assumed to be constant.

Further suppose that in the range of production from 6,000 to 10,000 pairs of edges, fixed costs can be expected to be $33,000. Under these assumptions, the Swiss offer of $24,000 for 1,000 pairs of edges should not be accepted because it is insufficient to cover both the differential variable costs of $20,000 and the differential fixed costs of $5,000 that will be incurred in accepting the offer. The foregoing example demonstrates some important points, including the following:

- That variable costs are differential and fixed costs non differential *when the decision alternatives being considered are alternate levels of activity within a "relevant range,"* and
- That in other cases *fixed costs can be differential* costs (e.g., when decision alternatives are alternate levels of activity in differert "relevant ranges" or when alternate production methods are being considered). Thus differential cost analysis is applied on a case-by-case basis, with the nature of the decision (alternatives) determining what is a differential and a non differential cost. Perhaps the only generalization that cuts across all decision situations is that past expenditures (often referred to as "sunk costs") are always non differential, since nothing that

a decision maker may do in the present or future can alter the level of past costs incurred.

Example: The Port Authority of Silver City purchased twelve hand-luggage screening devices for its airport security operations. The cost of these devices was $48,000.

Early in 19 × 7 the CAB (Civil Aeronautics Board) ruled these devices illegal as a hazard to public health. Recourse to the manufacturer of the devices was not available, since the manufacturer had acted in good faith in 19X6.

The Port Authority of Silver City had to decide immediately between screening by security guards and screening devices of an approved mechanical type. The $48,000 cost of the old devices is a non differential (sunk) cost to the new decision, even though this expenditure represented a bona fide cost in 19X6.

Analysis of differential cost can be refined for application in complex industrial equipment "make-versus-buy" decisions, leasing decisions, general plant replacement policies, and the like. It therefore ranks with cost behaviour analysis as an important tool of the management accountant.

Chapter 2

Planning and Control

MANAGEMENT DECISION CYCLE

Management decisions have two important distinguishing features:

- They are usually oriented toward a period of activity, and
- A distinct pattern of decisions is usually repeated each period (along with decisions necessitated by previously unanticipated developments).

PERIODICITY

The periodicity of short-run decisions is a result of their relationship to long-run courses of action that have been decided upon. Since the long-run programmes and product lines of an enterprise may be quite divergent in nature, time of origination, and life expectancy, there is a need for some unifying scheme to coordinate their implementation and execution.

One way of achieving this is to manage all projects and programmes on a one-period-at-a-time basis repetitively over the same calendar interval, such as a month, a quarter, or a year. Another reason for periodicity in short-run implementation and execution of long-run courses of action is the need for continuous evaluation and adaptation. Long-run courses of action are adopted in a state of uncertainty based on expectations of achievable results. As long-run programmes are implemented and executed, periodic surveillance is necessary to detect results that are significantly different from the expectations on which initial adoption of the programmes was based.

Furthermore, if needed alterations in a programme are to be made on a timely basis, experience indicates that the surveillance activity should not be left to chance. Therefore surveillance and evaluation of programmes is generally formalized as part of a periodic cycle of short-run management decisions.

Short-run Cycle

The preceding paragraph not only explains the periodicity of short-run management decisions, it also implies that there usually is a pattern of short-run decisions that is repeated with each new period. The pattern may be thought of as a cycle composed of two major phases-an *operations planning* phase and a *control* phase.

OPERATIONS PLANNING

Operations planning consists of all of the activities engaged in by management to initiate a programme of productive activity for a period, in accordance with established long-run enterprise objectives.

Control

Control consists of those activities engaged in by management to ensure that

- The programme of activities for a period is accomplished to the fullest, and
- Performance deficiencies are detected, their causes are determined, and remedial action is taken.

The cyclical aspect of short-run decisions results from the interrelationship of planning and control activities. Performance evaluation implied in the control phase of the short-run decision cycle is dependent on having a recognized plan with which to compare the results of actual activities. On the other hand, as one period's actual results are materializing and being evaluated, plans are made for the coming period's operations.

To be as realistic as possible, all new plans must incorporate the experience gained from current control activities. Thus there is a sequencing of activities with one period's control efforts based on the prior planning phase and leading into the next planning phase. Similarly, every period's plan is based on prior control experience and provides the basis of evaluation in the coming control phase.

OPERATIONS PLANNING

Accounting makes significant contributions to both phases. We first describe the planning phase step by step, including descriptions and illustrations of accounting's contributions.

The major steps in the planning phase of the short-run decision cycle that receive detailed attention are the following:

- Goals are assigned to responsibility centres.
- Plans are developed for responsibility centre operations.
- Production plans of responsibility centres are translated into budgets.
- Responsibility centre budgets are combined and coordinated: the master budget.
- Review of the master budget and replanning are undertaken.

Goals

Within the planning phase all requirements of long-run programmes, projects, and product lines are first interpreted and then broken down into specific descriptions of output goals or activity requirements corresponding to responsibility centres within the enterprise.

Responsibility Centre

A responsibility centre is any identified organizational unit, within the enterprise, that,

- Consists of one or more individuals,
- Is given responsibility for accomplishing a specific enterprise objective, and

- Is given authority (within limits) to accomplish that objective.

The overall output goals for the whole organization are decomposed into contributing goals to be assigned to various major responsibility centres, care is taken to allow for interactions between such centres. For instance, in a typical manufacturing situation, a realistic sales objective must usually be worked out with the sales staff first. This is followed by an evaluation of inventory requirements to determine whether finished goods on hand should be increased or decreased over the period to correspond to expected increases or decreases in sales.

Only after inventory requirements are known can demands be worked out which must be made on the production department. Production schedules, in turn, are used to derive demands for labour to be scheduled by the personnel department, along with demands for materials and supplies required for production (or for various inventory stocks) to be acquired by the purchasing department.

After goals are assigned to the large responsibility centres that perform major functions in the organization, each major responsibility centre further divides and subdivides its goal. The total sales goal is divided by territories and then again by salesmen within territories.

Similarly, the production goal is divided by factories, and then again by departments within the various factories. To illustrate this and other steps in the planning phase of the short-run decision cycle, we introduce a simple but comprehensive example.

Example: National Marketing Corporation (NMC) is a small publicly owned manufacturer of an adult game called Block. Block resembles Monopoly in format but is based on the rules of professional football.

The company entered the field a number of years ago with a capital investment in plant and equipment capacity to produce 120,000 sets of Block per year.

So far Block is NMC's only product. The company's research programme is expected to produce several new games in the next few years. Like other adult games, Block is expected to have several years of growing sales followed by many years of steady but modest sales.

Sales projections in units for the next five years are as follows:

Year	1	2	3	4	5
Block sales	100,000	120,000	90,000	50,000	50,000

All Block sales over the foreseeable future are expected to be at $10 per set. Last year's sales were only 50,000 units. But production was greater than sales by 10,000 units, building inventory up to 20,000-in partial anticipation of the coming year's increase in sales.

The company has followed a policy of ending each year with an inventory of finished goods equal to 20 per cent of the next year's sales estimate.

Based on this policy and the sales forecasts of the coming year and the following year, the production schedule for the coming year can be worked out.

Block Production Schedule

Sales (coming year)	100,000 units
Sales (following year)	120,000
Inventory requirements 20 per cent of following year sales	24,000
Total sales and inventory requirements	124,000
Less present inventory level	20,000
Production requirement (coming year)	104,000 units.

The production of every Block game requires the fabrication of sets of wooden pieces. They are the responsibility of the fabrication department. Each game also requires assembly of a play board and the wooden pieces, along with a set of instructions, into colorful boxes that the company uses to package the game.

This is the responsibility of the assembly department. Since the company's operations are not too complicated, it is a simple matter to pass along the same production schedule of 104,000 units to both the fabrication and the assembly department. Both departments consist of only one foreman and a crew of hourly laborers. Hence there is no further subdivision of the production goal. Assuming that production methods, level of labour skill, and quality of materials are all predetermined, the assignment of production goals will determine the materials and labour acquisition requirements placed on the purchasing and personnel departments, respectively.

Plans for Responsibility Centre Operations

The first step in working back toward a total plan for the organization is devising the "best" (least cost) plan of operations for accomplishing the goals assigned to each of the smallest individual responsibility centres. At the lowest responsibility centre levels within an organization, where a goal may be to perform just one or two operations on each product produced, success usually hinges on minimization of costs. Thus the accountant's skill in bringing together cost data and engineering or production data often facilitates the selection of the "best" plan of operations at that level.

Example: The primary problem is in the production of the wooden pieces. The fabricating department uses direct material in the form of soft white pine, which machine operators cut into sets of pieces. Besides direct materials and labour, whose use varies proportionately with the number of sets of pieces produced, the process requires certain indirect inputs called overhead items, such as machine time, lubricants, gloves for the workers, heat, light, and power. Some of these items vary proportionately with the numbers of labour hours of activity, averaging $1.50 per hour worked (under good conditions). Other overhead inputs are fixed, amounting to approximately $20,000 *per year* (under good conditions) for the whole fabricating operation, regardless of activity. Presently, the production of one set of pieces requires two feet of 1" by 10" pine board and 35 hours of labour. The engineers feel that there are two basic ways of altering the process for better or worse:

- Change the quality of wood used,
- Increase or decrease the level of skill of the machine

operators (presently all are about medium in skill). Management has rejected lower-quality wood because it might affect sales of the game. But it wishes to consider various combinations of labour skill and either pine (now in use) or birch (a better-quality wood).

One foot of 1" by 10" pine of proper quality can be purchased for $.30, whereas a one-foot length of birch costs $.50. *Including variable overhead* of $1.50 per hour, one hour of low-, medium-, and high-skilled labour costs $4.00, $5.00, and $6.00, respectively. Combining this cost data with the last two columns of the production data from, the accountant arrives at per-unit costs for each production combination.

Table. Costs of Alternate Production Possibilities Block Wood Pieces

Combination	**Input Requirements**	**Input Cost**	**Cost per**	**Set of pieces**	
Wood (ft.)	**Labour (hrs.)**	**Wood**		**Labour**	
1	2.5	.40	$.30	$4.00	$2.35
2	2.0	.35	.30	5.00	2.35
3	2.0	.25	.30	6.00	2.10
4	2.0	.35	.50	4.00	2.40
5	1.5	.30	.50	5.00	2.25
6	1.5	.25	.50	6.00	2.25

The best (lowest-cost) combination is combination 3, which requires the use of the same pine wood but higher-skill labour. The engineers had already indicated that a switch in labour force could be made almost immediately by rescheduling employees around the factory plus a small amount of on-the-job training, causing a minimum of layoffs and rehiring. Management adopts the new production plan.

Production Plans Are Translated into Budgets

After the best feasible production plan is determined for each responsibility centre, a financial representation of that plan, called a *budget,* is formulated. Accountants assist operating personnel at all levels in formulating budgets. The process consists of combining

- Individual unit resource requirements, based on a selected plan, with
- The assigned production activity goal. The budget process relies heavily on prediction of cost behaviour patterns.

Example: Based on the "least-cost" production combination selected for the fabrication department the budget for production of 104,000 sets of pieces for Block games for the coming year.

Table. National Marketing Corporation
Fabricating Department

Expected production level	**104,000 units**
Expected costs:	
Direct material:	
2' of 1" by 10" pine $.30 per ft.,	
or $.60 × 104,000	$ 62,400
Direct labour:	
.25 hours × 104,000,	
or 26,000 hrs. $4.50	117,000
Variable overhead items:	
26,000 direct labour hours $1.50	39,000
Total variable costs	$218,400
Fixed overhead costs	20,000
Total expected costs	$238,400

Responsibility Centre Budgets

At NMC, the fabricating department, along with the assembly, purchasing, and personnel departments, all come under the authority of the responsibility centre labeled "manufacturing." To get the total budget for manufacturing, we have to combine the budgets of all of the responsibility centres subordinate to it. The manufacturing budget for NMC for the coming year. Notice that total budgeted costs for the whole manufacturing activity are greater than the sum of the budgeted costs for separate subunits of responsibility within it. This is a common phenomenon in budgeting. The reason, of course, is that some costs incurred at the higher level (like the salary, secretarial help, and supplies for the factory superintendent) are not the responsibility of lower-level managers and, therefore, are not included in their individual budgets.

After the budgets of the various responsibility centres have been combined at successively higher levels, they are finally put together into a coordinated whole called the *master budget*.

Master Budget

A master budget consists of a coordinated set of financial estimates for the budget period, including a balance sheet, an income statement, and whatever other statements are considered useful. The master budget differs from the budgets of such high-level responsibility areas as sales and manufacturing in that it is not a "summing up" of lower-level budgets.

Instead, it allows for the financial consequences of divergent volumes of such major activities as production and sales. The income statement included in the master budget for NMC for the coming year might look something like the statement. Notice particularly that the statement is an income statement and therefore oriented toward sales activity rather than production activity.Thus total cost of units manufactured is adjusted to get the total *cost of units sold*.

Review of Master Budget and Replanning

Since the master budget integrates the plans for all activities of the enterprise in financial terms, it provides a check on all of the individual plans. The master budget does not pinpoint potential production bottlenecks and other technical planning defects.

But it is useful in other ways. For instance, if several areas of responsibility have been careless in seeking optimal plans of operation, the lack of rigor may not be discernible in their individual budgets. But when all budgets are combined in the master budget, the result will be a less-than-satisfactory estimated income figure.

If the master budget produces unsatisfactory results, some form of adaptation is desirable before operations start. The exact form of the adaptation depends on the cause of the disappointing outcome. If it is felt that the cause is lack of rigorous planning on the part of the various responsibility centres or selection of overambitious goals on the part of management, the entire planning process must be reiterated. In the former case, more attention must be devoted to selecting the best (least-cost) plans for each subunit.

In the latter case, more realistic goals must be assigned throughout. On the other hand, if the cause of the disappointment is beyond the control of management in the short run, that is, if it is due to some identifiable internal or external constraint, the problem becomes a matter for the long-run consideration of management; the initial plan of operation, though disappointing, is not necessarily abandoned—unless adaptation could lead to a better plan *under the circumstances.*

Control of Operations

The scope of control activities encompasses virtually every effort made by management to ensure that accepted plans are executed to the fullest. Because most control activity is preventive it goes on more continuously than short-run planning, which is distinctly cyclical.

Control of operations includes all of the following types of activities to some degree:

- Organizational control
- Standard conditions and procedures for operations and related cost standards
- Selecting, training, informing, and motivating employees
- Performance measurement, evaluation, and remedial action

Although accountants become heavily involved as information specialists only in the second and the fourth activity, all of the activities tend to blend together. They interact in achieving the purpose of control. We therefore comment below on each kind of activity in turn. Special attention is given to points of substantial accounting contributions.

Organizational Control

Essentially, organizational control means creating recognized lines of authority and responsibility throughout the business enterprise.

If plans are to be carried out properly, it is imperative that some individual within the organization be responsible for every activity included in the plans. It is equally imperative that the individual responsible for a particular activity have sufficient authority to accomplish his or her goal.

But organizational control is also a matter of balance and coordination. Obviously, no single segment of the enterprise should pursue success in its own activities in such a way as to restrict other segments from accomplishing their goals according to plan.

Two important techniques of organizational control are:

- Built-in redundancy, and
- Separation of duties in certain areas susceptible to serious malfunction. Redundancy means that more than one individual is able to perform key functions. Even though only one individual may be given responsibility for a specific function at any given time, the other qualified individual is available if an emergency arises. He or she may also notice impending difficulties that escape the attention of the person with primary responsibility.

Separation of duties is another label for building in "checks and balances." In a business enterprise, separation of duties takes such forms as assigning one individual the responsibility of recording all cash receipts from customers (to reduce respective account balances), while another individual counts the customers' checks and makes the bank deposits.

Neither individual is given control of both the records and the cash. This tends to ensure accuracy, and in the absence of a conspiracy of at least two employees, protects against misappropriations of enterprise resources.

Standard Conditions and Procedures

Although the input requirements (and their costs) of any given plan of operations largely determine its desirability, many more factors determine whether a given plan can be successfully implemented and executed.

Two things that embody these "other factors" are:

- Well-conceived sets of standard conditions and procedures for combining input resources to achieve the desired output at the lowest cost, and
- Sets of standard input costs which characterize the level of resource sacrifice achievable through use of standard operating conditions and procedures. The former serve as guides to action for employees; the latter serve both as goals to be striven for and as a basis for evaluating actual employee performance.

To see the importance of a set of standard or recommended conditions and procedures to the success of an operation, think of the features that make up a good recipe in cooking. A list of ingredients and quantities, by itself, is usually inadequate.

Without instructions on how to combine the ingredients, and in what order, the outcome of any given attempt at preparation is likely to be disastrous. The same is true of most productive activity, particularly manufacturing activity calling for specific product outputs while utilizing limited resource inputs.

To ensure success of any plan of operations, appropriate methods must be worked out in advance. As weaknesses become apparent, these methods should be corrected. Over time, the effect will be to continually move each operation in the enterprise toward its simplest, safest, lowest cost, and most easily learned form. This means that not only will the goal of low cost be achieved over the long run, but in any given period the likelihood is minimal that planned activities will go seriously awry.

Earlier we noted that the selection of a best plan of operations is usually based on the *expected* costs of production, employing that plan. But the expected costs of production under a particular plan may not be the same as the *standard costs* of production under the same plan.

Standard Cost

Estimated costs will differ from (usually exceed) standard costs whenever management expects that standard conditions and methods will not be achieved at all times. But, although management may not expect its employees to perform consistently according to standard procedures in a given planning period, standard cost is relevant for control purposes. If standard procedures are attainable by reasonably competent and conscientious employees, then the standard cost level of efficiency ought to be held out as a goal that employees should strive for and against which their performance may be fairly compared.

Example: The important distinction between estimated and standard costs for an operation, reconsider the National Marketing Corporation case. Recall that in planning the activity of the fabricating department for the coming budget period, one of six possible combinations of material and labour skill was chosen on the grounds that it had the lowest expected cost. The combination selected was *expected* to consume two feet of pine board at $.30 per foot and.25 hours of highly skilled labour at $6.00 per hour ($4.50 labour; $1.50 variable overhead) for a variable cost per unit of output of $2.10.

Now, it is likely that if all the standard procedures in the fabrication operation were followed to the letter, a lower level of cost per unit could be achieved with the combination of material and labour skill selected. We can realistically assume, for instance, that if everything goes according to standard engineering design of the operation, only 1.9 feet of wood and.24 hours of labour would be required to complete each unit. Thus, standard cost for each unit of output is (1.9 × $.30) + (.24 × $6.00) = $2.01. Provided the standard engineering design of the operation is actually achievable by reasonably motivated and industrious employees, this standard cost, not the estimated cost of $2.10, ought to be the goal for which employees should be striving. In addition, actual employee productivity should be measured relative to the achievable standard, not the expected, costs of production. Otherwise some real potential for improved performance may be overlooked.

If standard costs are the proper target and basis for evaluation of employees performing an operation, then why bother with expected costs of production in the first place? The answer is, of course, that a realistic estimate of resource consumption for each responsibility centre is necessary to coordinate planning of the various functions within the enterprise.

*Example:*In order for the fabricating department of NMC to produce 104,000 sets of Block pieces in the coming period, the purchasing department must acquire the proper amount of materials. If the standard materials quantity per set were used as the basis for the purchasing plans, 197,600 board feet (104,000 × 1.9') of pine lumber would be purchased. But it is realistically expected that actual usage will be 2.0 feet per set, or 208,000 feet in total.

A purchasing plan based on standard performance would, therefore, result in a shortage of materials. At expected input levels and with standard materials purchased, actual production might be restricted to 98,800 finished units (197,600 ÷ 2.0), or 5,200 units short of the output goal of the fabricating department.

Thus both estimated costs and standard costs are relevant to short-run management decisions. Estimated costs form the basis for planning. Standard costs are held out as models for employee performance and are established as a basis for performance evaluation-provided the standards are considered reasonably achievable by competent and conscientious employees.

Before leaving the topic of standard procedures and standard costs, an important qualification should be made.

Standardization of procedures and costs in and of itself can be harmful as well as beneficial for an organization. If standard procedures and costs become outdated, they may no longer be useful.

If standard procedures are too rigid-if they do not allow for variations among employees in physical characteristics, disposition, or tolerance of fatigue-they may not necessarily produce the desired result and may even damage employee morale.

In turn this may lead to costly employee turnover. A wise management will not deny latitude or flexibility in operating procedures if the variations adopted by employees result in achievement of output goals at reachable standard costs.

Selecting, Training, Informing and Motivating Employees

To assign a task to an unqualified employee reduces the likelihood of successful performance. It may jeopardize the morale of the employee or perhaps even his physical safety. If an employee is to be qualified to perform a given task, his selection should be based on possession of any innate qualities required for the task. Then the person must become thoroughly acquainted with the demands of the task, and, through training, innate ability should be refined into specific competence for the job.

The more successful the enterprise is with respect to selecting and preparing employees, the greater the probability that they will successfully carry out planned operations. Presumably every employee's goal in working for an enterprise is to contribute the most to the satisfaction of personal wants and needs. The purpose of the enterprise in employing a person is to use the person's resources to the fullest in satisfying enterprise goals. The best results for both parties are obtained when there is a maximum of *goal congruence* between the two.

Goal Congruence

Goal congruence is said to exist between an employee

and the enterprise (management) if by working in the manner most satisfying to himself or herself, the employee is at the same time most likely to produce desired results for the enterprise.

Clearly it is essential to the success of any plan of operations that the goals of the employees who perform the operations be as congruent as possible with successful performance from the enterprise's point of view. At one time during the development of business management it was assumed that man was a purely economic being, motivated wholly by wealth.

Hence it was further assumed that an employee could be induced to perform in any manner desired by management, within his or her physical and mental capability, if a sufficiently high wage or salary was offered. Experience, however, has been largely inconsistent with that theory. It is now widely recognized that human motivation is a much more complex phenomenon. Therefore, *employee motivation* is another aspect of control activity.

Employee Motivation

To be sure, in most cases *some* employee motivations fall within the realm of economic incentives that are tied directly to a desired level of productivity.

Example: The company performs several kinds of machining operations on various metal parts sent to it by its customers. Since Job Shop has a limited number of machines, its profitability depends on its full use of the capacities of the available machines. Rather than pay its machinists on an hourly basis, it pays them a fixed amount for each satisfactory piece of work completed.

To maximize their own wages, therefore, the machinists simply produce as many satisfactorily completed pieces per hour as possible, thus maximizing the output (and the revenues) from the machines they operate. Assuming that all machinists working for Job Shop are primarily interested in maximizing their wages, this sort of "piece-rate" incentive system might work quite effectively in inducing them to maximize output from the machines. But evidently many factors other than wage incentives are also important in motivating employees. Actually, the possible factors are so numerous that space limitations do not permit exhaustive coverage. We can only list several kinds that seem to influence employee motivation:

- Employees seem to relate to small, informal groups of fellow employees and to be influenced by the values of those groups, as well as by the policies and incentives offered by management.
- Some employees seem to thrive in very authoritarian environments, while others seem to chafe under an authoritarian management.
- Some employees are challenged to excel by very high performance standards, while others may become frustrated or despondent because of the seeming impossibility of ever succeeding when such high standards are set.
- Many employees respond more favorably to standard methods and costs if they have participated in devising the methods and therefore accept the standard cost levels as "achievable" (fair) standards for measuring their performance.

The list could go on and on. And the reader can no doubt add to the list as well by imagining what things he or she would respond to favorably or unfavorably in various types of job situations. Not only is our list incomplete, but knowledge about human motivation is still so inadequate that it is difficult to predict how various individuals will respond to the many different incentives that management may offer. It is for this reason that both practicing and academic accountants are turning more and more to behavioural sciences for relevant insights.

Measurement, Evaluation, and Remedial Action

For ensuring the success of any plan of operations, the old adage "An ounce of prevention is worth a pound of cure" is very appropriate. But management cannot anticipate every problem in advance of implementing the plans for a given budget period. Periodic surveillance and adjustment of operations are also necessary and important parts of management's control activities.

They are control activities to which accounting contributes significantly. Because control activities are costly in the sense that they consume scarce management resources and perhaps employee time that would otherwise be devoted to production, the concept of *management by exception* has evolved.

Management by Exception

Management by exception is the process of detecting and devoting remedial attention to only those facilities, employees, and operations that are not performing according to plan. The great advantage of management by exception is that time and efforts are not wasted on operations that are performing satisfactorily. But management by exception implies that management can locate trouble spots without detailed on-the-spot review of every responsibility center's activities. To do this, management typically relies on two sources.

The first source and, indeed, the first line of defence and correction, is the employee. A well-selected, well-trained, and well-motivated employee who understands the standard conditions and procedures for his operation will detect and correct many problems directly. Furthermore, he will seek help in correcting problems that are seemingly beyond his immediate control, thus bringing them to the attention of management. Management's second source for detecting performance problems lies in performance reporting systems.

Performance Reporting Systems

Performance reporting systems are formal information systems for periodically gathering data on actual production activities, comparing actual data with standard performance, and thereby highlighting problem areas for management attention. Formal performance reporting is conducted on either a physical-data or a cost-data basis. The advantage of physical data, like quantities of material and labour consumed, is that they are stated in terms of the things that employees manipulate directly during operations.

But a possibly greater comparative advantage of cost data is that they pinpoint problems in various operations in uniform (money) terms. This may have relatively greater economic significance to both management and employees.

Example: The result is that he has been *using 5 per cent less of his time* per unit of output while he has been *using 5 per cent more materials* than standard. The trade-off may seem reasonable to him when stated in percentages of physical inputs. But he may be shocked at the results on a cost basis if, for instance, standard material costs per unit of output are $100 while standard labour input is one hour at $5 per hour.

What seems to be a one-for-one trade-off in input percentage utilization is really a twenty-to-one cost trade-off. Formal performance reporting based on cost data usually falls within the special area of expertise of the accountant.

As with other contributions of accounting for management decisions, performance reporting on a cost (or money) basis involves association of costs (and revenues) with various kinds of real economic activities, such as the consumption of resources in production. Cost behaviour patterns are therefore applicable to performance reporting, just as they are applicable to other major managerial accounting contributions. One reason that cost behaviour patterns are a valuable tool for performance reporting is that it is useful to divide performance reporting into two major measures of performance called *effectiveness* and *efficiency*.

Effectiveness

Effectiveness is the degree to which a particular output or activity goal has been achieved.

Efficiency

Efficiency refers to the inputs consumed (measured in quantities or costs) *for a given level of output*.

Example: Suppose that the fabricating department actually completed 100,000 sets of pieces. It would be judged efficient if it incurred costs *less than or equal to* the standard input costs for 100,000 units; inefficient if it incurred more than standard costs *for that level of output*.

Whereas effectiveness is measured against a goal that is set in advance, efficiency is measured with respect to actual output, which is not known until a particular performance period is over. Thus accounting performance reporting, which is mainly oriented toward measuring efficiency, must be flexible. The source of that flexibility is the use of cost behaviour patterns. Relying on cost behaviour patterns that have been determined in advance, accountants can construct standard cost levels for *actual* levels of output immediately after those levels are known.

Accounting performance reporting usually follows these steps:

- As operations progress during a reporting period, quantities and costs of resources used in production are recorded for each responsibility centre.
- At the end of the reporting period, a performance report is prepared for each responsibility centre on which actual costs of production are compared with standard costs *for the achieved level of output*, and variances are noted.
- Variances are analyzed to highlight the nature of inefficiencies.
- Significant variances are investigated to determine the cause and appropriate action.

The level of *actual variable* costs is usually a function of two influences, the *quantity* of the variable input used and the average *price* paid per unit used.

Thus, variable cost variances can be due to either:

- Differences between standard and actual prices or rates paid (called price, rate, or spending variances) or
- Differences between standard and actual quantities used to achieve the actual level of output (called usage or efficiency variances).

Example: Suppose that we have the additional information (besides total actual cost of materials used) that the fabricating department used an average of 2.0 feet of wood or 200,000 board feet in total to produce its output of 100,000 sets of pieces. Now we can separate the total unfavorable material cost variance of $5,000 into two parts.

Table. National Marketing Corporation Fabricating Department Performance Report

Planned output: 104,000 units					
Actual output: 100,000 units					
Level of effectiveness: approximately 96%					
Cost Categories			**Standard Cost**	**Actual Costs**	**Variances**
Materials at standard			$ 57,000	$ 62,000	$ 5,000 (U)
$30 × 1.9' × 100,000 sets					
Labor at standard			108,000	119,600	11,600 (U)
$4.50/hr. × .24 hrs. × 100,000 sets					
Variable overhead (standard)			36,000	38,000	2,000 (U)
$1.50/hr. × .24 hrs. × 100,000 sets					
Fixed overhead			28,000	26,000	2,000(F)
			-------------	-------------	-------------
		Totals	$229,000	$245,600	$16,600 (U)
			======	======	=======

We recall that the total cost of 100,000 units at standard input quantity and standard price is $57,000. By multiplying the actual materials usage of 200,000 board feet by the standard price of $.30 per foot, we find that if all wood actually used in production were purchased at standard prices, actual cost would have been $60,000. This means that the variance due only to excess usage of wood is $3,000(U) or ($60,000 - $57,000). Now, since the $60,000 figure represents the actual quantity of wood used, times the standard price, it differs from actual cost of wood used only insofar as actual prices paid differed from standard prices.

Subtracting the $60,000 from the actual cost of $62,000 gives a price variance of $2,000(U).

These calculations are summarized below:

Standard cost of material	$3,000(U)
1.9' × 100,000 units × $30 = $57,000	Usage variance
Standard cost of actual material used	$2,000(U)
200,000 feet × $30 = $60,000	price variance
Actual cost of materials used	
(from supplier invoices) = $62,000	

The same reasoning as that used in the above example is applicable to other variable inputs besides material. The analysis of variable cost variances helps to focus management's attention on possible causes responsible for nonstandard performance even before costly investigations are begun. Once a significant performance variance is noted and it is determined that it should be investigated, management first consults with the individual who is responsible for the activity that is not measuring up to standard.

Frequently it will be found that the cause for the off-standard performance has already been discovered and eliminated. If it has not, the investigation will start with those most familiar with and most responsible for the troublesome activity. In any case, performance reporting's role will have ended.

The solution to problems highlighted by the performance report will come from one of the other three types of control activities outlined above or from revising plans and standards for the next period. Those problems that do not have satisfactory short-run solutions become inputs to long-run decision activities of management. In this fashion, management can strive continually for an improvement of overall enterprise performance.

Chapter 3

Organizational and Behavioural Foundations

ORGANIZATIAL FOUNDATIONS

Management accounting is built on organizational foundations. First, elements of organizational structure shape its techniques, approaches, and role in the firm. Second, it is a function of the theories of organization to describe and explain organizational behaviour. Robert Golembiewski was among the first authors to point to the problem of adapting accounting to organization theory and vice versa: It seems appropriate that organization theory receive considerable attention by members of the accounting profession, which is presently in the throes of rethinking its scope and methods. For an inappropriate organization structure can frustrate the most worthy of intentions and, in any case, any fundamental changes in accountancy will require changes in the traditional theory of organization.

Thus, management accounting requires a good grasp of the elements of organizational structure and theories of organization. Identifying the elements of an organization structure most prevalent and essential to a proper functioning of a management accounting system allows the tailoring of the internal reporting system to that structure or the suggestion of a more appropriate organization structure. Similarly, the theories of organization point to significant elements that approximate the patterning and order inherent in organi-zations. Determination of these characteristics guides manage-ment accounting to more effective ways of providing its services. Elements of organizational structure and theories of organization most relevant to a proper functioning of management accounting.

ELEMENTS OF ORGANIZATIONAL STRUCTURE

Formal organizational structure is the aspect of the organization that management often seeks to change in order to improve the functioning of the organization. The elements of this structure affect the ways the management accounting function will be exercised and they need to be fully understood by a management accountant. Before presenting the elements or organizational structure most relevant to a proper functioning of management accounting, the nature of an organization will be examined.

Nature of an Organization

Organizations can be viewed for various perspectives, and the choice of a perspective leads to different organizational topologies or taxonomies. Each typology calls for different management accounting systems to accommodate the informational needs of each type of organization included. A more general depiction of an organization is that of a "relatively permanent and relatively complex discernible interaction system." In other words, the organization is an observable result of the interaction rather than the group of actors. The three components of the definition deserve more clarification.

First, the organization is a *going concern* in the sense that the interaction system is relatively stable. Second, the organization is an *exclusive entity*. It is different from a group or a society in terms of structural complexity.

Structural complexity refers to both horizontal and vertical integration. Finally, the organization is an *interaction system*. It assumes the existence of two or more persons who have independent relationships.

With these in view, three problems appear:

- Organizational membership;

- Organizational boundaries; and
- Organizational environments.

George Homans chose to associate organizational membership with the frequency of interaction. If members interact more with each other than with subject *E*, then *E* is not considered a member of the group. To this definition, Eugene Hass and Thomas Drabeck added two criteria for organizational membership: the frequency of interaction and the content of interaction. In brief, "those interaction units that are perceived high in frequency and similar in content constitute the interaction system."

The organizational boundaries depend on the analyst (for example, the management accountant) and the questions asked by the analyst. Assembling the interaction units in a system on the basis of their frequency and content leads to a delimitation of the boundaries of the organization. The predominant school of thought is that boundaries ought to be viewed as flexible rather than rigid. In recent works of Donald Katz and Robert Kahn and James Thompson, organizations are perceived as "open systems."

The functioning of the organization is affected by a multitude of environments.They define the major constraints within which the organization is called to function. The idea is stated well in the following passage from Sherman Krupp: The range of behaviour which the business firm's internal variables will have depends, among other things, on the structure of the market. Under conditions of oligopoly (let us assume the firm is large), phenomena that might appear external and compelling to the smali competitive firm become themselves internal and susceptible of manipulation.

Thus, the large firm in oligopoly is much more independent of external constraints than is the firm under competition. In a competitive market, on the other hand, the behaviour of the firm is largely determined by environmental conditions.

The firm in a world of oligopoly is a more self-contained empirical structure than the firm in competition. The independence of the firm from external factors is an empirical matter; empirical structure defines the bounded units of the world of observables. These environments are characterized by their instability and exclusivity.

The nature of an organization as a relatively complex and relatively permanent interaction system places management accounting in the role of an organizational process intended for strengthening these interactions. More specifically, the management accountant will provide essential services that will concretize the interaction between individuals and their membership in the organization, define the boundaries of the organization to include all the interaction units, and structure all analyses, taking into account the constraints imposed by the organizational environments. In brief, interaction units, organizational membership, boundaries, and environment are important organizational concepts that define the scope and nature of the management accountant's activities.

Organizational Structure

It results from a deliberate and conscious planning of the areas of responsibility, specialization, and authority for each of the organizational members. In general, it takes a hierarchical form where authority and responsibility are differentiated along a vertical dimension, and units, such as departments or divisions, along a horizontal dimension. What results is a pyramid-shaped organization, usually referred to as an organization chart. Each vertical level in the hierarchy depicts different levels of authority. For example, each of the manufacturing centres is responsible to the manufacturing superintendent.

In turn, the latter, with all the other organizational units on the same horizontal line, is responsible to the manufacturing vice president. Finally, the latter, with all the other vice presidents, is responsible to the board of directors. Let us note again that each horizontal dimension is differentiated by specialization rather than by authority. This process is termed *departmentalization*, whereby employees are grouped into organizational units on the basis of similar skills and specialization. Growth and environmental change are usually the main determinants for departmentalization. In general, the departmentalization in organizations takes four major forms: by function, by location, by process, and by product. A firm may departmentalize or differentiate horizontally according to one of several of these forms.

First, firms may departmentalize by function. For example, a typical manufacturing firm may include sales, production, accounting, finance, personnel, research and development, and purchasing as necessary functions to be departmentalized. Second, firms may departmentalize by process. Most production activities include different technological processes that require different organizational units. The finishing, foundry, stamping, machining, welding and assembly are "housed" in different organizational units.

Third, firms may departmentalize by location. A large corporation may be differentiated on the basis of territories, districts, regions, and such. The relatively independent units are referred to as divisions. Hence a multinational corporation may divisionalize by location to adapt to different legal, taxation, and market environments. Finally, firms may departmentalize by product. This is beneficial to those firms producing different products for different markets.

Vertical differentiation by authority and responsibility and horizontal differentiation through departmentalization or divisionalization lead to the creation of periodic planning and control. This need is met only by the management accounting system in general and responsibility accounting in particular. Management accounting will produce accounting reports of performance and budgets that will serve as the means of communication between these units.

Similarly, by making the smallest areas of responsibility the main foundations of the management accounting system, responsibility accounting allows definition and consolidation of the decisions and the nature of the responsibility of each of the organizational units, and may facilitate effective communication. In brief, while organizational structure is concerned with authority, responsibility, and specialization relations aimed at assuring effective and efficient performance, management accounting, through responsibility accounting, represents the design and implementation of the accounting system for the purpose of better defining and consolidating these relations.

Types of Organizational Structure

Most theorists believe that organizational structure is developed as a response to the problem of control. Basically, control can be achieved by the type of organizational structure adopted. Those aspects of the organizational structure most effective as tools of control have been identified as the span of control, the functional specialization, vertical and horizontal differentiation, centralization, and formalization and standardization. The same structural dimensions can be combined in various ways to constitute an organizational structure. Henry Mintzberg argued that most organizational structures can be classified as belonging to one of five ideals of "pure" structural types, which he called "simple structure, machine bureaucracy, professional bureaucracy, divisionalized form, and adhocracy." Other hybrids are possible. Mintzberg argued, however, that "there are times when we need to caricature, or stereotype, reality in order to sharpen differences and so to better understand it."

The Simple Structure

According to Mintzberg, the basic simple structure can be summarized as follows. It has little or no technostructure, few support staffers, a loose division of labour, minimal differentiation among its units, and a small managerial hierarchy. Little of its behaviour is formalized, and it makes minimal use of planning, training, and the liaison devices. It is above all organic. Basically, the simple structure is a non-structure where a strong entrepreneur manager holds all of the decision powers, including planning and control. Most organizations, especially small and young organizations, pass through the simple structure in their formative years. The entrepreneurial firm fits best in the simplestructure category. It depends on the health and whims of one individual and generally has a sense of its mission. The simple structure, although ideal for the small and entrepreneurial firms, may be criticized for being paternalistic, unfashionable in contemporary society, and sometimes autocratic.

The Machine Bureaucracy

According to Mintzberg, the basic structure of a machine bureaucracy can be summarized as follows. It has highly specialized, routine operating tasks, very formalized procedures in the operating core, a proliferation of rules, regulations, and formalized communications throughout the organization, large-sized units at the reoperating level, reliance on the functional basis for grouping tasks, relatively centralized power for decision making, and an elaborate administrative structure with a sharp distinction between line and staff.

The machine bureaucracy is ideal when an integrated set of simple repetitive tasks must be performed well by human beings. It requires direct supervision by first-line managers and standardization of work processes. It depends on strict sets of rules and regulations governing every aspect of the enterprise's life. In fact, the machine bureaucracy is obsessed with control to contain all possible conflicts created by the structure. In fact, decision making in general and planning and control in particular are a top-down affair. The machine bureaucracy is generally found to prosper in a mature organization, large enough to have been able to settle on the standards it is going to use. It is the second stage of structural development following the aging and growing of simple structures.

Mass-production firms are the best-known machine bureaucracies. The main problem of the machine bureaucracy lies in its treatment of people as means or categories of status and function rather than as individuals. A machine bureaucracy also has to deal with the conflict between engineering and efficiency and individual satisfaction. To solve these problems it relies heavily on control and direct supervision.

The Professional Bureaucracy

The professional bureaucracy is an organization that is bureaucratic without being centralized. It calls for standardiza-tion and decentralization at the same time. According to Mintzberg, it "relies for coordination on the standardization of skills and its associated design parameters, training and indoctrination.

It hires only trained and indoctrinated specialists-professionals—for the operating core, and then gives them considerable control over their own work." The professional bureaucracy structure fits best the personal service organizations, like universities and accounting, law, and consulting firms. The structure of these firms is essentially bureaucratic, in that its coordination—like that of machine bureaucracy—is achieved by design or standards that determine what is to be done. The standards came from the external self-governing organizations that regulate all aspects of the given profession.

The professional bureaucracy is composed of an operating core of professionals serving and backed by a support staff to aid them and do whatever routine work can be formalized. This calls for parallel administrative and control hierarchies, one democratic and bottom-up for the professionals and another bureaucratic and top-down for the support staff.

The professional bureaucracy is not without its problems and limitations. It has no mechanisms for correcting deficiencies that have been ignored by the profession. It cannot easily deal with incompetent or unconscious professionals. As Mintzberg put it, "discretion not only enables some professionals to ignore the needs of their clients; it also encourages many of them to ignore needs of the organization."

The only way to bring effective changes in the professional bureaucracy is by causing effective changes in the professional organizations themselves, the professional schools that educated the professionals, and the oversight bodies that regulate them.

The Divisionalized Form

According to Mintzberg, the basic structure of a divisionalized concern can be summarized as follows: The Professional Bureaucracy, the Divisionalized Form is not so much an integrated organization as a set of quasi autonomous entities coupled together by a central administrative structure. But whereas those "loosely coupled" entities in the Professional Bureaucracy are individuals—professionals in the bureaucratic core—in the Divisionalized Form, they are units in the middle line. These units are generally called *divisions*, and the central administration, the *headquarters*. And here the flow of power is not bottom-up, but top-down.

The divisionalized concern is the most widely used structure by the large corporations in the United States and the world. It is basically a structure superimposed on others, where each division has its own structure and where the focus is on the structural relationship between the headquarters and divisions. In general the divisionalized form uses the markets for products as a basis for grouping units or divisions that will have full control of the operating functions to serve these markets. These divisions have practically full autonomy to make their own decisions and then monitor the results of these decisions. They have their own set of goals and work most of the time as machine bureaucracies, characterized by their own technical systems. They work best in environments that are neither very complex nor very dynamic—the same type of environment that leads to the machine bureaucracy. In fact, the structural response to machine bureaucracies that started out working in a simple, stable environment moved to the divisionalized form when the companies diversified into new product or service lines horizontally or when older age and/ or large sizes led to diversification.

The Adhocracy

According to Mintzberg, the basic structure of an adhocracy can be summarized as follows: It has a highly organic structure, with little formalization of behaviour; high horizontal job specialization based on formal training; a tendency to group the specialists functional units for housekeeping purposes but to deploy them in small, marketbased project teams to do their work; a reliance on the liaison devices to encourage mutual adjustment, the key coördination mechanism, within and between these teams; and selective decentralization to and within these teams, which are located at various places in the organization and involve various mixtures of line managers and staff and operating experts.

Adhocracy is essential to sophisticated innovation because it allows experts from various disciplines to work mostly together on ad hoc project teams. It tends to use the functional and market basis for grouping concurrently in a matrix structure. Coordination is possible by the mutual adjustment of one team member to another. Adhocracy is ideal for an environment that is both dynamic and complex. The dynamism for the environment calls for the need to decentralize selectivity to differentiated work constellations. In short, it calls for "emphasis on expertise, organic structure, project teams and task forces, decentralization without a single concentration of power, matrix structure, sophisticated and automated technical systems, youth, and environments that are complex and dynamic." It is generally considered the structure of the future.

Line and Staff Relationships

In the organization chart of the nature of the relationships implied by the lines connecting the organization unit boxes has not been explicitly defined. These relationships may be either line or staff. Line implies a basic hierarchical subordinate-superior relationship as defined by the line of authority or chain of command. Line managers are directly responsible for the particular tasks entrusted to them. Staff implies that a part of the managerial task has been assigned by an executive to someone outside the chain of command. Thus, staff managers facilitate the work of the line managers, providing them with essential services. The authority relationships between the staff member and employees of the line at the same or lower levels may be of four types: staff advice, compulsory advice, concurring authority, or limited company authority. Let us examine each type.

The "staff advice" is purely advisory. In general, people are inclined to accept the advice of staff managers when they are regarded as technical experts, when they have impressive titles, when they are skilled in presenting ideas, when they have potential backing by a senior operating executive, and when their views may influence the reward and penalty system. In short, "even though a staff man may have no command authority whatsoever, he may still get his recommendations accepted if he is smart, persuasive, impressive, and influential."

Staff managers may have a "compulsory advice" relationship in the sense that they must always be consulted before action is taken.

Staff managers may have a "concurring authority" relationship in the sense that no action can be taken until a designated staff manager agrees to it.

Finally, staff managers may have a "functional authority" or "limited company authority" relationship in the sense that they are authorized to personally give direct orders to operating personnel rather than merely making recommendations to line managers. For example, the financial accounting department may decide that certain production statistics ought to be disclosed in the annual reports, forcing the production department to produce them periodically.

The concepts of line and staff are another element of organizational structure of relevance to management accounting. First, management accounting is a process that provides services and assistance to other units in the organization. Its role is supportive by nature. It is basically a staff function.

Second, as a staff manager the management accountant's authority may range from purely advisory to limited company authority. Third, because of the great need for the specialized knowledge provided by the management accounting department, it is likely to be positioned rather highly in the organization. In any case, management accounting is a decision support system.

The Controllers in the Organization

The managers in charge of accounting departments are known as controllers. They are staff members of the top management team and are line managers in their own departments. As a member of the staff, they advise management in the areas of corporate reporting, planning, and control. Controllers' activities include mainly the following:

They are responsible for the supervision of all facets of financial accounting leading to the publication of annual reports. They coordinate all the activities leading to the establishment of the master budget and long-term plan of the firm. They promote maintenance of a system of control through proper circulation of performance reports.

As designers and activators of the basic organizational communication system, the electronic data processing system, controllers act as the essential persons for proper collection, diffusion, and channeling of relevant and timely information.

The role of controllers varies, however, from one firm to another, covering the total continuum of staff work. In other words, their role may be a purely advisory relationship, a "compulsory advice" relationship, a "concurring authority" relationship, or an effective "functional authority" relationship.

Because of their position in the top management team, controllers are overseers of the work of others. They initiate and direct the preparation of specific reports for internal or external reporting, and they advise top management on key issues.

Generally reporting to controllers are the staff departments of electronic data processing, taxes, financial analysis and budgeting, financial services, corporate accounting, management services, and payroll. This shows that corporate controllers have moved to the important and central stage. Consider the following quotation:

As the controller's job has changed so have the tools of the trade. In the old days, the controller simply worked up the profit and loss statement and the balance sheet. Today the job involves elaborate monitoring and cross checking of scads of financial data from profits and expenses to return on investment and the cost of capital. Instead of the adding machine and ledger books, the controller works with increasingly complex, sophisticated computer programmes that keep him in almost daily touch with almost every facet of the business.

The increase in the size and complexity of business entities, the growth in the use of the planning and control technique, and the new enlarged scope of management accounting activities are the reasons for this new controller concept. It is a top-level function with a primary responsibility for the detailed analysis and interpretation of operating results, policies, procedures, and proposals of major importance.

The job of controllers is difficult to define and depends on the particular organizational structure of the firm and the role and scope of the accounting activities. In any case, the job is a complex one. The large list of activities implies that controllers must have personal, educational, and experience qualifications in order to handle all these duties properly. These requirements are very important, given the new expanded role of management accounting in the organization as the "director of management information." Controllers are also essential to the acceptance of the new nature and uses of management accounting. Some of their tasks may involve teaching and convincing the rest of the organization about the new scope of management accounting.

The Role of the Controller in the Design and Operation of the Control System

The controller plays the most important role in the design and operation of the control system, which raises fundamental questions and suggests various solutions. There are misconceptions about the respective roles of the controller and the treasurer, to the point where in many firms the jobs described as falling under the responsibility of one of them belongs in fact under the responsibility of the other. In general, the treasurer is responsible for money-management activities, and the controller acts as chief accountant and financial planner. To clear up this dichotomy, the Financial Executives Institute approved a formal official statement of the controllership and treasurership functions, which is depicted.

There are also misconceptions about the staff function of the controller. The authority relationship between the staff member and employees of the line at the same or lower levels may be of four types: staff advice, compulsory advice, concurring authority, and limited company authority.

The controller functions best when he or she has a "functional authority," meaning a form of direct involvement in business decisions. The determinants of the degree of involvement of controllers in business decisions remains an empirical question. Vijay Sathe's empirical study of the control function in large ($300 million plus), multidivisional U.S. corporations revealed seven determinants of the degree of involvement of the typical controller in business decisions.

The degree of corporate management's financial orientation, with its emphasis on financial goals and on a "portfolio approach" type of management. The degree of corporate management's emphasis on the company's financial planning, budgeting, and capital-expenditure-review system.

The duration of sustained emphasis on development of controllership personnel, in terms of career planning, job rotation, or other programmes concerned specifically with the development of personnel in the controllership function. The working capital intensity of a business (inventories plus receivables divided by net sales).

Corporate management's expectations regarding controller involvement in business decisions. The emphasis that the corporation places upon transfers from the line organization to the controller function as part of the management development strategy. The emphasis the corporate controller organization places on the advisory role.

To be effective at being involved in business decisions and at exercising "functional authority," it is important for the controller to be a "strong controller." The definition of the controller role differs generally from the traditional definition of a functional role. An empirical study by Dale Henning and Roger Moseley indicates that controllers do not have the same authority in all of their functions or in the various decisions within those functions. They concluded as follows:

The role of the controller appears to be much more complex than the literature suggests. He is assigned certain functional responsibilities, yet as he attempts to fulfill those responsibilities, he finds himself with different degrees of authority as he moves from one function to another and from one decision to another. His superior, who has considerable say about his destiny, and his executive peers, with whom he must establish good relationships if he is to successfully fulfill his responsibilities, observe his behaviour with different expectations about his authority.

The controller might be looked upon in one instance by his superior as being too aggressive, and, at the same time, as not aggressive enough by his peers, or just the reverse. The profile of the controller is that of an executive with substantial authority in some functions and more limited authority in others: with varying degrees of authority in different decisions within a function, many times as making unilateral decisions and often sharing in the making of decisions; perceiving himself as having more authority than he is seen to have by his superior and his peers.

He occupies a role with great opportunity, yet is both ill-defined and fraught with potential conflict. While still in its infancy, research findings point to a number of significant relationships between the nature of the controller's department and characteristics of the overall organization. For example, K. Rosenzweig found size and unionization to be important considerations in the design of a controller's department structure.

Although the case for active involvement of the controller in management may be easily made and defended, it raises, however, the question of controller independence. The issue is important to both society and the corporation. Inaccurate reporting will undermine public confidence and distinct internal resource allocation. Can the controller wear two hats, one for being actively involved and one for keeping his or her sense of objectivity and independence?

Most people would argue that the answer is no. One solution lies in using the internal audit function in general and internal and external compliance auditing to ensure overall organizational control, including the controller's department.

Another unresolved organization design question is whether the division controller should report directly to the decision manager or to the corporate controller. If the division controller reports to the division manager, one may question his or her "independence." In fact, M. Schiff and A. Y. Lewin reported that in those cases, the division controller appears to have undertaken the task of creating and managing division slack and is most influential in the internal allocation of this slack. The solution seems to lie again on the role of the internal audit function. J. G. San Miguel and V. Govindarajan found a contingent relationship between the division controller's independence from the division manager and the duties and responsibilities assigned to the internal audit function. Basically, in firms where the division controller was less independent, the internal audit functions were employed to perform a significantly greater amount of financial, compliance auditing than firms with more independent division controllers. This contingent relationship appears to have evolved quite naturally because of top management's concern for maintaining effective organizational control to satisfy the firm's and their own objectives.

THEORIES OF ORGANIZATION

The theories of organization represent different attempts in the literature to describe and explain organizational behaviour. Each of these theories attempts to determine the significant elements that may approximate the patterning or order existing in organizations. Because these elements comprise the key organizational variables or the ways they are related, they define the ways management accounting will better provide its services to the organization. Although not exhaustive, the theories examined comprise those that currently reflect organizational literature: the rational perspective, the classical perspective, the human relations perspective, and the natural system perspective. Management accounting is thought to rest on elements provided by each of these formulations, rather than on any single one, because none provides an entirely adequate theory organization on its own.

The Rational Perspective

Max Weber argued that the social behaviour and social interaction of individuals depend on their "ideas" of the existence of a *legitimate authority*. He distinguished between three pure types of legitimate authority, each dependent on a different source of legitimation:

Traditional authority, legitimated by time and resting "on established belief in the sanctity of immemorial traditions and the legitimacy of the status of those exercising authority under them."

Charismatic authority, legitimated by the appealing personality of the leader and resting on the "devotion to the specific and exceptional sanctity, heroism or exemplary character of an individual person, and of the normative patterns or order revealed or ordained by him."

Bureaucratic or rational-legal authority, legitimated by rules and resting "on a belief in the 'legality' of patterns of normative rules and the right of those elevated to authority under such rules to issue commands."

The last type of authority was viewed by Weber as an ideal characteristic of modern organizations. He drew attention to the fact that in modern society the bureaucratic type has become dominant because of its alleged greater efficiency. The bureaucratic organization is composed of a bureaucratic administrative staff. The position occupied by the chief of such an organization is by virtue of appropriation, election, or succession. The individuals comprising the organization conform to the following ten criteria:

They are personally free and subject to authority only with respect to their impersonal official obligations.

They are organized in a clearly defined hierarchy of offices. Each office has a clearly defined sphere of competence in the legal sense. The office is filled by a free contractual relationship. Thus, in principle, there is free selection. The candidates are selected on the basis of technical qualifications. In the most rational case, this is tested by examination or guaranteed by diplomas certifying technical training, or both. They are appointed, not elected.

They are remunerated by fixed salaries in money, for the most part with a right to pensions. Only under certain circumstances does the employing authority, especially in private organizations, have a right to terminate the appointment, but the official is always free to resign. The salary scale is primarily graded according to rank in the hierarchy; but in addition to this criterion, the responsibility of the position and the requirements of the incumbent's social status may be taken into account.

The office is treated as the sole, or at least the primary, occupation of the incumbent. It constitutes a career. There is a system of promotion according to seniority or achievement, or both. Promotion is dependent on the judgment of superiors.

The official works entirely separated from ownership of the means of administration and without appropriation of his position. He is subject to strict and systematic discipline and control in the conduct of his office. The organization under a rational perspective is viewed as a highly efficient machine where members strive together in an orderly fashion to complete a given objective. Empirical evidence related to the organizational effectiveness of the Weberian type of organization was provided by James Price.

The rational perspective stresses both goal specificity and formalization. As A. W. Gouldner notes, fundamentally, the rational model implies a "mechanical" model, in that it views the organization as a structure of manipulable parts, each of which is separately modifiable with a view to enhancing the efficiency of the whole. Individual organizational elements are seen as subject to successful and planned modification, enactable by deliberate decision.

Robert Merton also appropriately notes that "formality facilitates the interaction of the occupants of offices despite their (possibly hostile) private attitudes toward one another."

Different points of criticism appear in the literature against the rational perspective in organizational structure and behaviour. Organizations tend to change from bureaucratic to charismatic during crisis situations. Weber uniquely assumed a formal behaviour existing in the organization. People within the organization were assumed to behave rigidly and mechanistically according to established rules. Thus, informal behaviour, group norms, environmental changes, and internal conflict are not discussed by Weber, who provided the first of the original studies designed to examine the nature and functioning of bureaucracy and organization in general. Weber in fact was confused between two analytically distinguishable bases of authority by once arguing that authority is based on incumbency in a legally defined office and later arguing that it is based on technical competence. Gouldner, again, notes:

Weber, then, thought of bureaucracy as a Janus-faced organization, looking two ways at once. On the one side, it was administration based on discipline. In the first emphasis, obedience is invoked as a means to an end; an individual obeys because the rule or order is felt to be the best known method of realizing some goals.

In his second conception, Weber held that bureaucracy was a mode of administration in which obedience was an end in itself. The individual obeys the order, setting aside judgment either of its rationality or morality, primarily because of the position occupied by the person commanding. The conduct of the order is not examinable.

Despite its apparent limitations, the rational perspective designates significant elements approximating the patterning or order inherent in organizations and of relevance to management accounting. Organizations may be seen as a deliberate, rational arrangement of means to accomplish a desired end. Rules are established in order to regulate the organization's structure and processes. Finally, legal authority is used to coordinate all the elements of an organization in order to allow their efficient functioning. In response to these patterns, management accounting will focus on the legally prescribed structures and the mechanisms by which they are maintained. For example, control will focus on whether persons comply with organizational rules given that each person's actions are essential to the accomplishment of the organizational goals. Similarly, management accounting as a form of organizational behaviour will be consciously and rationally administered with the organizational goals in mind.

The Classical Perspective

The classical school originated with Frederick Taylor and his *"Principles of Scientific Management."* The concern was with insuring the most efficient utilization of the physical resources of the organization. Taylor's aim was to replace the arbitrary and capricious work of managers with analytical, scientific procedures: Under scientific management arbitrary power, arbitrary dictation, ceases and every single subject, large and small, becomes the question for scientific investigation, for reduction to law....The man at the head of the business under scientific management is governed by rules and laws which have been developed through hundreds of experiments just as much as the workman is, and the standards which have been developed are equitable. Scientific management was based on four main principles:

The development of an ideal or best method primarily through time and motion study. The selection and development of workers. The combination between the best method and the best selected and trained workers. The close cooperation of managers and workers. Taylor's approach led to major advances in industrial efficiency and influenced the works of Henry Gantt and Frank Gilbreth.

The main goal of scientific management is to use scientific methods to establish a standard for completing a job in the best manner.

The productive processes are concerned with the ratio of output to input, *the criterion of efficiency*. To accomplish these objectives, the work force is to be organized so that each person is assigned a standard for his or her highly specialized job, based on the most efficient method of completing the work and rewarded on the basis of task accomplishment.

From these objectives stem two basic characteristics of the organization. It is *work centered and authoritarian*. The central characteristic of an organization is work and, given that work is considered distasteful by some, authority is necessary for insuring the accomplishment of organizational objectives. Authority is centralized and flows from the owners to the board of directors to the workers. The authority of the president lies in POSDCORB. The acronym stands for Planning, Organizing, Staffing, Directing, Coordinating,

Reporting, and Budgeting. Work is specialized in units, leading to what is known as the departmentalized approach to the problem of management. These units are coordinated in a hierarchical structure.

The authority in each unit is defined by the "span of control" of each manager. All these characteristics reflect a facet of the traditional school known as "the principles of management" or "administrative management theory." Henri Fayol, in particular, viewed the principles of management as follows:

- Division of work
- Authority
- Discipline
- Unity of command
- Unity of direction
- Subordination of individual interests to the general interests
- Remuneration
- Centralization
- Scalar chain (line of authority)

- Order
- Equity
- Stability of tenure of personnel
- Initiative
- Esprit de corps

The classical school has also had its share of criticism. It has been labeled as normative rather than analytical. Like the Weberian model, it has ignored the impact of the external environment, the existence of internal conflict, and the behavioural idiosyncracies resulting from the different cognitive make-up of organization members.

Like the Weberian perspective, the classical perspective identifies elements approximating the patterning or order inherent in organizations and of relevance to management accounting. Organizations are viewed only as means in the pursuit of a specific end, defined as optimal organizational efficiency. The accomplishment of this objective lies in the arrangement of the employees and machines. This arrangement relies on scientific means of associating the best person and/or machine to the ideal job. It requires developing scientific standards rather than rules of thumb for each individual and each task.

The work of every workman is fully planned out by the management at least one day in advance, and each man received in most cases complete written instructions, describing in detail the task which he is to accomplish, as well as the means to be used in doing the work.

Briefly, the classical perspective rests on management accounting by calling for both planning and control: planning by the setting of rigid scientific standards for each job, and control by insuring the realization of *optimal organizational efficiency*. Let us note, however, that the classical perspective calls for planning and control primarily at the operative or worker level and is essentially shortrange and specific. What may then be learned and extrapolated from the classical perspective is the requirement of planning and control at all levels of management, short-term and long-term, toward the realization of the optimal organizational efficiency.

The Human Relations Perspective

As a counterpoint against the impersonality of classical theory, the human relations perspective emphasizes the human dimension of management. The major thrust of this perspective is that the dominant focus of organization was transformed from a rational model, free from the friction of man's emotions, to a model which appears to be less determined and unfathomable.

That is, the new look in organizational theory took cognizance of the unanticipated consequences of organizations: workers' feelings, beliefs, perceptions, ideas, and sentiments—exactly those elements of passion Weber believed escaped calculation. Administrators began to take seriously in part through the seminal work of several social scientists not only their formal organizational chart, but workers' feelings about the structure and hierarchy. This model of organization... took as its major assumption that man could be motivated to work more productively on the basis of fulfilling certain psychological needs. This "new look" of organization was no less rational than the earlier machine model, except that man's motivation was a tricker and more elusive concept than the machine.

The essence is to distinguish between the formal organization and the informal organization. The founders of the human relations school, proposed that the patterns of human interrelations, as defined by the systems, rules, policies, and regulations of the company, constitute the formal organization. It includes the systems, policies, rules, and regulations of the plant which express what the relations of one person to another are supposed to be in order to achieve effectively the task of technical production.

By contrast, the informal organization is described as follows: Many of the actually existing patterns of human interaction have no representation in the formal organization at all, and others are inadequately represented by the formal organization. Too often it is assumed that the organization of a company corresponds to a blueprint plan or organization chart. Actually, it never does.

This perspective started when Elton May and other Harvard University professors were invited to study new ways to increase plant productivity at the Hawthorne plant of the Western Electric Company. Known as the Hawthorne Studies, they showed that workers are complex social creatures with feelings, desires, and fears, and they react to change in terms of the meaning change has for them. What change meant to workers depended on their social conditioning (feelings, fears, hope, etc.) and their social situation at work where group pressures determined attitudes and sentiments. Other similar findings were included in *Management and the Worker*, the publication resulting from the Hawthorne experiment. This line of research was pursued through the empirical works of such theorists as Rensis Likert, Chris Argyris, and Douglas McGregor. What stems from the human relations perspective is that workers as social creatures are motivated by attitudes formed through interactions in the formal group rather than uniquely by economic factors.

Group norms act as a major regulatory tool, affecting member behaviour given that persons desire group acceptance. Thus, the organizations become essentially sets of interlocked functioning groups.

Likert suggests that these groups may be linked together to create a working organization where each individual will increase a sense of participation because each individual is more aware of the congruence between personal goals and the company's objectives. In fact, Likert advocated the use of the participative group type of management system as the most effective, rather than the exploitive-authoritative, benevolent-authoritative, and consultative systems. These characteristics of the human relations perspectives have great implications for management accounting. First, management accounting concepts and techniques, in general, and planning and control, in particular, have to take into account the individuals and what motivates them. "Each of us wants appreciation, recognition, influence, a feeling of accomplishment, and a feeling that people who are important to us believe in us and respects us." Second, it implies that workers should be involved in some participatory ways in the setting of standards. Preferably group norms should be considered in the setting of standards with an emphasis on cooperation rather than competition among group members.

The best performance, lower costs, and the highest level of earnings and of employee satisfaction occur when the drive for a sense of personal worth is used to create strong motivational forces to *cooperate* rather than *compete* with one's peers and colleagues.

The use of this motive in ways which yield cooperative rather than competitive relationships appears to yield stronger motivational forces oriented toward achieving the organizations' objectives and is accompanied by positive rather than negative side effects. Subordinates aid each other and share leadership tasks rather than putting immediate selfinterest ahead of long-range self-interest and organizational success. Third, performance reports used for control should not be limited to financial data and should be expanded to include a measure of the "organizational atmosphere" or climate that determines workers' productivity.

The Natural System Perspective

The natural system perspective views organizations as continually adapting to a changing environment in order to maintain equilibrium. Once created, the organizations acquire a life of their own and behave in unplanned and spontaneous or "natural" ways. This perspective is best illustrated in the works of three sociologists: Robert Michels, Talcott Parsons, and Philip Selznick.

For example, Selznick emphasizes "coaptation" as a predominant adaptive process of organization; that is, "the process of absorbing new elements in the leadership or policy-determining structure of an organization as one means of averting threats to its stability or existence." These continuous attempts at adapting to their environments lead the organizations to modify their basic structures and create a character or personality. The structure of an organization, therefore, is inseparable from the functioning of the organization. Viewed as a system, the organization stresses the interdependence of parts or subsystems.

These are:

- The productive subsystem responsible for the technical processes,
- The supportive subsystems responsible for the efficient flow of inputs in the organization and output of the organization,
- The maintenance subsystem responsible for the maintenance of the organization by recruiting and rewarding the members,
- The adaptive subsystem responsible for responding to the environmental changes, and
- The managerial subsystem responsible for directing and controlling all other subsystems.

The natural system perspective, like the other perspectives, identifies elements and characteristics of importance to management accounting. First, each organization acquires a given personality that will require specific management techniques different from those adopted by other organizations. "Every structure has a set of basic needs and develops systematic means of self-defence." Second, because the organization faces a given changing environment, it must change and adapt to the new environmental conditions requiring management accounting to be dynamic in the sense of continuously absorbing new elements and information into its reporting function, adapting old techniques, and adapting new techniques to avert threats to the stability or existence of the organization.

Third, the control process should rely on feed forward techniques that precipitate internal changes. Fourth, because the organization is a collection of systems, each trying to maintain its own equilibrium, management accounting should be designed to serve the subsystems and to maintain their autonomy. Deliberate changes can be made without affecting other subsystems, because each subsystem is part of an organic whole. Under the natural system perspective, management accounting adopts a structural-functional model of analysis that assumes that the organization, as a social unit, has needs and requirements to be met if it is to survive. Accordingly, information about salient changes in the environment of the firm must be produced and communicated by the management accounting system. Given that the structural elements of the firm are mutually interdependent, management accounting information should play the crucial role for these systems to tend toward a state of equilibrium.

ORGANIZATIONAL DESIGN

Toward a Contingency Model for the Design of Management Accounting

The contingency approach to the design of accounting systems assumes that a general strategy applicable to all organizations does not exist. On the contrary, it assumes that the design of various components of accounting systems depends on the specific contingencies that can create a perfect match. It is then the perfect link or match between the design of accounting systems and the specific contingencies that is the scope of contingency theory.

To date, the contingency formulations have considered the effects of technology, organizational structure and theory, and the environment in attempting to explain how accounting systems differ in various situations.

All of these formulations point to the accepted thesis that there is no universal "best design" for a management accounting information system, and that "it all depends upon situational factors." These formulations adopt a general framework depicted, which links

The formulations are either empirical or theoretical. The literature includes various theoretical speculations about the nature of a contingency theory of accounting-information systems and/or control systems. L. A. Gordon and D. A. Miller identified environment, organizational characteristics, and decision making styles as the main classes of contingent variables, similarly, J. H. Waterhouse and P. A. Tiessen proposed environment and technology. A more elaborate contextual model of information system, provided by N. B. Macintosh, combines both personal decision style and organizational technology to derive four distinct information-system styles—concise, cursory, diffuse, and elaborate—each of which is suited to a particular technology.

The four distinct information-system styles are defined as follows:

- Some contingent variables (that is, variables that cannot be influenced by the organization) to
- Any components of an organizational control package (consisting of accounting information design, other management information design, organizational design, or organizational control arrangements), and then through
- Some interviewing variables provide a link to
- A measure or organizational effectiveness.

The concise information system. Small to moderate amounts of information that is precise and unambiguous, and is used in a quick and decisive way.

The elaborate information system. Large amounts of information, frequently in the form of data bases or stimulation models, which tend to be detailed or precise; recipients normally use such information in a slow and deliberate manner. The cursory information system. Small amounts of information, neither precise nor detailed and frequently superficial, that is used in a casual yet decisive way.

The diffuse information system. Moderate to large amounts of information, covering a wide range of material, frequently ill-defined and imprecise, that typically is used in a slow, deliberate manner. All of these attempts at formulating a contingency theory of accounting information systems and/or control systems fail to provide a more exhaustive list of the main classes of contingent variables.

A summary of the structural features affecting accounting system design. A wide range of potentially influential factors is shown in these empirical studies. The most significant factors are technology, environment, size, strategy, and culture. The two most important factors of technology and the environment are reviewed next.

Impact of Technology

Technology includes not only machines and equipment but also all of the techniques used to transform materials in a prescribed manner. Harold Leavitt defined *technology* as direct problem-solving inventions like work-measurement techniques or computers or drill presses.

However, Charles Perrow defined technology as the "actions that an individual performs upon an object, with or without the aid of tools or mechanical devices, in order to make some change in that object." He saw as dimensions of technology both *variability*, which is the number of exceptional cases that must be handled in work, and *analyzability*, which is the nature of the search process that must be used when exceptions occur.

Various ways of classifying organizations in terms of their technology have been used. Most theories disagree with the Standard Industrial Classification System, which classifies firms on the basis of their primary function, and argue for a classification that conforms to the technical systems.

For example, the following three groupings:

- *Unit production*: Units or small batches produced to customer specifications
- *Mass production*: Making large batches of the product at one time
- *Continuous process*: A steady flow of inputs into a continuous process.

She also identified three aspects of organizational desi to structure, the findings indicated that structural characteristics of firms tended to vary from group to group. More explicitly, successful large-batch or mass production firms tended to be organized along classical lines, with duties and responsibilities clearly delineated, a unity of command, a clear distinction between line and staff, and a narrow span of control.

With respect to control mechanisms, the type of control found in the technical subsystem of an organization is directly related to the type of technology employed. Although unit technology puts an emphasis on personal controls, continuous-process technology focuses on impersonal controls, and mass-production technology relies on a mix of personal and impersonal controls.

With respect to information systems, the findings indicate that the impact of technology extends to the production tools that can alter the flow of material through the system. Of new interest to this book is the finding that technology plays a major role in dictating the type of control system that is feasible or practical.

More explicitly, it states that with routine and repetitive production recesses, task uncertainty is relatively low, and organizational coordination requires only programmed interactions; also, impersonal controls in the form of budgeting and accounting-performance measures are easier to use.

Impact of the Environment

The type of control system is generally developed as a response to the environment. In effect, the external environment is the societal context for the organization and its members. D. Silverman, for example, perceived it as the source of meaning, providing the stock of knowledge in guiding the behaviour of the organization and its members.

The impact of the environment on control has been examined by various researchers. E. G. Flamholtz identified three broad classes of environmental factors likely to be potential mechanisms of control on the behaviour of organizational members: the dominant work values in the temporal social setting, the level of professionalism, and direct demands from clients and customers.

Hence there is an emerging need for active involvement and increased responsibility, professionalism is growing in many occupations, and the demand for quality service or products from customers and clients may act as potential mechanisms of control. Organizations are "hiring purposeful" or "adaptively rational" systems whose survival depends on their ability to interact successfully, on a continuous basis, with the surrounding environment.

Based on that assumption Kweka Ewusi-Mensah identified three states of the external organizational environment controllable, partially controllable, and uncontrollable and discussed the information characteris-tics of each state.

The environments are characterized by mostly homogeneous factors in the controllable state, both homogeneous and heterogeneous factors in the partially controllable state, and uncertainties with respect to events and changes in the environment in the uncontrollable state.

The external organizational environment may also be classified as static or dynamic. This last classification depends on the degree of stability in the environmental factors. The static environment can be characterized by a high level of stability, calling for the use of formalized procedures for dealing with environmental factors or elements.

The dynamic environment can be characterized by "an increasing rate of interconnection and/or interaction among environmental factors, resulting in a higher degree of uncertainty and complexity" and calling for the use of sophisticated strategies for monitoring the environment to collect pertinent data.

Both classifications of the external environment (static or dynamic; controllable, partially controllable, or uncontroll-able) may be combined to describe the total external organizational environment, with the relevant characteristics identified in each cell. Each of the cells calls for an appropriate control system and different information characteristics.

Different types of competition may lead to a different use of management controls. Basically, the greater the competition, the greater the need to control costs and to evaluate production, marketing, finance, and so on as operating according to expectations.

One of the implications follows:

- This implies that as competition intensifies, the expected benefits from the application of these controls tend to outweigh their costs.
- Thus, for those entrusted with the planning of control systems, it is important to know the degree of competition faced by the firm.
- Other things being equal, an elaborate control system for a firm not facing serious competition can produce net benefits, but a sophisticated control system in a firm which does not face intense competition may do more harm than good.

Models of sectorial economic differentiation derived from theories of economic dualism include various perspectives such as theories of dual economy, dual labour markets, and labour-force segmentation, Common to all of these perspectives is the proposal of a division of the industrial structure of the economy into two distinct sectors (at least in the two-sector model), consisting of the core and periphery sectors.

Theories of dual economy suggest that these sector differences have important implications for the opportunity structures and environment faced by individual firms. Firms in the periphery sector face a more restricted opportunity structure and a higher degree of environmental uncertainty than firms in the core sector.

Therefore, firms in the periphery sector may need a more complex and exhaustive management accounting system than firms in the core sector. The implications of the line/staff relationships, and the new role of controllers—provide management accounting with different organizational concepts that define and shape some of its techniques and approaches.

BEHAVIOURAL FOUNDATION

Management accounting is built on behavioural foundations. Its explicit aim is to affect the behaviour of individuals in a desirable direction. To accomplish this purpose, management accounting has to be adapted to the different characteristics that shape the "cognitive make-up" of individuals within an organization and affect their performance.

In general, these characteristics pertain to three factors:

- The perception by the individual of what should be the objective function or goals in the firm;
- The various factors likely to motivate the individual to perform; and
- The decision-making model most relevant to particular contexts and most preferred by the individual. Although these factors do not constitute an exhaustive list of the behavioural concepts likely to affect the performance of an individual within an organization, they have been identified in the literature of various disciplines as essential factors to be considered for an understanding of an individual behaviour within an organization and the design of any information system.

Thus, management accounting requires a good grasp of the behavioural concepts; namely, the objective function in management accounting, motivation theories, and models of decision making. Each of these concepts identifies factors and situations that influence the individual behaviour and indicates avenues for management accounting to adapt its services.

FUNCTION IN MANABGEMENT ACCOUNTING

Many authors in the field of complex organizations define an organization as a social system that is created to achieve certain specific goals or objectives. For example, Amitai Etzioni defines organizations as "social units (or human groupings) deliberately constructed and reconstructed to seek specific goals."

Richard Hall states: An organization is a collectivity with a relatively identifiable boundary, a normative order, authority ranks, community systems, and membership coordinating systems; this collectivity exists on a relatively continuous basis in an environment and engages in activities that are usually related to a goal or a set of goals.

The concept of organizational goal and/or objective has not, however, been clearly defined in the literature. The general goals refer to the intentions or wishes espoused by those persons who develop them.

It is the decision to commit resources for certain activities and to withhold them from certain others that operationally defines the organization's goals. Verbal pronouncements are insufficient for defining goals; the speaker must put his resources where his mouth is if something is to be considered a goal.

Different typologies of goals have also been proposed. First, J. D. Thompson differentiated between goals held for an organization and goals of an organization. The former are held by persons who are not members of the organization but have a given interest in the activities of the firm, such as clientele, investors, action groups, and so on. The latter are held by persons who are part of the "dominant coalition" in terms of holding enough control to commit the organization to a given direction.

Each discipline conceives a different goal or objective in its examination of profit-oriented organizations. The discipline of economics, for example, in its neoclassical approach views profit maximization as the single determinant of behaviour. In management accounting, as in corporate finance, neither the economic model nor the behavioural model appears entirely suitable. In fact, both models have influenced three held views of business behaviour applicable to management accounting: the shareholder wealth maximization model, the managerial welfare maximization model, and the social welfare maximization model. Each of these models constitutes an acceptable objective of profit-oriented organizations in the field of management accounting. Because the scope and practice of management accounting is heavily influenced by these assumptions, each of them will be examined next.

The Shareholder Wealth Maximization Model

In most textbooks in the field of corporate finance and specifically in management accounting, authors operate on the assumption that management's primary goal is to maximize the wealth of its stockholders. This view is referred to as the shareholder wealth maximization (SWM) model. According to this model, the firm accepts all projects yielding more than the cost of capital, and in equity financing prefers retaining earnings to issuing new stocks. It also assumes that earnings are objectively determined to show the true financial position of the firm to its owners and other users. In fact, the SWM model translates into maximizing the price of the common stock.

Management is assumed to use decision rules and techniques that are in the best interests of the stockholders. In a management accounting context, SWM implies an acceptance by management of budgeting and control standards, a rejection of slack budgeting, any sub-optimizing behaviour, and an adoption of management accounting techniques that are in the best interests of the owners of the firm. If management behaves otherwise, its right to manage may be either questioned or revoked, given that stockholders own the firm and elect the management team. E. Solomon made a similar suggestion as follows:

But what if management has other motives, such as maximizing sales or size, growth or market share, or their own survival, or peace of mind? These operating goals do not necessarily conflict with the operating goal of wealth maximization. Indeed, a good case could be made for the thesis that wealth maximization also maximizes the achievement of these other objectives. But the point of issue is what if there is a conflict? What, for example, if management's quest for its own peace of mind or for some other goal consistently leads it to reject operating decisions that should be accepted by the wealth-maximizing criterion? The traditional answer is that such a management will be replaced sooner or later, and this is the only answer possible. Legally, management governs only as the appointed representatives of the owners. It may reject over-all goals so long as it substitutes goals which are designed to promote that of society as a whole. But if it rejects owner-oriented goals and socially-oriented goals in favour of goals that are solely management-oriented and which lead to substantially different courses of action, its right to govern is open to question.

Managerial Welfare Maximization Model

Another school of thought maintains that a different objective function other than shareholder wealth maximization exists for the firm—namely, that managers run firms for their own benefits. It is maintained that because the stock of most large firms is widely held, the managers of such firms have a great deal of freedom. This being the case, they may be tempted for personal benefits to pursue an objective other than shareholder welfare maximization.

This school of thought is generally referred to as the managerial welfare maximization (MWM) model. So rather than maximizing profits, the managers may maximize sales or assets, the rate of growth, or managerial utility. As a consequence, managers may engage in sub-optimization schemes as long as they contribute to their own welfare. For example, an entrenched management may avoid risky ventures even though the returns to stockholders would be high enough to justify the endeavor.

In a management accounting context, MWM implies a lesser acceptance by management of budgeting and control standards, a recourse to slack budgeting and any sub-optimization behaviour, a manipulation or avoidance within legality of full disclosure in order to present the firm's operation favorably (i.e., income smoothing), and, finally, adoption of management accounting techniques that are in the best interest of managers.

In a recent survey, B. Branch concludes as follows:

The evidence to date may be summarized as follows. Many managers have considerable discretion to substitute their own interests for that of the stockholders. Stockholder and manager interests can conflict or be independent in significant respects. The extent to which firms are managed in stockholder interests vary considerably. Most of the empirical work suggests that firms managed in stockholders' interests tend in some sense to outperform management-oriented firms.

That managers may elect to substitute their own different interests raises the question of how goals within MWM are "determined" or "set" in decisions to commit the organization to a particular course of action.

Three distinct models have been identified to represent the goalsetting processes: the bargaining model, the problem-solving model, and the coalition model. Because they present good conceptualizations of the goal determination process under MWM.

The Bargaining Model

The bargaining model depicts goal determination as the result of an open-minded negotiation process among all interested parties leading to a series of trade-offs and compromises.

It is based on three important assumptions:

- There is an active group of participants (internal or external) who impose demands on the organization.
- These demands are conflicting; they cannot be accommodated simultaneously.
- The individuals or groups are interdependent.

The Problem-Solving Model

The problem-solving model describes goal determination as the result of successive decisions made by high level administrators.

It is based on three important assumptions:

- Policy commitments are made within a set of constraints or requirements that are known to decision makers.
- These constraints can be ranked and a preferred set accommodated.
- The goals of different individuals or groups can be simultaneously satisfied.

The Dominant Coalition Model

Given the existence of controlling interests in the firm, the dominant coalition model describes goal determination as the result of decisions made by those who control the ends to which policies and resources are committed.

It is based on two assumptions:

- There are many persons or groups who hold goals for an organization. These goals are frequently in conflict and cannot all be accommodated.
- One individual or group does not have sufficient power alone to act unilaterally. Power is dispersed. Collective behaviour is required to secure support for goals.

The Social Welfare Maximization Model

The climate in which businesses operate is changing with pressures on organizations to be more sensitive to the impact of behaviour on society. In adopting a more socially responsible attitude and responding to the pressures of new dimensions social, human, and environmental organiza-tions may have to alter their main objective, whether SWM or MWM, to include as an additional constraint the welfare of society at large. This view may be referred to as the social welfare maximization (SOWM) model.

Thus, under SOWM the firm is not only liable to the shareholders and managers, but also to the society at large. Given the different interest groups in the society at large, the organization may have to develop different corporate purposes.

For example, it was reported that one group has defined eight corporate purposes: "profit, sensitivity to natural and human environment, growth, responsiveness to consumer needs, equitable distributions of benefits, dynamic business structure, fair treatment of employees, and legal and ethical behaviour." In a management accounting context, SOWM implies the developing of a social reporting system oriented toward the measurement of social performance, including not only social costs but also social benefits. It suggests the development of a new concept of organization performance that will be more indicative of the firm's social responsibility than is provided by conventional accounting. For example, the AAA Committee on Measurement of Social Cost suggested a total organization performance, which is a function of "five outputs":

- Net income, which benefits stockholders and provides resources for further business growth
- Human resource contribution, which assists the individual in the organization to develop new knowledge or skills
- Public contribution, which helps the organization's community to function and provides services for its constituency
- Environmental contribution (closely allied with public contribution), which affects "quality of life" for society
- Product or service contribution, which affects customer well-being and satisfaction

While a theory of social accounting is still emerging in the new public interest accounting paradigm, the proposed objectives and concepts for social accounting offer an interesting beginning.

However, regardless of the objective function adopted by managers, social reporting and particularly social reports are needed by management for relevant decision making and to comply with both social pressures and legal requirements.

MOTIVATION THEORIES

Motivation is related to the intrinsic forces within the individual—namely, the motives and unsatisfied needs of the individual. More explicitly, motivation is concerned with "how behaviour gets started, is energized, is sustained, is directed, is stopped, and what kind of subjective reaction is presented in the organization while all this is going on." For this reason, motivation is important for an organization and for management accounting.

It basically refers to an individual's needs or motives that make that individual act in a specific manner. It relates all aspects of individual behaviour where a deliberate and conscious action is initiated in the organization to direct individuals so that they can satisfy their needs as much as possible while they strive to accomplish the objectives of the organization.

These actions may be initiated either directly by the managers' actions or through the adoption of appropriate management accounting techniques. Thus, management accounting techniques necessitate a good grasp of motivation in organizations.

The identification of the factors and situations that may influence and coordinate employee action allows the management accountant to adapt the services to offer to the realities of human behaviour.

The literature on motivation identifies five theories of motivation: the need theory, the two-factor theory, the value/ expectancy theory, the achievement theory, and the inequity theory.

Each of these theories identifies what factors within the individual and his or her environment activate high performance, or attempts to explain and describe the process of how behaviour is activated, what directs it, and how it is controlled and stopped. Let us examine each of these theories of motivation and their implications for management accounting.

Theory

Originally advanced by Abraham Maslow, need theory holds that people are motivated to satisfy a "hierarchy" of needs. These needs are as follows (in ascending order of prepotency):

Objectives and Concepts

Objective 1

An objective of corporate social accounting is to identify and measure the periodic net social contribution of an individual firm, which includes not only the costs and benefits internalized to the firm, but also those arising from externalities affecting different social segments.

Objective 2

An objective of corporate social accounting is to help determine whether an individual firm's strategies and practices which directly affect the relative resource and power status of individuals, communities, social segments and generations are consistent with widely shared social priorities, on the one hand, and individuals' legitimate aspirations, on the other.

Objective 3

An objective of corporate social accounting is to make available in an optimal manner, to all social constituents, relevant information on a firm's goals, policies, programmes, performance and contributions to social goals.

Relevant information is that which provides for public accountability and also facilitates public decision making regarding social choices and social resource allocation.

Optimality implies a cost/benefit-effective reporting strategy which also optimally balances potential information conflicts among the various social constituents of a firm.

Concept 1

A *social transaction* represents a firm's utilization or delivery of a socioenvironmen- tal resource which affects the absolute or relative interests of the firm's various social constituents and which is not processed through the market place.

Concept 2

Social overheads (returns) represent the sacrifice (benefit) to society from those resources consumed (added) by a firm as a result of its social transactions. In other words, social overheads is the measured value of a firm's negative externalities, and social returns is the measured value of its positive externalities.

Concept 3

Social income represents the periodic net social contribution of a firm. It is com- puted as the algebraic sum of the firm's traditionally measured net income, its aggregate social overheads and its aggregate social returns.

Concept 4

Social constituents are the different distinct social groups (implied in the second objective and expressed in the third objective of social accounting) with whom a firm is presumed to have a social contract.

Concept 5

Social equity is a measure of the aggregate changes in the claims which each social constituent is presumed to have in the firm.

Concept 6

Net social asset of a firm is a measure of its aggregate nonmarket contribution to the society's well being less its nonmarket depletion of the society's resources during the life of the firm.

- The physiological needs: food, shelter, warmth, and other bodily wants.
- The safety needs: security and protection.
- The need for love and belongingness: desire to both give and receive love and friendship.
- The need for esteem: self-respect and the respect of others.
- The self-actualization need: "What a man can be, he must be."

Thus, individuals strive to satisfy these needs in a sequential fashion, starting with the physiological needs. The process of deprivation-dominationgratification-activation continues until the self-actualization need has been activated. This suggests that once the basic physiological and safety needs are satisfied, individuals will respond better to rewards leading to self-respect and self-actualization than to economic rewards, which are primarily related to the satisfaction of lower-level needs.

What this implies for management accounting is that assuming individuals in the organization are well paid, the emphasis should be on the introduction of management accounting techniques, in general, and control techniques, in particular, that are consistent with the satisfaction of higher-level needs.

This view is also shared by E. H. Caplan when he states that "it may be more important to concentrate on the development of organizational structures, leadership practices, and control systems which are consistent with satisfaction of the higher level needs."

Two-Factor Theory

In a series of studies, F. Herzberg and his associates developed the "motivation hygiene" theory. Briefly, they found two factors affecting a job situation, which they labeled *satisfiers* and *dissatisfiers*. The satisfiers were related to the nature of the work itself and to rewards that flowed directly from the performance of that work:

- Perceived opportunity for achievement on the job,
- Recognition,
- A sense of performing interesting and important work,
- Responsibility, and
- Advancement. The dissatisfiers were related to the context rather than the content of the job:
- Company policies that foster ineffectiveness,
- Incompetent supervision,
- Interpersonal relations,
- Working conditions,
- Salaries,
- Status, and
- Job security. The satisfiers were classified as "motivators" and the dissatisfiers as "hygiene" factors.

According to Herzberg, the satisfiers contribute very little to job dissatisfaction; and conversely, the dissatisfiers contribute very little to job satisfaction. Similarly, motivation to work is created by the satisfaction of the individual's needs for the satisfiers and not from an elimination of the dissatisfiers. The implications of Herzberg's theory for management accounting are twofold.

First, to contribute to the motivation of employees, management accounting techniques should focus on better measurement and reporting of achievement, recognition, work, responsibility, and advancement. Second, given that the key to motivation is to make jobs more meaningful, management accounting techniques should focus on job enrichment. Job enrichment is the attempt by managers to design tasks in such a way as to affect employees' positive feelings about their job and to build in the opportunity for personal achievement, recognition, challenge, and personal growth. It gives the employees a greater amount of responsibility in carrying out complete tasks and insures a timely feedback on their performance. Martin Evans suggests several steps to insure job enrichment of relevance to management accounting:

- Eliminating controls from the job while keeping accountability.
- Increasing the individual's accountability for his or her job.
- Providing each individual with a complete and natural work module (or elements of work).
- Allowing greater job freedom for an individual's own work.
- Providing timely feedbacks on performance to the employee instead of the supervisor.
- Improving old tasks and introducing new tasks.
- Assigning specific tasks so the employee can develop expertise in performing them.

Value/Expectancy Theory

The theories of Maslow, McClelland, and Herzberg are

content theories in the sense that they attempt to identify what factors within the individual and the individual's environment induce high performance. The value/expectancy theory is a process theory in the sense that it attempts to explain and describe the process of how behaviour is initiated, maintained, and terminated. Originally developed by K. Lewin, and later specially applied to motivation to work by V. H. Vroom, the basic tenet of the value/expectancy theory is that an individual chooses personal behaviour on the basis of:

- Expectations that such behaviour will result in a specific outcome, and
- The sum of the valences—that is, personal utilities or rewards, derived from the outcome. Vroom advances the following theoretical proposition:

The force on a person (motive) to perform a given act is based on the weighted value (or utility) of all the possible outcomes of the act multiplied by the perceived usefulness of the given act in the attainment of these outcomes. Whenever an individual chooses between alternatives that involve certain outcomes, it seems clear that his behaviour is affected not only by his preferences among outcomes, but also by the degree to which he believes these outcomes to be probable.

Hence, an individual's motivation may be expressed as:

$$M = S[(E®O)\ (V)]$$

where,

E = Effort

O = Outcome

V = Values placed on the outcome

The above expression may be reformulated to include both an effortperformance linkage and a performance-reward linkage. The new model will include two expectancies. The first one refers to the probability that the effort will lead to a task accomplished or performance. The second one refers to the probability that the accomplishment will result in the desired outcomes. hence, the individual's motivation may be expressed as:

$$M = (E \rightarrow P)]S\ [(P \rightarrow O)\ (V)]$$

where,
P = Performance

L. W. Porter and E. E. Lawler have extended the value/expectancy theory by arguing that poor performance may result if abilities are lacking and the individual's role perceptions are erroneous. Thus, for preferences and expectations to affect performance, adequate ability and accurate role perceptions are necessary.

This formulation shows some of the implications of expectancy theory for management accounting. Appropriate management accounting techniques may be chosen to affect the independent variables of the model in the following ways:

- By determining what extrinsic rewards ($EV_{i)}$ follow work-goal accomplishment.
- By increasing through timely reports the individual's expectancy ($P_{2)}$ that work-goal accomplishment leads to extrinsic rewards.
- By increasing the intrinsic valence associated with work-goal accomplishment ($IV_{a)}$ through a greater role of the individual in goal-setting and task-directed effort.
- By recognizing and supporting the individual's effort thereby influencing P_i.
- By increasing the net intrinsic valences associated with goal-directed behaviour ($IV_{b)}$.

Achievement Theory

The concept of "achievement motive" was first introduced by McClelland, Atkinson, and their associates. It is based on the desire of people to be challenged and to be innovative and adopt an '"achievement-oriented behaviour"-that is, a behaviour directed toward meeting a standard of excellence.

The achievement-oriented individual likes to assume responsibility for individual achievement, seeks challenging tasks, and takes calculated risks depending on the probabilities of success. Therefore, he will take small risks for tasks serving as stepping stones for future rewards, take intermediate risks for tasks offering opportunities for achievement, and will attempt to find situations falling somewhere between the two extremes, providing the highest probability of success, and hence maximizing his sense of personal achievement.

According to the theory, the individuals will particularly behave in an achievement-oriented way in situations that enable them to strive for a standard of excellence, require the use of skills, present a challenge, and allow the individuals to appraise their performance.

Another important contention of the theory is that all motives are learned, including the achievement motive. As a result, the high achiever is experienced in making maximizing decisions, is less affected by anxiety, and proceeds in an efficient way in any endeavor.

What these contentions imply for management accounting is:

- The necessity of constructing ways of developing the achievement motive at all managerial levels, and
- The need to introduce management accounting techniques and to report management accounting information that encourages and facilitates the performance of high achievers.

Inequity Theory

Elaine Walster, Stacey Adams, and their colleagues have advanced that individuals in a relationship have two motives: to maximize their own gains and to maintain equity in the relationship. Inequity results when a person's rewards from a relationship are not proportional to what that person has put in the relationship. More explicitly, inequity theory is based on the premise that when individuals compare their own situations with other situations and have a feeling of inequity, in terms of feeling either under rewarded or over rewarded for their contributions, they experience increased tension and strive to reduce it. Hence, overpaid workers will increase their efforts by producing more as a way of reducing inequity, while underpaid workers will produce less to achieve a contribution-reward balance.

Other methods of restoring equity may be used also. Walster et al. state that individuals can restore actual equity by altering either their own payoffs or those of other participants. Similarly, a psychological equity can be restored when individuals change their perceptions of either rewards or contributions so that their contributions appear greater or lower than originally thought. They may also restore equity by quitting their jobs, severing relationships with comparison persons, or by forcing comparison persons to leave the field.

The inequity theory suggests, then, that rewards must appear to the employees to be fair or equitable. An appeal to equity norms can be used to reduce conflict. The role of management accounting in restoring equity is in insuring correct and accurate measurement and reporting of performance and the corresponding rewards. To avoid creating feelings of inequity, the methods of measuring performance and rewards should be made public to the employees.

MODELS OF DECISION MAKING

The identification of the decision-making models most relevant to particular contexts and most preferred by particular individuals allows the management accountant to adapt the services to offer to the realities of the decision situation. The literature on decision making identifies five main perspectives: the "rational" manager view, the "satisficing" process-oriented view, the organizational procedures view, the political view, and the individual differences perspective.

Before analyzing each of these models, it is appropriate to mention the excellent analysis of the Cuban missile crisis by G. T. Allison using three of these models: the rational actor view, the organizational procedures view, and the political view. Addressing the central issues of the crisis from one of the three perspectives "lead [s] one to see, emphasize, and worry about quite different aspects of events." By analogy, addressing management issues from any of the five perspectives leads one to have different perceptions and understanding of events and place on the management accountant different demands for services. Let us examine each of these models and its importance to management accounting.

The Rational View

The rational view of decision making is a normative model that refers to a consistent value-maximizing choice process in the presence of specific constraints.

This process may be summarized as follows:

- Individuals assume that there is a set of alternative acts or courses of action displayed before them in a particular situation.
- They associate a set of possible outcomes or consequences with the set of possible acts.
- They have a preference ordering over the consequences or payoff function that allows them to rank the consequences and select that act which ranks highest in their payoff function.

This view is used and relied upon as the model of the "economic man" in neoclassical economic theory and as the model of the "rational man" in game theory and statistical decision theory. Both make optimal choices in the presence of well-defined specific constraints.

As a defence of the rational view of decision making, one of the two assumptions has been made. On the one hand, there is the assumption of comprehensive rationality where individuals have perfect knowledge of all alternative acts, all the consequences, and the corresponding payoff function. On the other hand, there is the assumption of limited rationality with its inherent restricted claim on "optimal choice." Whatever the assumptions, the rational view of decision making requires the management accountant to define all the possibilities in terms of acts, consequences, and payoff function, and to evaluate the costs and benefits associated with rational decision making.

The rational view of decision making, although normative and rigorous, has been criticized as being descriptively unrealistic. H. A. Simon, in particular, advanced the principle of bounded rationality of the human decision maker:

When the limits to rationality are viewed from the individual's standpoint, they fall into three categories: he is limited by his values and conceptions of purpose, which may diverge from the organizational goals; he is limited by the extent of his knowledge and information. The individual can be rational in terms of the organization's goals only to the extent that he is able to pursue a particular course of action, he has a correct conception of the goal of the action, and he is correctly informed about the conditions surrounding his action. Within the boundaries laid down by these factors, his choices are rationalgoal oriented.

In replacement of the "economic man," Simon suggests the notion of the "administrative" or "satisficing" man as more representative of what is in decision making.

Satisficing and Process-Oriented View

The satisficing and process-oriented view of decision making is a descriptive model that maintains that the administrative individual satisfices rather than optimizes when making most decisions. Thus, rather than searching the haystack for the sharpest needle, the objective of the administrative man is to find one sharp enough to sew with. Simon summarizes the assumptions of the satisficer's theory as follows:

In actual organizational practice, no one attempts to find an optimal solution for the whole problem. Instead, various particular decisions, or groups of decisions, within the whole complex are made by specialized members or units of the organization. In making these particular decisions, the specialized units do not solve the whole problem but find a "satisfactory" solution for one or more sub-problems, where some of the effects of the solution on other parts of the system are incorporated in the definition of "satisfactory."

Thus, the satisficing man makes a decision-making choice in the context of a simplified view of the real situation. Simon introduces a concept of "subjective rationality" as a challenge to the concept of "objective rationality" advocated by the rational view of decision making. Subjective rationality depends on the individual's personal values. Thus, an objectively rational decision calls for a maximizing behaviour given values in a specific situation, while a subjectively rational decision calls for maximizing attainment relative to the actual knowledge of the individual. To be able to satisfice, the individual's strategies will consist essentially of heuristics or rules of thumb that meet a subjective minimum standard with respect to the things being sought.

That managers satisfice rather than optimize, refer to subjective rather than objective rationality, and rely on their heuristics places distinctive demands on the management accountant. To be able to service managers and facilitate their decision-making process, an understanding of their heuristics is essential. It is not an insurmountable task, given the general evidence suggesting how simple and how few are the heuristics used by managers. It also implies a good working relationship between managers and management accountants.

Organizational Procedures View

The organizational procedures view of decision making is a descriptive model that maintains that individuals comply with an act according to a fixed set of standard operating procedures and programmes. They make their choice in terms of goals and on the basis of expectations. The organization as a coalition of individuals with different demands, priorities, goals, focus of attention, and competencies. Decision making within the organization requires bargaining among the coalition members, resulting in de facto agreements and standard procedures for dealing with problematic situations.

Thus, individuals will act according to standard patterns of behaviour established in their particular organizational unit to achieve its stated goals.

What results in the organization is:

- A permanent goal conflict between the units with possibly the dominant coalition imposing its independent constraints,

- A quasi resolution of conflict marked by a sequential attention to problems,
- Uncertainty avoidance,
- Problematic search where the search is triggered by a specific problem and motivated to finding a solution to the problem, and
- Organizational learning leading to changes in goals, expectations, and standard procedures.

This process-oriented view of decision making has been applied with some success to simulate the working of a retail department store by Cyert and March, the trust investment process used by officers in a bank by G. E. Clarkson, and the behaviour of government units in municipal budgeting by John Crecine, and the foreign investment decision process of businesses by Lair Aharoni.

That managers may belong to coalitions that rely on programmes and standard procedures places distinctive demands on management accountants. These coalitions and their standard procedures should be identified by management accountants to be able to service managers and facilitate their decision making. This implies that management accountants must be careful not to be identified with any of these coalitions, but as support agents providing the necessary information for an efficient resolution of problems. Following P. R. Lawrence and J. W. Lorsch's appeal for a balance between integration and differentiation within complex organizations, management accountants may act as integrating agents between the subunits of the organization.

The Political View

The political view of decision making is a descriptive model that maintains that decisions are due partly to political processes. In this process, different groups committed to different courses of action interact and arrive at decisions through the "pulling and hauling that is politics." The differences between this view and the rational and process views are summarized by Allison as follows: "what moves the chess pieces is not simply the reasons that support a course of action or the routines of organizations that enact an alternative but the power and skill of proponents and opponents of the action in itself."

Thus, each individual in the firm is a player in a competitive game called politics, where persuasion, accommodation, bargaining, and the constant search for support are the determinants of decision making. This may be justified because managers [government leaders] have competitive, not homogeneous interests; priorities and perceptions are shaped by positions; problems are much more varied than straightforward strategic issues; management of piecemeal streams of decisions is more important than steady-state choices; making sure that management [the government] does what is decided is more difficult than selecting the preferred solution.

This political view resulted in the concept of incremental change advanced mainly by C. W. Lindblom. According to this view, labeled as "the art of the possible," managers attack rather than solve problems incrementally through "successive limited comparisons."That managers may be motivated by political positions and disagree with other political positions in the firm, that they may favour managing through incremental muddling rather than comprehensive, satisfactory, or procedural choice is very relevant for the management accountant and should not be ignored. The acceptance and use of either management accounting techniques or information suggested by the management accountant is very much a function of the political dimensions existing in the firm.

The Individual Differences View

The individual differences view maintains that individuals have specific decision-making styles appropriate for some cases and less so for others. This view emerged from the recognition in psychology of the concept of cognitive style as a hypothetical construct to explain the mediation process between stimuli and responses.

Five approaches have been reported for the study of

cognitive style: authoritarianism, dogmatism, cognitive complexity, integrative complexity, and field dependence.

- Authoritarianism arose from the focus by T. W. Adorno et al. on the relationship between personality, antidemocratic attitudes, and behaviour. They were primarily interested in individuals whose way of thinking made them susceptible to antidemocratic propaganda. Two of the behavioural correlates of authoritarianism—rigidity and intolerance of ambiguity—were reflections of an underlying cognitive style. For example, J. Dermer investigated the relationship between intolerance of ambiguity and subjective cue usage. His result showed a significant positive correlation between intolerance of ambiguity and the amount of information perceived to be important.
- Dogmatism arose from M. Rokeach's efforts to develop a structurally based measure of authoritarianism to replace the content-based measure developed by Adorno and his colleagues. His interest was in developing a measure of cognitive style that would be independent of the content of thought.
- Cognitive complexity as introduced by G. A. Kelly and J. Bieri et al. focuses on the psychological dimensions that individuals use to structure their environments and to differentiate the behaviour of others. The more cognitively complex individuals are assumed to have a greater number of dimensions available with which to construe the behaviour of others than the less cognitively complex persons. Another clarification of decision makers in the literature is made in terms of two cognitive styles: heuristic and analytic. Based on terms and meanings used by Jan Huysmans, they may be defined as follows: Analytic decision makers reduce problem situations to a more or less explicit, often quantitative, model as a basis for their decision. Heuristic decision makers refer instead to common sense, intuition, and

unquantified feelings about future development as they apply to the totality of the situation as an organic whole rather than as built from clearly identifiable parts.

Huysmans's findings show particularly that cognitive style may operate as an effective constraint on the implementation of operations research recommendations, and that operations researchers perceive their own analytic style as self-evident and tend to ignore the impact of cognitive style on the acceptance and use of analytic techniques. Similarly, in an experimental study of the relationship between different information structures, decision approaches, and learning patterns, T. Mock, T. Estrin, and M. Vasarhelyi found that analytics significantly outperformed heuristics in terms of profit and decision time.

- Integrative complexity as presented by O. J. Harvey et al., and later expanded by H. M. Schroder et al., results from the view that people engage in two activities in processing sensory input: differentiation and integration. Differentiation refers to the individual's ability to place stimuli along dimensions. Integration refers to the individual's ability to employ complex rules to combine these dimensions. Then a person low on both activities is said to be concrete, while a person high on both activities is said to be abstract. The continuum from concrete to abstract is referred to as an integrative or conceptual complexity. To the concept of integrative complexity is usually added the concept of environmental complexity and the level of information processing. It is expressed by the "U-Curve Hypothesis". As the level of information processing increases and reaches a maximum level at an optimal level of environmental complexity beyond which it begins to decrease. H. M. Schroder et al. extended the concept of the inverted U-shaped curve to the study of integrative complexity. The differences between the concrete and the abstract individual. The more abstract the individual, the higher the maximum level of infor-mation processing.

- Finally, field dependence as presented by H. A. Witkin and his associates is a measure of the extent of differentiation in the area of perception. Field-dependent individuals tend to perceive the overall organization of a field and are relatively unable to perceive parts of the field as discrete. Field-independent individuals, however, tend to perceive parts of the field as discrete from organized parts rather than fused with it.

That managers have specific cognitive styles in terms of authoritarianism, dogmatism, cognitive complexity, integrative complexity, and field dependence, which give them specific styles of decision making, has strong implications for management accounting. First, management accounting reports should be compatible with the cognitive structures of its users.

They should be designed on the basis of realistic assumptions about the users' decision styles. Second, the utilization and the acceptance of management accounting techniques and information depend on their suitability to the cognitive style of the users. Thus, management accountants should be aware of the cognitive style constraint in the implementation of management accounting. Quantitative-based management accounting techniques may be more attractive to the analytic rather than the heuristic decision makers. Finally, the analytic management accountants should not assume that all users are and should be like themselves.

HEURISTICS AND BIASES

Research in behavioural decision theory suggests that individuals seem to employ heuristics and biases in order to reduce complete cognitive processes to simpler judgmental obligations that are more manageable. Research in behavioural accounting has tried to verify the existence of these heuristics and biases in judgments in an accounting setting. To date, this type of research has examined the following heuristics: representativeness, availability, confirmation bias, anchoring and adjustment, the conjunction fallacy, hindsight bias, illusory correlation, and the Weber-Fechner law. That managers resort to these heuristics in making professional and business judgments also has strong implications for management accounting. Management accountants have to take these heuristics into account when devising the content and format of management accounting reports. To understand the differences in information needs, the various types of heuristics are explicated.

Representativeness

A frequent heuristic in probability assessment appears to be representativeness. "A person who follows this heuristic evaluates the probability of an uncertain event, or a sample, by the degree to which it is: (i) similar in essential properties to its parent population; and (ii) reflects the salient features of the process by which it is generated." According to this heuristic, a person will estimate the probability that subject A belongs to class B by the extent to which A resembles B. This heuristic, where class membership is assessed by the degree of its similarity to a stereotypical class member, has been found to lead to the following systematic biases in probability estimation:

- Insensitivity to prior probability or base rate
- Insensitivity to the impact of sample size on the variance of the sampling distribution
- Misperception of the likelihood of different sequences resulting from a random process
- Insensitivity to the predictability of data

The neglect of the base rate was investigated a number of times, varying base rates, problem content, information order, and response mode. The results confirmed the findings that base rates were ignored. When other experiments were used within subject experimental designs rather than between subjects, the findings showed that base rates were not ignored, in the sense that the subjects modified their judgments in the appropriate direction as the base rate was changed. Where the base rate was neglected, it was attributed to the fact that people lacked good schemata for working with probabilistic information, and the "abstract, pallid, and remote" nature of the base rate contrasted to the generally "concrete, vivid, and salient" character of individuating information.

In fact, three situations characterize the base rate fallacy case:

- People tend to rely on the base rate in making their judgments when case-specific evidence doesn't suggest a hypothesis (i.e., is not diagnostic and therefore not informative).
- People ignore the base rate when case-specific evidence strongly favours a particular hypothesis (i.e., is not diagnostic and therefore not informative).
- People rely on the base rates when the experimental case wording or format make them appear causal or specific. This naturally follows from the findings that different framings of short cases will provide different results and the suggestion by Tversky and Kahneman that in the preliminary analysis of a decision problem, the decision maker frames the effective acts, contingencies, and outcomes: "Framing is controlled by the manner in which the choice problem is presented as well as by norms, habits and expectancies of the decision maker."

Availability

Availability of information is argued to be an important clue that people use in making judgments. It has been considered as a bias whereby people make a probabilistic judgment on an event by the ease with which similar events are recalled. "A person is said to employ the availability heuristic whenever he estimates frequency or probability of the case with which instances or complications can be brought to mind." That is, frequent events are easier to recall than infrequent ones, making availability a valid cue for the assessment of frequency and probability. Availability is also influenced by factors unrelated to likelihood, such as familiarity, recency, and emotional saliency and imaginability. S. Lichtenstein et al. asked their subjects to compare the frequency of occurrence of pairs of lethal events and found that they overestimated the relative frequency of diseases or causes of death that are much publicized. What seems apparent is that emphasis on some aspects in the environment affects judgment by making it easier to recall instances and estimate their frequency.

Michael Ross and Fiore Sicoly postulated that an egocentric bias in availability of information in memory could produce biased attribution of responsibility for a joint product because of significant processes that may be operating to increase the availability of one's own contributions: selective encoding and storage of information, differential retrieval, informational disparities, and motivational influences. Three experiments confirmed the prevalence of self-centered biases in availability and judgments of responsibility.

In everyday life these egocentric tendencies may be overlooked when joint endeavors do not require explicit allocations of responsibility. If allocations are stated distinctly, however, there is a potential for discussion, and individuals are unlikely to realise their differences in judgment could arise from honest evaluations that are differentially available.

Confirmation Bias

It is an accepted normative view of scientific inference that disconfirmation and testing of alternative hypotheses have major roles. More particularly, Karl Popper's philosophy of science centres around the concept of disconfirmation or refutation. He maintained that hypotheses can be disconfirmed only by evidence and never confirmed. J. R. Platt also argued that successive generations of alternative hypotheses should be disconfirmed—a strategy he labels "strong inference." Popper asserted that the purpose of science is not the verification but the falsification of theories. The falsification can be achieved by deductive logic. If one adopts a rationalist view of humanity, then deductive logic is a necessary and natural part of human thought. The behaviorist view would argue that the use of logical knowledge depends on whether or not the appropriate reinforcement contingencies have been applied. People are generally presented with conditional relationships between propositions that may be represented as "if *p*, then *q*," where *p* is the antecedent and *q* is the consequent. A typical deductive reasoning problem is to entertain alternative hypotheses with respect to the truth or the falsity of the rule. Given *p*, *q*, *p*2 (not *p*) and *q*2 (not *q*), the problem of deciding whether the rule "if *p*, then *q*" is true or false becomes a deductive reasoning problem. The selection may be accomplished using either a verification or falsification principle, depending on the degree of weight, and as follows:

- A subject with no insight will select the options that verify the rule. That is, they will choose *p* or *p* and *q*.
- A subject with partial insight will appreciate the need to select potential falsifiers, but only choose options that could only verify. *p*2 will be considered irrelevant because it should neither verify nor falsify.

All other options will be chosen because they could either verify, falsify, or both.

- A subject with complete insight will select only the options that could falsify. That is, *p* and *q*2 will be chosen.

Which strategies will be used has been the subject of experiments using either abstract or thematic problems, with the evidence showing only 10 per cent of the subjects capable of solving the problem using the falsification principle. The results were consistent with undergraduates as well as more sophisticated subjects and with abstract as well as thematic tasks. Which of these three strategies will be used by the accountant? The auditor's concern is mainly with verification—the examination of financial data for the purpose of judging the faithfulness with which they portray events and conditions.

In the business world, the act of verification is the trade of auditors, both internal and external. This philosophical truth about the necessity of verification is so well accepted that the business world has adopted a general practice of submitting such propositions to a verification process before they are given any serious consideration for many purposes. This verification consideration takes many forms; sometimes it is the continuous examination of procedures and data performed by an internal audit staff, sometimes the annual examination of an independent auditor, sometimes the investigation of an Internal Revenue Agent. Whatever the form, the importance and fact of verification are well accepted.

Therefore, while deductive logic dictates the use of falsification in a deductive reasoning task, the emphasis on verification in auditing will lead the auditors to rely on a verification principle.

A. Belkaoui examined the use of logical knowledge in deductive reasoning by students and auditors. One abstract and two thematic tasks were used and subjects were asked to test the truth or falsity of an implication rule. The results in the abstract test verified the dominance of the verification principle rather than the falsification principle for both students and auditors.

No thematic effect was observed as the use of thematic effects showed a worsening of the falsification principle. In addition, the strong results on the dominance of the verification principle were found to be independent of the level of education, affiliation with a given accounting firm, position in the firm, years of experience as an auditor, years of application with the firm, or age of the subjects. While there is strong evidence both in accounting and psychology for this "confirmation bias," J. Klayman and Y.-W. Ha showed that many phenomena labeled confirmation bias are better understood in terms of a general "positive test strategy." In addition, confirmation bias has meant different things to different researchers.

Examples include the findings that people pay undue attention to the frequency of occurrence of two events, while underweighting instances in which one event occurs without the other; the findings that people tend to discredit or reinterpret information counter to a hypothesis they hold; and the findings that people may conduct "biased" tests that pose little risk of producing disconfirming results.

Anchoring and Adjustment

In many situations, people make estimates by thinking of an internal value or "anchor" that is suggested by the formulation of the task or as a result of partial computation, and then make some adjustment to it to yield the final answer. This heuristic has been termed "anchoring and adjustment."

For example, if a purchasing agent is asked to estimate next year's purchases, he may start with last year's purchases before making some adjustments to them to reflect new environmental conditions.

Therefore, people starting from different anchors end up with different answers. In addition, this heuristic has been found to lead to the following systematic biases in probability estimation:

- Insufficient adjustment
- Biases in the evaluation of conjunctive and disjunctive events—"the chain-like structure of conjunctions leads to overestimation, the funnel-like structure of disjunctions leads to underestimation"
- Anchoring in the assessment of subjective probability distributions

P. Slovic also found evidence of anchoring in the subjective valuation of gambles. Subjects finding a gamble basically attractive use the amount to win as an anchor, then adjust it downward to take into account the less-than-perfect chance of winning and the possibility of losing a small amount. The adjustment was insufficient and Slovic pointed out that it may be the reason why people price gambles inconsistently with straight choices between pairs of gambles where a monetary response is not required.

The anchoring heuristic was also observed in an experiment by M. Albert and H. Raiffa. They asked subjects to give the 1st and 99th percentile values for various quantities of items. It amounted to asking the subjects to estimate the 98 per cent confidence intervals for the population value of the various quantities. The evidence showed that, on average, the subject's 98 per cent confidence intervals included the true value only 40-50 per cent of the time.

Conjunction Fallacy in Probability Judgment

The conjunction rule, a qualitative law of probability, specifies that the probability of a conjunction, *P(A & B)*, cannot exceed the probabilities of its constituents, *P(A)* and *P(B)*, because the extension (or the possibility set) of the conjunction is included in the extension of its constituents. In other words, *P(A & B)* d" min *[P(A), P(B)]*

But intuitive judgments of probability are generally not extensional. People instead use a limited number of heuristics. The natural assessments of representativeness and availability do not conform to the extensional logic of probability theory. "In particular, a conjunction can be more representative than one of its constituents, and instances of a specific category can be easier to retrieve than instances of a more inclusive category."

One would expect, therefore, that representativeness and availability will make a conjunction appear more probable than one of its constituents. Indeed, Tversky and Kahneman present convincing evidence that people often violate the conjunction rule of probability theory when assessing the joint probability of two events. They showed that both sophisticated and naive people, in many different substantive problems, often judge the conjunction of events to be larger than one of its components ("single violation") or as large as both of its components ("double violation"). Their experimental task included the following components:

A = the judged probability of an event *A* given model *M*

J = the judged probability of an event *B* given model *M*

A & *J* = the judged probability of the conjunction of *A* and *J* given model *M* The violations to the conjunction rule were,]*B* <*J* <*A* or B <*A* <*J*.

For example, they gave their subjects the following task: " Bill is 24 years old. He is intelligent, but unimaginative, compulsive, and generally lifeless.

In school he was strong in mathematics. Please rank order the following statements by the degree to which Bill resembles the identical mem'ver of that class."

- Bill is a physician, who plays poker for a hobby.
- Bill is an architect.
- Bill is an accountant. (*A*)
- Bill plays jazz for a hobby. (*J*)
- Bill surfs for a hobby.
- Bill is a reporter.
- Bill is an accountant who plays jazz for a hobby. (*A* & *J*)
- Bill climbs mountains for a hobby.

The risk included:

- A model *M* (the description of Bill),
- An event *A* similar to the description (Bill is an accountant),
- A dissimilar event *J* (Bill plays jazz for a hobby), and
- The conjunction of the two events (event *A* and *J*: Bill is an accountant who plays jazz for a hobby). The subjects ranked the conjunctive event (*A* & *J*) as more probable than one of its constituents in this task as well as for other tasks in a variety of contexts using a number of different methods.

One explanation of this phenomenon may be derived from Tversky's feature matching model, which suggests:

$S(a, b) = J(A\&B) - J(A - B) - J(B - A)$

where $A\&B$ = the features that are common to both A and B

$A - B$ = the features that belong to A but not to B

$B - A$ = the features that belong to B but not to A

J = an interval scale measure of feature salience

S = an interval scale measure of similarity

The model stipulates that the addition of a common feature to the stimuli produces an increase in their judged similarity and probability while the addition of a distinctive feature to either of the two produces a decrease in their judged similarity and probability. In the Tversky and Kahneman experiments the addition of event *A* with common features to the prototypical outcome of the description and event *J* with distinctive features led the subjects to rank conjunctive event (*A&J*) as more probable than *J* but not more than A. H. J. Einhorn provides a more formal representation of the conjunction fallacy. More examinations of judgments of event conjunctions were provided in various studies.

Hindsight Bias

The hindsight bias or hindsight illusions were studied by B. Fischhoff and Fischhoff and R. Byeth. Basically, hindsight bias stipulates that subjects who have a knowledge that an outcome has occurred give that outcome a higher prior probability of occurrence than subjects who do not have any knowledge of the outcome. Fischhoff explains as follows:

In hindsight, people consistently exaggerate what could have been anticipated in foresight. They not only tend to view what has happened as inevitable, but also to view it as having appeared "relatively inevitable" before it happened. People believe that others should have been able to anticipate events much better than was actually the case. They even misremember their own predictions so as to exaggerate in hindsight what they know in foresight.

In addition, subjects seem to be unaware of the influence of outcome knowledge on assessed probabilities. As stated by Fischhoff: "Making sense out of what he is told about the past seems so natural and effortless a response that one may be unaware that outcome knowledge has had any effect at all on him." Hindsight bias was observed in experiments by Fischhoff employing psychotherapy cases, by Slovic and Fischhoff employing the outcomes of scientific experiments, and by Fischhoff and Byeth, Fischhoff, and G. Wood, employing general knowledge events. It was also observed in a number of medical settings involving judgments by nurses, patients, surgeons, and physicians. Various arguments were provided to explain the hindsight bias. First, that outcome knowledge restructures memory. R. Hogarth, for example, states: The knowledge that an event has occurred seems to restructure one's memory.

Our memory of the past is not a memory of the uncertainties of the past, rather it is a reconstruction of past events in terms of what actually occurred. Furthermore, that past is structured in a way that makes some kind of coherent sense to the individual, for example, concerning the relationship between what actually happened and particular (but not all) antecedent events.

Second, it stems from the difference between foresight and hindsight, with the first requiring more powers of imagination.

Prediction requires considerable powers of imagination and both the ability and willingness to entertain several hypotheses simultaneously. Keeping one's options open is not a tidy exercise and can induce considerable anxiety.

Postdiction or hindsight, on the other hand, requires little imagination and is an invitation to impose a causal structure on a sequence of past events. Furthermore, subjectively there is less uncertainty than in prediction problems concerning the events that "caused" what happened. One can believe any claim that seems plausible since it was seen to precede the event.

Third, hindsight bias results from the limited availa-bility of causal scenarios for alternative outcomes vis-a-vis scenarios for the reported outcome. Fourth, hindsight bias is a result of the individual's "fluency of diagnostic thinking." In other words, outcome information makes possible the generation of a coherent story and what follows in terms of forward inference (i.e., prediction of outcomes) involves less uncertainty, given the reduction in the multiplicity of causation.

Fifth, hindsight bias is a result of motivating factors given that subjects, eager to preserve their self-images and how they are perceived by others, may be motivated to act as if they always knew what was going to occur. The hindsight bias raises a number of important issues with regard to judgments of the apparent failures (and successes) of others, distortions in memory, overcoming bias, and learning from experience.

- With regard to judging others, hindsight makes it

easier to judge the mistakes of others without considering that at the time a decision was made, it might have been quite reasonable.

- Distortions in memory result from hindsight bias. We may fail to blame people who make the wrong decision but get away with it.
- Fischhoff was able to "debias" distortions in memory caused by the knowledge of outcomes by giving the subject knowledge of the true outcomes following the false information provided earlier. That created a stimulus capable of overcoming hindsight bias.
- The hindsight bias raises questions concerning the ability of people to learn from experience and to make predictions.

Illusory Correlation and Contingency Judgments

Illusory correlation refers to the belief that two variables covary when, in fact, they do not. L. J. Chapman defined it as "the report by observers of a correlation between two classes of events which, in reality,

- Are not correlated,
- Are correlated to a lesser extent than reported, or
- Are correlated in the opposite direction from that which is reported.

" In fact, Chapman and Chapman provided subjects with information concerning hypothetical mental patients, which included a clinical diagnosis and a drawing of a person made by the patient. The drawings and symptom statements were combined in such a way that "each drawing occurred as often with one statement as another." Therefore, no relationship existed between drawings and symptom statements. The subjects were then asked to estimate the frequency with which each diagnosis (e.g., suspiciousness or paranoia) had been accompanied by various features of the drawings (e.g., peculiar eyes). The results showed that the subjects markedly overestimated the frequency of co-occurrence of pairs commonly believed to exist by society, such as suspiciousness and peculiar eyes.

Similar results in,

2 × 2 Joint Frequency Table	Presence of Y	Absence of Y
Presence of X	a	b
Absence of X	c	d

Illusory correlations were provided by Chapman and Chapman, Golding and Rorer, and Starr and Katkin.

Illusory correlation studies point to the tendencies of finding nonexistent relationships. Studies of contingency judgments, however, point to sensitivity to certain relationships and not to others. If X_1 and X_2 represent two events like the presence or absence of cloud seeding, and Y_1 and Y_2 represent two other events like the presence or absence of rain, then a contingency exists between X (cloud seeding) and Y (rain) to the extent that the probability of Y_1 given X_1 differs from the probability of Y_1 given X_2.

A contingency exists between X and Y to the extent that $a/a + b$ differs from $c/c + d$. In contingency studies, subjects are generally asked to make a judgment J about the degree to which the variables X and Y covary. The normative or objective covariation, N, is measured by organizing the data in a 2 × 2 joint frequency rule and applying one of the following correct data-integration rules:

- N_1 (difference in diagnosis) = $[a + d] - [b + c]$
- N_2 (delta coefficient) = $[a/(a + b)] - [c/(c + d)]$
- N_3 (contingency coefficient) = $[X/(n + X)]^{1/2})]$
- N_4 (lambda coefficient) = $[\max (a, c) + \max (b, d) - \max (a + b, c + d)] / [n \max (a + b, c + d)]$
- N_5 (phi coefficient) = $[ad - bc] / [(a + c)(b + d)(a + b)(c + d)]^{1/2}$

The correlation between J, the judgment about the degree to which the variables X and Y covary, and the data integration rule N is a measure of accuracy.

The results of experiments point to the following:

- Subjects fail to appreciate that all four frequencies are required.
- Subjects make errors in estimating cell frequencies when factors unrelated to frequency influence the

availability of data retrieved from memory or produced by imagination.

- Subjects concentrate on the number of positive confirmatory data of a cell *a* and occasionally cell *d*, and ignore or underestimate the number of disconfirmatory data.
- Studies of manipulatory task difficulty indicate that the covariation judgment accuracy decreases as establishing a data set becomes more difficult.

Weber-Fechner Law

The Weber-Fechner law suggests that a just noticeable difference is uniquely related to the standard for which it was established. More explicitly, given a standard *S* and a just noticeable difference *S*, then change in *S*/*S* = *K* for all *S* (where *K* = constant)

In other words, the change in intensity of a stimulus that is necessary before it can be detected is a constant function of the amount of stimuli present. To measure the just noticeable difference, the method used is the method of constant stimulus differences.

Under this method, subjects are presented with a standard, followed by a series of changes above and below the standard. The subjects are then asked to judge the pairs of stimuli. For the responses, three curves are drawn representing the relative frequency of judgments of larger, equal, and smaller for the different magnitudes of the comparison stimulus.

Accordingly, J. Rose et al. made the hypothesis that people do respond to data stimuli as to sense stimuli and these stimuli obey the Weber-Fechner law. They asked the subjects to judge whether a stock should sell for more than, less than, or the same as a series of comparison stocks, based on comparison of earnings-per-share (EPS) figures. The results showed that judgments of numerical stimuli could be represented by the Weber-Fechner law. In effect, the Weber ratios ranged from 6.6 to 7.0 per cent of the standard stimulus across two experiments and two standards.

John Dickhaut and Ian Eggleton continued this line of research on the Weber-Fechner law of examining comparative judgments of numerical information, especially accounting information.

Unlike the study by Rose et al., they manipulated the stated setting in which judgments were made, the sequence of data presentation, and the format in which standards and comparison stimuli were presented. The results showed that the subjects' perceptions of the data were consistent with the Weber-Fechner law. Examination of individual plots raised serious doubts about a similarity of the psychophysical process of comparing numerical stimuli. A second experiment was conducted followed by a questionnaire designed to elicit heuristics the subjects used in making similarity judgments.

The results suggested that subjects used single decision rules, formulated either early in the task or possibly before the task was undertaken, applied inconsistently and defined as percentage functions of the expectations.

STRATEGIC FOUNDATIONS

Management accounting is built on strategic foundations. First, management accounting provides a framework and a language of discourse for the three stages of strategy: reenactment, resolution, and implementation. Second, the conduct of management accounting differs for different distinctions in the strategic process and the strategic decision-making process.

Third, it works best when there is consequence between the design of management control systems and types of control strategies. Finally, the new area of strategic management accounting requires management accounting to focus on the firm's value added compared to its competitors and to monitor the firm's performance using strategic rather than tactical indicators.

These relationships between strategy, strategic process distinctions, strategic archetypes, and strategic management accounting on one hand and management accounting on the other hand are exhibited.

NOTIONS OF STRATEGY

The Greeks refer to strategy as the "art of the general." It evolved in the Harvard mold into an imaginative act of integrating numerous complex decisions. A. D. Chandler, Jr. was the first to use strategy as a managerial tool. He defined it as "the determination of the basic long-term goals and objectives of the enterprise and the adoption of courses of actions and the allocation of resources necessary for carrying out these goals." The influence of this definition is clear in R. N. Anthony's depiction of strategic planning as "the process of deciding on objectives of the organization, or changes in these objectives, or the resources used to attain these objectives, and on the policies that are to govern the acquisition, use, and disposition of resources." According to the last two definitions, the concern of strategy is the link between the organization and its environment through both ends (objectives and goals) and means (courses of action and allocation of resources).

Other theorists prefer to restrict strategy to only the objectives and goals and excludes the means to achieve them. C. W. Hofer and D. E. Schendel make the restriction by defining strategy as "the fundamental pattern of present and planned resource deployments and environmental interactions that indicates how the organization will achieve its objectives."

Another limitation is provided by M. E. Porter's concept of competitive strategy as "the search for a favorable competitive position in an industry... It aims to establish a profitable and sustainable position against the forces that determine industry competition." This school of thought is more in line with the argument that firms act to create their own environments by making a strategic choice regarding markets, products, technologies, desired scale of production, and so on. K. E. Weick refers to this concept as *environmental enactment*.

This interpretive view of organization assumes that organizations are socially constructed systems of shared meanings. The environment is neither objective nor perceived but enacted through the social interaction process of their organizational participants. "Theories involving objective or perceived 'environments' envision concrete, material 'organizations' that are within, but separate from real material 'environments.'" The relationships between the two are expressed in terms of cause and effect. On the other hand, enactment theory abandons the idea of concrete, material "organizations/environments" in favour of a largely socially created symbolic world." This view of enacted environment changes drastically the view of strategy and the role of the strategist from the old role of the one devoted to environmental scanning and data and fact collecting to a more imaginative and creative one best depicted as follows:

In the chaotic world, a continuous stream of ecological changes and discontinuities must be sifted through and integrated. Relevant and irrelevant categories of experience must be defined.

People make sense of their situation by engaging in an interpretive process that forms the basis of their organized behaviour. This interpretive process spans both intellectual and emotional realms. Managers can strategically influence this process. They can provide a vision to account for the streams of events and actions that occur—a universe within which organizational events and experiences take on meaning. The best work of strategic managers inspires splendid meanings.

In any case the identification of strategies is needed to impose order in whatever environment. The decisions selected to be interpreted are then infused with meanings. What may happen is that different organizations will assign different meanings to a particular environmental event, resulting in different responses to similar environmental events. As stated by Jane Dutton and Susan Jackson; "meanings attached to strategic issues are imposed by categories that decision makers employ to describe an issue.

Categories are engaged by using linguistic labels. Two labels most frequently applied to strategic issues are focused on: threat and opportunity. Once applied, labels initiate a categorization process that affects the subsequent cognition and motivations of the decision makers; these, in turn, systematically affect the process and content of organizational actions.

Accounting plays a role in the three stages of strategic change: Preenactment, resolution, and implementation. Accounting provides "a framework for and a language of discourse [and] the power to establish and maintain the credibility of issue allocations through its authority structures, accountability measures, and performance evaluations." Basically, strategies need to be framed in an accounting language and supported by the authority of accounting techniques, indicators, and reports.

STRATEGIC PROCESS DISTINCTIONS

The strategic process is a complex phenomenon that calls for theoretical and practical distinctions. One distinction generally made is between *strategy formulation* and *strategy implementation*. Charles Snow and Donald Hambrick say "the advantage of making this distinction is that the cognitive aspects of strategy (formulation) can be viewed as an important phase apart from the action component (implementation). A second distinction made is between *business-level strategies* ("How should we compete in this business?") and corporate-level strategies. The difference between these two levels is explicated as follows:

The term business level refers to that level in an organization at which responsibility for the formulation of a multifunctional strategy for a single industry or product-market arena is determined; the term corporate level refers to the top level of the organization regardless of the number of industries in which it competes. Thus, for a multiindustry company, the business level normally would correspond to the divisional level. In a single product line company, however, the business and corporate level would be the same.

The difference between the two strategies is important as corporate-level strategy precedes the enactment of the business-level strategy. In addition, the success of the business-level strategy in one period determines the corporate-level strategy in future periods. The two strategies are linked and equally important to each other's formulation and implementation.A third distinction made by Mintzberg is between intended *strategy, deliberate strategy, realized strategy, unrealized strategy,* and *emergent strategy.* Basically strategy is planned, qualifying as intended strategy, and if the exercise is successful they are realized strategies rather than unrealized strategies. If in addition a stream of decisions is made in a consistent way, it defines an emerging strategy that becomes a realized strategy.

As stated by Mintzberg:

- Intended strategies that get realized; these may be called *deliberate strategies.*
- Intended strategies that do not get realized, perhaps because of unrealistic expectations, misjudgments about the environment, or changes in either during implementation; these may be called *unrealized* strategies.
- Realized strategies that were never intended, perhaps because, as in
- Those that were got displaced along the way; these may be called *emergent* strategies.

The difference between the intended and deliberate strategies on one hand and the emergent strategy on the other hand are a result of the differences between the teleological and the ecological views of strategy. The teleological view presumes that the strategic agenda is the sole responsibility of management. Under this perspective, management uses strategies to control the organization. It is a prescriptive view of the strategic process., The ecological view presumes that the organization is a conflicting arena of different shareholders, each striving to impose and/or suggest an agenda. Under this view, strategy is the untamed of these organizational struggles, our expression of what the organization does rather than should do., It is a descriptive approach similar to the emergent strategy approach. As stated by Jerry Dermer:

Thus, from an ecological perspective, the strategic agenda emerges from the reconciliation of conflicting rationalities, not from the imposition of management's global scheme.

And because neither issues nor support can be controlled, managerial plans do not necessarily determine what the agenda contains. Consensus can originate anywhere and the role of "change entrepreneur" can be assumed by any shareholder with the motivation and ability to do so. Each change entrepreneur is free to operate within his/her own rationality, albeit constrained by the contingencies arising out of inescapable interdependencies.

The dynamics of what determines the composition of the agenda is not the intentions of any particular player but rather the fit among concerns, capabilities and support. An issue gains the agenda when a concern is recognized, a resolution proposed and support sufficient to generate action aroused. This may be achieved through managerial control or it may be the result of other processes.

Strategic Research

One important research theme has been to link strategy and structure of firms. The evidence is used to bolster either the argument "structure follows strategy" or the argument that "strategy follows structure."

The proposition that structure follows strategy followed from Chandler's historical analysis of 70 large American firms. Basically, multi product growing firms solved their administrative problems by the implementation of new structures. The strategies adopted by these firms included either horizontal, vertical, or diversification in related or unrelated markets.

Chandler maintained that a horizontal strategy called for a unitary structure, one characterized by manufacturing, sales and marketing, and finance departments; a vertical strategy called for a functional structure, one characterized by departments along discrete task lines; a diversification strategy called for a multidivisional structure, one in which a firm is organized into product divisions and each division contains a unitary structure. A heroic view of top management is presented. As stated by Robert Burgelman,

Chandler's case data suggest that multiple layers of management were involved in the strategic initiatives that produced the extensive diversification, and in response to which the new strategy and the new structure eventually emerged. The theoretical generalizations, however, collapse this strategic process into a top management activity. Even though the influence of lower levels in the determination of the context of the strategy is recognized, the major emphasis is on the role of top management.

The proposition that strategy follows structure follows from J. L. Bower's study of strategy making as a multilayered process, spread over the management hierarchy. The process is viewed as a culmination of a bottom-up and topdown multilayered process where strategy adopts itself to the particular structure of the firm.

A second line of research has been connected with the strategic decision making process. One line of research views strategic decision making as a linear, sequential, orderly activity originated by powerful executives. "It relies on rational techniques for analyzing environments and organizational resources, generating action alternatives and appraising these against unitary, consistent preferences." A second line of research views strategic decision making as a disorganized, noisy, and uncoordinated activity resulting from the conflictual and political climates of firms, where primacy is given to personalities, power, context, and the untidiness of chance.

STRATEGIC ARCHETYPES

Management accounting in general and management control systems in particular include formalized procedures for cost accumulation, product costing, budgeting, performance evaluation, and resource allocation. Business strategies define how a firm decides to compete in a given business and positions itself among its competitors. The strategy style adopted needs to be supported by adequate and appropriate management accounting techniques. Therefore, the strategic style chosen is an important determinant of the principles, techniques, and systems of management accounting adopted.

The determination of the appropriate strategic style is important to both internal and external users of management accounting information of a given firm as it may show the nature of the "fit" between the strategic style and the management accounting system supporting its enactment, formulation, and implementation.

Mintzberg's Strategic Archetypes

Mintzberg's model of strategic archetypes falls into three distinct groupings or modes: entrepreneurial, adaptive, and planning. The *entrepreneurial mode* is modeled after the actions, attitudes and behaviour of the individuals who sought opportunity, founded firms, took bold decisions, focused on growth, and sought high uncertainty. *Four characteristics are identified for the entrepreneurial mode of strategy-making*:

- In the entrepreneurial mode, strategy-making is dominated by the active search for new opportunities.
- In the entrepreneurial organization, power is centralized in the hands of the chief executive.
- Strategy-making in the entrepreneurial mode is characterized by dramatic leaps forward in the face of uncertainty.
- Growth is the dominant goal of the entrepreneurial organization.

Four characteristics are identified for the adaptive mode:

- Clear goals do not exist in the adaptive organization; strategy-making reflects a division of power among members of a complex coalition.
- In the adaptive mode, the strategy-making process is characterized by the "reactive" solution to existing problems rather than the "proactive" search for new opportunities. The adaptive organization makes its decisions in incremental, serial steps.
- Disjointed decisions are characteristic of the adaptive organization.

Three characteristics are identified for the planning mode:

- In the planning mode, the analyst plans a major role in strategy-making.
- The planning mode focuses on systematic analysis, particularly in the assessment of the costs and benefits of competing proposals.
- The planning mode is characterized above all by the integration of decisions and strategies.

Utterback and Abernathy's Strategic Archetypes

The performance-maximizing firm faces an uncertain environment in which it is one of the first to introduce new products in the anticipation that new capabilities will expand customer requirements. As emphasized by Utterback and Abernathy, a majority of innovations produced by performance-maximizing firms would be expected to be market-simulated with a high degree of uncertainty about their ultimate market potential. Technology to meet market needs may come from many sources.

Characteristics and Conditions of the Three Modes

Innovation may often arise from unexpected sources or directions of inquiry. Performance maximizing firms would be expected to rely more heavily on external sources of information, and on more diverse sources of information than would others. The *sales-maximizing firm* uses other firms' innovations to offer new product variation and features, thus reducing market uncertainty and ensuring more stable environments through the product differentiation. The *cost-minimizing firm* enters the market at the end of the product life cycle with less complex and less expensive products.

Strategic Archetypes

The first three are viewed as "stable" forms of organization, while the last one is viewed as essentially "unstable." Each type is assumed to have its own strategy for reacting to the environment and its own mix of strategy, technology, structure, and process that is consistent with the strategy. *Defenders* are organizations that have narrow product-market domains. Top managers in this type of organization are highly expert in their organization's limited area of operation but do not tend to search outside of their domains for new opportunities.

Characteristic	Entrepreneurial Mode	Adaptive Mode	Planning Mode
Motive for Decisions	Proactive	Reactive	Proactive & Reactive
Goals of Organization	Growth	Indeterminate	Efficiency & Growth
Evaluation of Proposals	Judgmental	Judgmental	Analytical
Choices made by	Entrepreneur	Bargaining	Management
Decision Horizon	Long-Term	Short-Term	Long-Term
Preferred Environment	Uncertainty	Certainty	Risk
Decision Linkages	Loosely Coupled	Disjointed	Integrated
Flexibility of Mode	Flexible	Adaptive	Constrained
Size of Moves	Bold	Incremental	Global
	Decisions	Steps	Strategies
Vision of Direction	General	None	Specific
Condition for Use			
Source of Power	Entrepreneur	Divided	Management
Objectives of Organization	Operational	Nonoperational	Operational
Organizational Environment	Yielding	Complex, Dynamic	Predictable, Stable
Status of Organization	Young, Small or Strong Leadership	Established	Large

As a result of this narrow focus, these organizations seldom need to make major adjustments in their technology, structure, or methods of operation. Instead, they devote primary attention to improving the efficiency of their existing operations.

Analyzers are organizations that operate in two types of product-market domains—one relatively stable, the other changing. In their stable areas, these organizations operate routinely and efficiently through use of formalized structures and processes. In their more turbulent areas, top managers watch their competitors closely for new ideas, and then they rapidly adopt those that appear to be the most promising.

Prospectors are organizations that almost continually search for market opportunities, and they regularly experiment with potential responses to emerging environmental trends. Thus, these organizations often are the creators of change and uncertainty to which their competitors must respond. However, because of their strong concern for product and market innovation, these organizations usually are not completely efficient.

Reactors are organizations in which top managers frequently perceive change and uncertainty occurring in their organizational environments but are unable to respond effectively. Because this type of organization lacks a consistent strategystructure relationship, it seldom makes adjustment of any sort until forced to do so by environmental pressures.

Porter's Strategic Archetypes

M. E. Porter identified and defined three generic strategies: cost leadership, differentiation, and focus strategies. *Cost leadership* focuses on the production of a standardized product at a low price for a high market share under conditions of economies of scale and tight cost control. As stated by Porter; "cost leadership requires aggressive construction of efficient-scale facilities, vigorous pursuit of cost reductions from experience, tight cost and overhead control, avoidance of marginal customer accounts, and cost minimization in areas like R&D, service, sales force, advertising, and so on." *Differentiation* focuses on the production of industry-unique products for loyal and relatively price-insensitive clientele, with emphasis on marketing and research.

Approaches to differentiating can take many forms: design or brand image, technology in stereo components; Coleman in camping equipment), features; customer service, dealer networks, or other dimensions.

Focus strategy centres on the production of products that are needed by a defined buyer group, on a segment of the product line, or on a geographic market in the search of the appropriate niche. Porter says that although the low cost and differentiating strategies are aimed at achieving their objectives industry-wide, the entire focus strategy is built around serving a particular target very well, and each functional policy is developed with this in mind. The strategy rests on the premise that the firm is thus able to serve its narrow strategic target more effectively or efficiently than competitors who are competing more broadly.

Miller and Friesen's Archetypes of Strategy Formulation

D. Miller and P. H. Friesen examined undisguised cases of business organizations to look for simultaneous associations among a large number of variables to determine archetypes of strategic formulation. Ten archetypes are identified.

The successful archetypes are:

- The adaptive firm under moderate challenge
- The adaptive firm in a very challenging environment
- The dominant firm
- The giant under fire
- The entrepreneurial conglomerate
- The innovator

The *specialization ratio* is defined as the proportion of the firm's revenues that is attributable to its largest discrete product market activity. The *related ratio* is defined as the proportion of firm revenues that is attributable to the largest group of businesses that are related to one another in some way. The *vertical ratio* is defined as the proportion of revenues attributable to all the by-products, intermediate products, and final products of a vertically integrated sequence of manufacturing operations.

The primary diversification strategies and their subcategories are:

- Single business
- Dominant business as either
- Dominant vertical
- Dominant constrained
- Dominant linked.or
- Dominant unrelated
- Related business as either
- Related constrained or
- Related linked
- Unrelated business as either
- Multibusiness or
- Unrelated-portfolio

A specialization ratio (SR) of less than.7 defines businesses as being either related or unrelated. If.7 d″ SR <.95, then the firm is classified as a dominant business. The firm is classified as a single business if SR e″.95. A related ratio (RR) greater than.7 defines a related business. A vertical ratio (VR) greater than.7 defines a vertically integrated business. Rumelt's ratios were used to classify firms as being in one of the three following categories:

- Primarily dominant vertical firms. Vertically integrated firms (VR e″.7) producing and selling different end products, no one of which contributes more than 94 per cent of total revenues.
- Related-constrained firms. Firms with.7 d″ SR <.95 and RR e″.7, which have diversified by relating new businesses to a specific central skill or resource and in which each business activity is related to almost all the other business activities of the firm.
- Unrelated business firms. Firms with.7 d″ SR e″ <.95 and RR <.7, which have aggressive programmes for the acquisition of new unrelated businesses.

STRATEGIC MANAGEMENT ACCOUNTING

John Shank and Vijay Govindarajan predicted that strategic accounting will supplant managerial accounting as a decisional framework because managerial accounting lacks strategic relevance. While cost analysis provides an assessment of the financial impact of managerial decision alternatives, strategic cost analysis will provide cost data for the development of the right strategy necessary to gain competitive advantage. As stated by Shank and Govindarajan, "a sophisticated understanding of a firm's cost structure can go a long way in the search for sustainable competitive advantage. This understanding is what we refer to as 'strategic cost analysis.' "

Underlying Shank and Govindarajan's concern is the failure of management accounting to explicitly consider strategic issues and concerns. Only strategic management accounting in general and strategic cost analysis in particular can fill that void.

Strategic cost analysis is broader than conventional cost analysis by bringing into the analysis the strategic elements necessary to gain a competitive advantage. As a result, accounting information gains an expanded role in the four stages of the strategic process:

- Formulation of strategies and stages,
- Communication of strategies,
- Development of tactics, and
- Implementation.

That role is defined as follows:

- *At stage 1*, accounting information is the basis for financial analysis, which is one aspect of the process of evaluating strategic alternatives. Strategies that are not feasible or do not yield adequate financial returns cannot be appropriate strategies.
- *At stage 2*, accounting reports constitute one of the important ways that strategy gets communicated throughout an organization. The things that are reported are the things people will pay attention to. Good accounting reports are those that focus

attention on the factors that are critical to success of the strategy adopted.

- *At stage 3*, specific tactics must be developed in support of the overall strategy and then carried through to completion. Financial analysis, based on accounting information, is one of the key elements in deciding which tactical programmes are most likely to be effective in helping a firm to meet its strategic objectives.

Finally, at stage 4, monitoring the performance of managers or business units usually hinges partly on accounting information. The role of standard costs, expense budgets, and annual profit plans in providing one basis for performance evaluation is well accepted in businesses worldwide. These tools must be explicitly adapted to the strategic content of the firm if they are to be measurably useful.

Another working definition of strategic management accounting is provided by M. Bromwich as "the provision and analysis of financial information on the firm's product markets and competitor's costs and cost structures and the monitoring of the enterprises' strategies and those of its competitors in these markets over a number of periods." With such a definition focusing on the provision of information concerning the firm's markets and on its competitors, Bromwich was successful in offering the vertical supports for the involvement of accountants in strategic management accounting.

The first theoretical support for the involvement of accountants in strategic management accounting is provided by Bromwich. This theoretical support is derived from the economic theory that sees economic goods as being a bundle of attributes.

The accountant is asked to cost these attributes and monitor their performance over time. Information about a number of demand and cost factors pertaining to these attributes is deemed important for optimal decision making. As stated by Bromwich:

Accountants may play a role here in costing the characteristics provided by goods and in monitoring and reporting on these costs regularly. Similarly, they may be involved in determining the cost of any package of attributes which is being considered for introduction in the market. However, where a strategic perspective is adopted by accountants, costs may have to be considered in the context of demand factors because of the likely interplay between costs and demand in determining successful strategic conduct when considering product attributes.

The second theoretical support is derived from the theory of contestable markets that gives the conditions for a firm's price and output strategy to be sustainable in the face of potential competition.

Following contestable market theory precepts, and the recommendation for monitoring cost advantages over rivals, strategic management accounting is oriented toward not only the cost structure of the firm but also the cost structures of all firms in the market and those likely to enter the market. What follows from this concern with strategic management accounting is a complete restructuring of the role of accounting toward an active role in the strategic process and an essential means to help achieving economic success. Consequently, Shank and Govindarajan suggest the following key management questions to ask about any accounting idea:

- Does it serve an identifiable business objective? (facilitate strategy formulation... assess managerial performance.
- For the objective it is designed to serve, will the accounting idea enhance the chances of attaining the objective?
- Does the objective whose attainment is facilitated by the accounting idea fit strategically with the overall thrust of the business?

Chapter 4

Industrial Learning

HISTORY

Instead, it describes a more complex organism—the collective efforts of many people, some in line and others in staff positions, but all aiming to accomplish a common task progressively more efficiently.

The improvement in labour time is generally referred to as resulting from productivity. If the improvement is, however, repetitive and predictable, it is considered as resulting from learning. In effect, progress depends on people learning, and a conventional hypothesis in industry is that they learn according to a predictable pattern often called the learning curve.

The learning curve describes the empirical relationships between output quantities and quantities of certain inputs (mainly directlabor hours) where learning inducement improvement is present.

It portrays the concept that the cumulative average unit cost decreases systematically by a common percentage each time the volume of production increases geometrically (that is, increases by doubling). The phenomenon is helpful in the investigation of the cost behavioural patterns, cost estimation, and decision making in general.

In effect the forecasting of labour input and its impact on various economic decisions has been a laborious and time—consuming job. The learning curve is intended to make such forecasting easier, quicker, and much more accurate. In brief, learning curves are applicable to all the aspects of production planning and control where there are tasks subject to improvement. A schematic representation of how learning curves can influence the use of production resources. Synonyms for the learning curve include the manufacturing progress function, cost-quantity relationship, cost curve, product acceleration curve, improvement curve, performance curve, experience curve, and efficiency curve.

THEORY

The learning curve was first recognized in the aircraft industry, where any reduction in the considerable number of direct-labour hours needed for assembly work is quickly recognized and formalized. However, the learning curve was not translated into an empirical theory curve until 1925, when it was observed in a military manufacturing operation. Some eleven years later, T. P. Wright disclosed the results of empirical tests of the learning curve. He observed that on the average, when output doubled in the aircraft industry, the labour requirements decreased by about 20 per cent; in other words, there was an 80 per cent learning factor. Interest in such a discovery applied to a wartime situation; the U.S. Defence Department commissioned the Stanford Research Institute to study the direct-labour input required for aircraft production in a number of firms.

The resulting learning curves had a common characteristic: an 80 per cent improvement rate. From 1909, when the first Model T Ford was produced, until 1926, productivity improved along an 86 per cent learning curve. Evidence of improvement over sixteen years and on sixteen million items was found in a human-paced operation that involved assembling candy boxes. The learning continued for the production of tens of millions of units in a machine-paced operation.

The learning curve theory is based on a simple principle of human nature: People learn from experience. As workers repeat a task, they become more efficient at it. The net result is a reduced use of direct-labour hours per unit. This improvement can be regular enough to follow a predictable pattern that should apply to any task or job in any industry. The early literature considered the learning improvement possible only in labour-intensive, discontinuous forms of manufacture, such as airframe assembly.

It was later proved, however, that the improvement could take place in continuous and capital-intensive forms of manufacture. Industries where the learning phenomenon is applicable include the petroleum, refining, and basic chemical industries.

Finally, learning was found to exist in process-oriented contexts as well as in job-order production, and in mature phases of production as well as in start-up phases. Industries in which the learning curve phenomenon was found applicable include machine-intensive manufacturing (steel mills and glass, paper, and electrical products), automotive assembly, apparel manufacture, large musical instruments and electromechanical assembly, housing construction, machine tools, petroleum refining, clerical operations, printing and typesetting, machine shop processes, electronic (radar), and electrical manufacture.

As an example of the learning phenomenon, assume that the average labour hours required per unit are reduced by 30 per cent as the quantity produced doubles. If the first unit takes 100 hours, then the average for 2 units is 70 hours (0.7 × 100 hours), or a total of 140 hours for 2 units. Therefore, the time required to complete the second unit equals 40 hours (140 - 100). Continuing this line of reasoning, 4 units would require an average of 49 hours per unit (0.7 × 70 hours), and a total of 196 hours (4 × 49 hours) for all 4 units. The third and fourth units require 56 hours (196 hours required for 4 units minus 140 hours required for 2 units). The basic doctrine of the learning curve can be summarized as follows:

Where there is life, there can be learning.

The more complex the life, the greater the rate of learning. Man-paced operations are more susceptible to learning or can give greater rates of progress than machine-paced operations.

The rate of learning can be sufficiently regular to be predictive. Operations can develop trends which are characteristic of themselves. Projecting such established trends is more valid than assuming a level performance or no learning.

What factors account for the learning curve phenomenon? It is appropriate to distinguish between the impact of two factors:

- The learning in the literal sense on the part of the workers, and
- Other factors, including management innovation. Although these factors operate together, the presence of a consistent behaviour indicates that of the various factors, learning in the literal sense is the predominant influence. The non learning factors, such as new machinery, time studies, or design changes, do bring some labour savings; however, they will probably have an irregular effect on the learning curve. Furthermore, the learning factors will be subject to two conditions:
- The predisposition of an operation to an improvement, and
- The extent to which the predisposition is used.

On one hand, the predisposition to an improvement is related to the human content of an operation. It is reflected in the ratio of assembly (human content) to machine work. In assembly work there are relatively large possibilities for learning; in machine work the improvement is

Constrained by the fact that the machines cannot "learn" to run any faster.

The following rates are often employed as possible benchmarks:

- *75% assembly labour, 25% machine labour: 80% curve*
- *50% assembly labour, 50% machine labour: 85% curve*
- *25% assembly labour, 75% machine labour: 90% curve*

On the other hand, the extent to which the predisposition is used may depend on the following two factors:

The effect of faith. A positive attitude toward the possibility of learning can reinforce progress. Winfred B. Hirschmann states: "If progress is believed possible, it will likely be sought; and if it is looked for, there is some possibility of finding it. Conversely, if improvements are considered unlikely, there will be little urge to seek them.

A defeatist philosophy can be engendered which so debilitates an effort that it helps to produce the very condition it assumes." The presence of open-ended expectations. The absence of "ceiling psychology" may create a predisposition to learning and permit improvement to continue. Some companies obtain more rapid progress when the workers are not informed of the target rate.

Learning Curve

Since the discovery of the learning curve and the publication in 1936 of the first article formulating the theory of learning curves, various geometric versions have been proposed.

The more well known are these:

The log-linear model

Pegels's exponential function

Levy's adaptation function

The Stanford-B model

DeJong's learning formula with an incompressibility factor

The S-curve

Glover's learning formula with a work commencement factor Common to all these models, however, is the need to estimate these two basic parameters: Input resources associated with the production of the first unit The learning curve characteristic or some measure of the rate reduction

These various models are described next. It is, however, appropriate to note that the log-linear model has been and still is, by far, the most useful model. The other models are described because they have been found and may be found in the future to be applicable to some manufacturing experiences.

The Log-Linear Model: The log-linear model or constant percentage model basically states that the improvement in productivity is fairly constant as output increases.

$$\gamma = KXn$$

where,

γ = the number of direct-labour hours required to produce the xth unit,

K = the number of direct-labour hours required to produce the first unit,

X = the cumulative unit number,

n = log ∏/log 2 = learning index,

∏ = the learning rate,

1 = the progress ratio.

Assume that a company's rate of learning, like the aircraft industry's, is 80 per cent. On an arithmetic chart with linear coordinates, the relationship between the cumulative average direct-labour hours and the cumulative units of production is portrayed by a curve showing a rapid decline that trails off. The same curve on a logarithmic chart will follow a straight declining rate. The portrayal of the learning phenomenon as a straight line is generally preferred for practical reasons.

Pegels's Exponential Function

As an alternative to the power function formulation of the log-linear model, various authors proposed models based on exponential functions. As an example, Pegels proposed an alternative algebraic function, an exponential-type function, to complement or replace the power function approach. The functions are expressed as follows:

The marginal cost per unit index for the xth unit, M·C(x) is as follows:

$$MC(x) = aax - 1 + b$$

where α, β, and a are empirically based parameters.

By integrating across x yields TC(x) which is the total cost index up to the xth unit in terms of the marginal cost per unit index, in other words where α, β, and a are empirically based parameters, and C is a constant to be derived after the parameters have been derived. In fact, the constant C can be derived by letting *MC* (1) = *TC*(1) = *AC*(1) which yields

The average cost AC(x) of the first × units produced in

marginal cost index terms or cumulative average cost can be derived as follows: The main assumption in the exponential function formulation is that the marginal cost of the first unit, MC(1) = y0, is assumed to be known and will be set equal to the index value of one. In other words, y0 = $\alpha + \beta = 1.00$.

In comparing the merits of his model to the other power function models, Pegels concluded as follows:

The proposed exponential model is only slightly more difficult to apply than the common power function model. Although there are three parameters to be estimated, one of these, ß, is based on subjective estimates or historically based subjective estimates. The other two parameters, *a* and *b*, can be as readily determined as the two power function parameters. Since the exponential function is based on a zero-to-one marginal cost index, applying the exponential function requires slightly more training and care. In addition, the basic power function has the disadvantage of showing both marginal and average costs decreasing with increasing output, while in the exponential function the marginal cost becomes constant after a certain number of units produced.

Levy's Adaptation Function

Levy cites two shortcomings of the log-linear model—namely, it does not recognize the leveling off of production rate, and it does not give insight into factors that may influence learning. The new type of learning function which he proposes is particularly useful in showing how a firm can adapt itself to the learning process and isolate the variables which influence learning.

Levy's function has the following form:

MC = [1/β - (1/β - xb/a)C-cx]-1 where MC = marginal cost, a and b are the parameters that are analogous to the power function parameters, C is a third parameter to be estimated, and ß is the production index for the first unit. The function of the parameter C is to flatten the curve for large values of x. In other words, Levy's learning function reaches a plateau and does not continue to decrease or increase as does the power function.

Stanford-B Model

The search for something other than the log-linear model stems from the fact that the linear model does not always provide the best fit in all situations. A Stanford study found that the linear formulations of the learning curve may be inappropriate for some World War II data. Instead the following equation, usually referred to as the Stanford-B formula or the learning formula with a B-factor, was found to be more representative:

$$y = a(X + B)n$$

where,

y = Direct-man hours required for cumulative unit number x,

a = constant, equivalent to the cost of the first unit when B = 0,

n = Exponent describes slope of the asymptote (-0.5 is a typical value),

B = Constant which may be expressed as the number of units theoretically produced prior to the first unit acceptance, or the equivalent units of experience available at the start of a manufacturing process (1 < B < 10 and 4 is a typical value).

The Stanford study found that n for 29 cases ranged between -0.397 and -0.599 (66.1% and 75.9% slopes) with a mean value of -0.499. In fact, the Boeing Company found that the Stanford-B model was the best for the manufacturing of the Boeing 707 if it is modified to incorporate design differences for special customers' requirements. The modified progress curve developed suffers, however, from the following limitations:

It assumes that the learning experienced on any component is fully retained, no matter how much time elapses before the same work is repeated. Modifying the assumption will lead to a more cumbersome formulation and has not been attempted.

- When the number of versions in a family of airplanes gets large, the computations become extensive. The difficulty is relieved if attention is restricted to a smaller number of versions in a combination with the version to be estimated. These will be ones which share the most work with this version and contribute the most experience.

The Stanford-B model includes as a main feature the B factor which measures design differences or complexities beyond the control of management know-how or the amount of engineering or retooling. Another explanation is that the Stanford-B model accounts for previous learning retained by using a scale of displacement B.

Note that setting n = 0.5, the Stanford-B model yields a unit learning curve equation as follows:

With B = 0, the same equation becomes y = ax-0.5 which is equivalent to a 70.7 per cent linear unit time reduction curve. A typical learning curve of the Stanford-B type is asymptotic to a straight line with slope n and approaches such a line over its entire length as B approaches zero. The main result of the B factor is that the curve tends to follow a convex shape in the early part of a programme.

There is at least one known attempt at evaluating the superiority of the Stanford curve over the conventional log-linear curve. Hoffman used the same data used by the Stanford Research Institute and concludes that there is little basis for choice between the two curves in spite of the fact that in several cases the inclusion of parameter B did result in smaller sums of squared deviations.

DeJong's Learning Formula with an Incompressibility Factor

DeJong proposed a version of the power function which suggests parameters to be assigned for the proportion of manual activity in a given task. When the activities are mainly controlled by manual operations, the time is compressible as successive units are completed. If machine time was dominant in the cycle of activities, the time will be less compressible as the number of units increases. Accordingly, DeJong introduced an incompressibility factor M in the log-linear model to take into account the man-machine ratio and the asymptotic behaviour of the curve when it approaches a limit of unit time as the number of units increases. This model generates, then, two components: a fixed component which is set equal to the irreducible portion of the task and a variable component which is subject to learning. It has the following form: MC = a [M + (1 - M)/Xn] where*MC* = marginal time for the xth unit,*a* and *n* are parameters analogous to the power function,*M* is the factor of incompressibility.

The incompressibility factor suggested by DeJong is often 0.25 for manually dominated activities and 0.50 for machine-dominated activities. When *M* is zero, the DeJong formulation becomes the log-linear model, which would happen in a situation of a completely manual situation. In a machine-dominated situation, *M* approaches 1, and the expected unit time is a constant, thus *MC* = *a*. A set of curves for various values of *M*, for all of which the learning exponent is *n* = 0.32.

The incompressibility factor indicates the inability to reduce production time as the number of cycles is repeated. A completely machine-dominated operation would be unlikely to improve and thus possess high incompressibility. In addition, the model demonstrates a practical limit to the amount of learning or improvement. The curve ultimately approaches a plateau as the number of units increases.

The S-Curve

Another curve useful when the data "miss" the straight learning curve is the somewhat S-shaped curve. For example, Carr proposed an S-type function which was based on the assumption of a gradual startup. An S-type function has the shape of the cumulative normal distribution function for the start-up curve and the shape of an operating characteristics function for the learning curve. Several factors appear to contribute to this pattern:

- The early stages of production are a time of partial experimentation by all personnel. Various approaches are tried in learning to use prescribed tooling and methods, which preclude rapid improvement. Further, last minute changes in design and materials sometimes hit during this period, and these prevent the solidification of techniques necessary for rapid learning or initial low cost.

- As corrections are made to toolings and methods, a rapid reduction in cost is possible for some time. For our assembly operation, the learning slope often reaches 50 per cent during the period, compared with a norm of 75 per cent.

3. Finally, however, the "water" has been taken out of the costs and we settle down to a more routine activity—the slope activity. The slope of learning now proceeds somewhat more slowly than average, say at 80 per cent for assembly.

Because the Stanford-B may better fit the early part of the curve and the DeJong model the latter part, one approach may be to combine these two models to obtain an S-curve such as:

$$MC = a [M + (1 - M) (x + B)n].$$

To solve this equation, however, assumptions have to be made to preselect the incompressibility M and equivalent experience units B and a to solve for a value of n. In other words, values for any of the unknown can be determined given a logical pre selection of the other three independent variables.

Another procedure for the determination of the coefficients of the Scurve is to look at it as a smooth "cubic curve." In such a case the model log MC = A + B(log x) + C(log X2) + D(log X3) represents the cubic curve on a log-log plot. The fitting of a cubic curve to actual time can then be accomplished by the use of any polynomial fit programme from the available computer library statistical routines.

GLOVER'S LEARNING FORMULA WITH A WORK COMMENCEMENT FACTOR

In contrast to other theories which were based on an analysis of the output of complete factories, Glover examined studies of the gain in speed skill of individuals before extending the model to complete departments of companies. A model derived for the learning of individuals in experimental psychology was found applicable to learning of all kinds in industry. It is expressed as follows: where yi and xi are interchangeable in the sense that either may represent time or quantity, C is a commencement factor, a is the time of the first cycle, and n is the index of the curve = 1 + b. If "y is used to represent the total elapsed time, then xi will normally be unity, that is,

The model differs from the conventional power function of the introduction of the work commencement factor C. The rationale for such adjustment is stated as follows:

The nature of logarithmic scales tends to exaggerate any early deviation from the straight line, and it is not surprising that, if only a few cycles of practice can upset a laboratory experiment, lack of understanding of the importance of recording exact times in industry can cause a curve to be obtained instead of a straight line.

The "work commencement" factor C in the model is, in effect, a factor of ignorance concerning the commencement of a job. As has been stated, there is reason to think that when C is not zero, the data relating to the time of commencement may be inaccurate. The reader may synthesize such inaccuracies by taking data which is known to yield a straight line relationship and introduce a fictitious constant error into either the time or practice scales.

Chapter 5

Learning Model

The learning curve is a well-accepted model in the production and managerial accounting literature. Although various mathematical models have been suggested as descriptive of the phenomenon, only one—the constant-percentage or log-linear model—is widely used and discussed in the managerial accounting literature. The log-linear model basically states that the improvement in productivity is fairly constant as output increases. A basic knowledge of the working of these models is important for an efficient implementation in actual managerial situations.

GENERAL MODEL

The learning phenomenon based on the constant-percentage model is generally expressed by the mathematical function,

$$(Y, I_* \text{ or } M) = ax$$

where the right side of the function is defined as,

a = the number of direct-labour hours required to produce the first unit of output,

where,

r = the rate of learning or improvement represented by the constant percentage decrease in hours,

f = the factor increase in output (usually discussed in terms of 2).

As can be seen from the formulae, the dependent variable is represented by either Y, I_* or M. This is due to the existence of three types of learning curve models which differ in their definition of the dependent variable. They are the average time model, the marginal time model, and the individual unit-time model. They may be defined as follows: The average time model specifies that the new cumulative average time per unit (Y) will decrease by a constant percentage (r) as the cumulative production doubles. The marginal time model specifies that the new marginal time per unit (M) will decrease by a constant percentage (r) as cumulative production doubles.

The individual unit-time model specifies that the new individual time per unit (I *) will decrease by a constant percentage (r) as cumulative production doubles. In what follows I will explain each of these models, present a synthesis of the three models, provide guidance for the choice of one of these models, and elaborate on the relationships between the percentage of learning and the b parameter (the learning exponent).

The Average Time Model

As stated earlier the average time model specifies the relationship between the cumulative average time per unit (Y) and the cumulative production (X).

More precisely, the basic formulae for the average time or average curve specifies that the new cumulative time per unit (Y) will decrease by a constant percentage (r) as the cumulative production doubles.

Besides the average time, the model provides formulae for the total time or total curve, the individual time or individual curve, and the marginal time or marginal curve.

Formula 1 computes the average curve Y (that is, the average cumulative labour hours, labour dollars, or material cost for all units produced up to any particular point):

Y = aXb

where,

Y = Average cumulative labour hours, labour dollars, or material costs for X number of units,

a = Theoretical value or actual value (if known) of the first unit,

X = Cumulative number of units produced,

b = Slope coefficient, exponent, or learning index. It is always negative, since the cost or number of hours is decreasing.

A much more used logarithmic version of formula 1 is,

$$\log Y = (\log a) + (b \log X).$$

Formula 2 computes the total curve T (that is, the total labour hours required to produce a predetermined number of units):

$$T = YX = XaXb = aXb\text{-}1$$

where T = total labour hours required to produce a predetermined number of units.

Formula 3 computes the individual unit time I (that is, the change in successive times):

$$I = aXb+1 - a(X - J)b + 1$$

Formula 4 computes the marginal curve M (that is, the relative change in total time to produce the xth unit, or slope of total time):

$$M = dt/dn = (b + 1)aXb$$

where M = marginal time to produce the xth unit.

To apply any of the four formulae, the value of the exponent b is first computed as follows:

$$b = \log r/\log 2 \text{ or } \log r = b \log 2.$$

To illustrate the average time model, let us assume that:

- It takes 800 hours to produce the first unit of a product, and
- An 80 per cent learning rate is found to exist in the average assembly time when cumulative production doubles. Determine the value of b and the cumulative average labour hours for 4 units of output by first determining the value of *b*:

  b = log (0.80)/log 2

Table. Common Logarithms of Numbers

No.	0	1	2	3	4	5	6	7	8	9	Avg. diff.
1.0	0.0000	0043	0086	0128	0170	0212	0253	0294	0334	0374	
1.1	0414	0453	0492	0532	0569	0607	0645	0632	0719	0755	
1.2	0792	0828	0864	0899	0934	0969	1004	1038	1072	1106	
1.3	1139	1173	1206	1239	1271	1303	1335	1367	1399	1430	

No.	0	1	2	3	4	5	6	7	8	9	Avg. diff.
1.4	1461	1462	1523	1553	1584	1614	1644	1673	1703	1732	
1.5	1761	1790	1818	1847	1875	1903	1931	1959	1987	2014	
1.6	2041	2068	2095	2122	2148	2175	2201	2227	2253	2279	
1.7	2304	2230	2355	2380	2405	2430	2455	2480	2504	2529	
1.8	2553	2577	2601	2625	2648	2672	2665	2718	2742	2765	
1.9	2788	2810	2833	2856	2878	2900	2923	2945	2967	2989	
2.0	0.3010	3032	3054	3075	3096	3118	3139	3160	3181	3201	21
2.1	3222	3243	3263	3284	3304	3324	3345	3365	3385	3404	20
2.2	3424	3444	3464	3483	3502	3522	3541	3560	3579	3598	19
2.3	3617	3636	3655	3674	3692	3711	3729	3747	3766	3784	18
2.4	3802	3820	3838	3856	3874	3892	3909	3927	3945	3962	17
2.5	3979	3997	4014	4031	4048	4065	4082	4099	4116	4133	17
2.6	4150	4166	4183	4200	4216	4232	4249	4265	4281	4298	16
2.7	4314	4330	4346	4362	4378	4393	4409	4425	4440	4456	16
2.8	4472	4487	4502	4518	4533	4548	4564	4579	4594	4609	15
2.9	4624	4639	4654	4669	4683	4698	4713	4728	4742	4757	15
3.0	0.4771	4786	4800	4814	4829	4843	4857	4871	4886	4900	14
3.1	4914	4928	4942	4955	4969	4983	4997	5011	5024	5038	14
3.2	5051	5065	5079	5092	5105	5119	5132	5145	5159	5172	13
3.3	5185	5198	5211	5224	5237	5250	5263	5276	5289	5302	13
3.4	53151	5328	5340	5353	5366	5378	5391	5403	5416	5428	13
3.5	5441	5453	5465	5478	5490	5502	5514	5527	5539	5551	12
3.6	5563	5575	5587	5599	5611	5623	5635	5647	5658	5670	12
3.7	5682	5694	5705	5717	5729	5740	5752	5763	5775	5786	12
3.8	5798	5809	5821	5832	5843	5855	5866	5877	5888	5899	11
3.9	5911	5922	5933	5944	5955	5966	5977	5938	5999	6010	11
4.0	0.6021	6031	6042	6053	6064	6075	6085	6096	6107	6117	11
4.1	6128	6138	6149	6160	6170	6180	6191	6201	6212	6222	10
4.2	6232	6243	6253	6263	6274	6284	6294	6304	6314	6325	10
4.3	6335	6343	6355	6365	6375	6385	6395	6405	6415	6425	10
4.4	6435	6444	6454	6464	6474	6484	6493	6503	6513	6522	10
4.5	6532	6542	6551	6561	6571	6580	6590	6599	6609	6618	10
4.6	6628	6637	6646	6665	6665	6675	6684	6693	6702	6712	10
4.7	6721	6730	6739	6749	6758	6767	6776	6785	6794	6803	9
4.8	6812	6821	683	6839	6848	6857	6866	6875	6884	6893	9
4.9	6902	6911	6920	6928	6937	6946	6955	6964	6972	6981	9

No.	0	1	2	3	4	5	6	7	8	9	Avg. diff.
5.0	0.6990	6998	7007	7016	7024	7033	7042	7050	7059	7067	9
5.1	7076	7084	7093	7101	7110	7118	7126	7135	7143	7152	8
5.2	7160	7168	7177	7185	7193	7202	7210	7218	7226	7235	8
5.3	7243	7251	7259	7267	7275	7284	7292	7300	7308	7316	8
5.4	7324	7332	7340	7348	7356	7364	7372	7380	7388	7396	8
5.5	7404	7412	7419	7427	7435	7443	7451	7459	7466	7474	8
5.6	7482	7490	7497	7505	7513	7520	7528	7536	7543	7551	8
5.7	7559	7566	7574	7582	7589	7597	7604	7612	7619	7627	8
5.8	7634	7642	7649	7657	7664	7672	7679	7686	7684	7701	7
5.9	7709	7716	7723	7731	7738	7745	7752	7760	7767	7774	7
6.0	0.7782	7789	7796	7803	7810	7818	7825	7832	7839	7846	7
6.1	7853	7860	7868	7875	7882	7889	7896	7903	7910	7917	7
6.2	7924	7931	7938	7945	7952	7959	7966	7973	7980	7987	7
6.3	7993	8000	8007	8014	8021	8028	8235	8041	8048	8055	7
6.4	8052	8069	8075	8082	8089	8096	8102	8109	8116	8122	7
6.5	8129	8136	8142	8149	8156	8162	8169	8176	8182	8189	7
6.6	8195	8202	8209	8215	8222	8228	8235	8241	8248	8254	7
6.7	8261	8267	8274	8280	8287	8293	8299	8305	8312	8319	6
6.8	8325	8331	8338	8344	8351	8357	8363	8370	8376	8382	6
6.9	8388	8395	8401	8407	8414	8420	8426	8432	8439	8445	6
7.0	0.8451	8457	8463	8470	8476	8482	8488	8394	8500	8506	6
7.1	8513	8519	8525	8531	8537	8543	8549	8555	8561	8567	6
7.2	8575	8579	8585	8591	8597	8603	8609	8615	8621	8627	6
7.3	8633	8639	8645	8651	8657	8663	8669	8675	8681	8686	6
7.4	8692	8698	8704	8710	8716	8722	8727	8733	8739	8745	6
7.5	8751	8756	8762	8768	8774	8779	8791	8791	8797	8802	6
7.6	8808	8814	8820	8825	8831	8838	8842	8848	8854	8859	6
7.7	8865	8871	8876	8882	8887	8893	8899	8904	8910	8915	6
7.8	8921	8927	8932	8938	8943	8949	8954	8960	8965	8971	6
7.9	8976	8982	8987	8993	8998	9004	9009	9015	9020	9025	5
8.0	0.9031	9036	9042	9047	9053	9058	9063	9069	9074	9079	5
8.1	9085	9090	9096	9101	9106	9112	9117	9122	9128	9133	5
8.2	9138	9143	9149	9154	9159	9165	9170	9175	9180	9186	5
8.3	9191	9196	9201	9206	9212	9217	9222	9227	9232	9238	5
8.4	9243	9248	9253	9258	9263	9269	9274	9279	9284	9289	5
8.5	9294	9299	9304	9309	9315	9320	9325	9330	9335	9340	5

8.6	9345	9350	9355	9360	9365	9370	9375	9380	9385	9890	5
8.7	9395	9400	9405	9410	9415	9420	9425	9430	9435	9440	5
8.8	9445	9450	9455	9460	9465	9469	9474	9479	9484	9439	5
8.9	9494	9499	9504	9509	9513	9510	9523	9528	9533	9538	5

No.	0	1	2	3	4	5	6	7	8	9	Avg. diff.
9.0	0.9543	9547	9552	9557	9562	9566	9571	9576	9581	9586	5
9.1	9590	9595	9600	9605	9609	9614	9619	9624	9628	9633	5
9.2	9638	9643	9647	9652	9657	9661	9666	9671	9675	9680	5
9.3	9685	9689	9694	9699	9703	9708	9713	9717	9722	9727	5
9.4	9731	97.6	9741	9745	9750	9754	9759	9763	9768	9773	5
9.5	9777	9782	9786	9791	9795	9800	9805	9809	9814	9818	5
9.6	9823	9827	9832	9836	9841	9845	9850	9854	9859	9863	4
9.7	9868	9872	9877	9881	9886	9390	9894	9899	9903	9908	4
9.8	9912	9917	9921	9926	9930	9934	9939	9943	9948	9952	4
9.9	9956	9961	9965	9969	9974	9978	9983	9987	9991	9996	4

$\log \pi = 0.4071$ $\quad \log \pi/2 = 0.1961$

$\log \pi 2 = 0.9943$

$\log \theta = 0.4343$ $\quad \log (0.4343) = 0.6378 - 1$

These pages give the common logarithms of numbers between 1 and 100, correct to four places. Moving the decimal point n places to the right [or left] in the number is equivalent to adding n [or - n] to the logarithm. Thus, log 0.017453 - 0.2419 - 222, which may also be written 2.2419 - 10.

$\log (ab) = \log a + \log b$ $\quad \log (a) = \log a$

Next, the four formulae—the average time, the total time, the individual unit-time, and the marginal time—may be used to determine the average labour hours, the total labour hours, the individual unit labour hours, and the marginal labour hours required for different numbers of units.

The Marginal Time Model

As stated earlier, the marginal time model specifies the relationship between the marginal time per unit (M) and the cumulative production (X).

More precisely the basic formulae for the marginal time or marginal curve specifies that the new marginal time per unit (M) will decrease by a constant percentages (r) as cumulative production doubles. Besides the marginal time, the model provides formulae for the total time or total curve, the individual time or individual curve, and the average time or average curve. Formula 1 computes the marginal curve M (that is, the marginal labour hours, labour dollars, or material cost for all units produced up to any particular point):

$$M = aX$$

where,

M = marginal time per unit for X *** numbers of units produced, a = number of hours to build the first unit, X = number of units completed, b = learning factor.

To apply these formulae, assume that:

- It takes 700 hours to complete the first unit of output,
- An 80 per cent learning curve exists in the marginal time when production doubles. As in the earlier example (in the average time model), b may be found to be equal to -0.3200. Inserting the proper values in the form formulae will yield the marginal time, total time, and average time for different levels of production.

The Individual Unit-Time Model

As stated earlier, the individual unit model specifies that the new individual time per unit (I_{*}) will decrease by a constant percentage (r) as cumulative production doubles. More precisely, the basic formulae for the individual unit-time or unit-time curve specifies that the new individual time per unit (I_{*}) will decrease by a constant percentage (r) as cumulative production doubles. Besides the individual time, the models provide formulae for the total time or total curve, the average time or average curve, and the marginal time or marginal curve.

Distinguishing among the Three Forms of the Constant Percentage Learning Curve Model

The three models differ in their definition of the dependent variable (the left side of the equation) which is subject to the learning phenomena.

- In the average time model, the dependent variable is the new cumulative average time per unit Y.
- In the unit time model, the dependent variable is the individual time per unit, I *.
- In the marginal time model, the dependent variable is the marginal time per unit, M **.

It is important to determine which is the correct dependent variable which is subject to the learning phenomena because it dictates the types of formulae to be used.

Which Model to Use

The process being studied determines whether the average time, the marginal time, or the individual unit time should be used.

The procedure consists of the following steps:

- Collecting average time, marginal time, and individual unit-time information and cumulative output information.
- Plotting the information on a log-log graph and the line providing the best visual fit between, on one hand, the average time, the managerial time, or the individual time information and, on the other hand, the cumulative output defines the model to be used.
- To be more exact in determining whether the average time, marginal time, or individual unit time applies, perform a logarithmic linear regression of either one of the possible dependent variables with the output, that is, log (time, average, total, or individual unit) = log a + b log (cumulative units).

The model which provides the best statistical fit in terms of the highest coefficient of determination, R, should be used as the right model for the observed learning phenomenon.

Relationships Between Percentage of Learning and Parameter b

To simplify the computations necessary in the applications of the learning curve, the relationships between the percentage of learning (r) and the exponent (b) can be established for all possible values of r. In general, the relationship is computed as b = log 2/log 2. For example, for 2 = 70 per cent, b = -0.51457. This relationship for all values of r ranging from 51 through 97, and it can be used as an expedient way to find the appropriate value of b.

FORMULAE FOR DETERMINING THE SLOPE

The average time model of the log-linear model is represented by the formula $Y = ax$. If production doubles, then the formula becomes $Y = a(2x)$. Given that learning (r%) takes place when production doubles, then. If we take the logarithm of both sides and solve for b, then we obtain For example, the slope b for a 50 per cent curve is

COST ESTIMATION

The learning curve can be used in cost estimation. Cost estimation when cumulative costs are known and when the learning phenomenon is in effect consists of estimating the coefficients of the learning curve from past data using the logarithmic linear equation $\log Y = \log a - b \log x$.

In one method, the regression analysis of the logarithmic data on y and x using the least-squares method will provide a regression line. Its slope coefficient, exponent, or learning constant can be determined using the least-squares method as follows: where N = number of observations for which cost and hours are available, XY = product of log y and log x, X = log of the cumulative production, Y = log of the cumulative labour hours.

For a first example, suppose you were provided the data disclosing only the first three columns:

- For the weeks, column.
- For total production, column.
- For direct-labour hours. On the basis of these data two new columns are added: column.
- For cumulative units completed and column.
- For cumulative direct-labour hours. The data for columns and

- Are then plotted on a log-log graph. If the scatter diagram indicates the presence of a learning phenomenon, then we need to determine the following information to insert in the formula for the slope coefficient:

  Inserting the correct values in the formula yields

  Next the learning rate
- Can be determined as follows: b = log 2/log 2 or log $r = b$ log 2 = -0.267(0.3010) = -0.080367 r = 83.3%

The other method of finding the learning rate is the doubling approach. Basically, it reads the gain time over any doubled quantity. The learning factor can be expressed as the ratio between the time taken to produce Z units and the cumulative time to produce 2Z units.

If double quantities are not available, use instead the following formula:Using the, the learning rate may be computed as follows. If the time to produce 10 units is 174 hours and the cumulative time for 20 units is 290 hours, the learning factor is equal to (290/20 ÷ (174/10) × 100% = 83.3%.

After determining the learning rate using either the regression approach or the doubling approach, any of the computational formulae can be used to compute the average cumulative labour hours, unit labour hours, total labour hours, or marginal hours required to produce a specific number of units. The results of these computations. Finally, assuming the rate of learning will continue beyond total estimated production of 80 units, the learning curve can be used to make cost estimates.

WARRANTY MAINTENANCE AND MAINTENANCE FORCE

The learning phenomenon has been used in both the areas of warranty maintenance and estimating the size of a maintenance force.

In the area of warranty maintenance, Kneip suggested that a progress function exists in the relationship of a product's maintenance requirement to cumulative production. Whereas in the conventional application of the learning phenomenon, the dependent variable (cost r labour time) is a production efficiency variable, in the maintenance progress function, the dependent variable is a quality, reliability, and serviceability characteristic.

The results of regression analysis on two products showed that the maintenance progress function exists, that it relates warranty period maintenance to cumulative production, and that the relationship is logarithmic. Kneip also made the following interesting note:

Progress in a product's maintenance requirement is thus a characteristic of the organization, dependent upon both its structure and personnel, as well as the nature of the product. It cannot be overemphasized that progress is neither automatic nor self-perpetuating, but is the result of continual effort toward improvement.

Furthermore, its use as a management control device involves the possibility of actually impeding progress that might otherwise have been attained through the selection of a progress rate too slow to provide challenging objectives. The selection of the progress rate is a critical decision in the application of the function. In the area of maintenance force, Clarke used the learning phenomenon to predict the required size of a plant's maintenance force.

MAKE OR BUY DECISIONS

Learning curves are very helpful in make or buy decisions, which involve a choice between the cost of producing an item and the cost of purchasing it. The learning curve can provide the data for determining the necessary labour hours and the cost of producing the item. There are other costs involved, of course, but the labour costs are usually considered more illustrative. Once they have been determined, the make or buy decision is reduced to simpler terms.

Andress gives the following illustration of the usefulness of the learning curve in make or buy decisions. An aircraft company is faced with an economic slowdown and the necessity of reconsidering some existing subcontracts. It produces a landing flap assembly in its own plant as well as subcontracting it to another company. An existing subcontract to be considered for cancelling was for 372 landing flap assemblies.

In examining its learning curve, the aircraft company noticed that it produced 165 assemblies with a unit time of 445 hours for the 165th unit and that it would take a total labour cost of 111,000 hours if it decides to make the 372 additional units. On the other side, the subcontractor relying also on the learning curve has produced the 165th unit with a unit time of 42 hours—43 hours less than the aircraft company.

However, he found that the additional 372 units would require 164,000 hours, or 53,000 more than the aircraft company. Obviously the short-run analysis using the learning curve argued in this case for making rather than subcontracting. Using the same example as the one used by Andress, Katz cautions that the decision may very well hinge on the nature of the future demand. He states:

In the short run (for the first 372 units) it would be more economical to cancel the subcontract. In the long run, however, it would be less expensive to leave the work with the subcontractor, as he could produce the product for 10% less labour once it fabricated as many units as the company. Therefore, this decision would hinge largely on the profitability of future demand for these products. Since, in the particular case under consideration, the future demand was considered very difficult to measure, the decision was to make the units in the house and cancel the subcontract.

To use another illustration of the use of the learning curve in make or buy decisions, let's assume that the XYZ Company purchases 800 pumps from the ABC Company.

The price was set last year at $70 per unit. Given the higher price, the XYZ Company decided to make some cost estimates to consider the feasibility of making rather than buying the pumps.

The following estimates were made for an assembly run of 100 units:

Purchased components	$ 1,300	
Assembly labour	4,000	
Variable factory overhead	4,000	(100% of assembly labour)
Fixed factory overhead	5,000	
General and administrative overhead	3,200	
	$17,500	

A conventional make or buy analysis would compare the incremental costs with the supplier's price. In this case the incremental price will include only the relevant costs, that is, purchased components, assembly labour, and variable factory overhead.

The incremental price is computed as follows:

	Cost of 100 pumps assembly run	**Per unit**
Purchased component	$1,300	$13
Assembly labour	4,000	40
Variable factory overhead	4,000	40
	$9,300	$93

In this case the XYZ Company must elect to buy the pumps rather than make them given that the supplier's price of $70 per unit is lower than the company's cost of $93.

If, however, the XYZ Company was experiencing an 80 per cent learning factor, the analysis used would be different. With an 80 per cent learning phenomenon the XYZ's assembly labour and variable overhead costs should decrease by 20 per cent every time there is a doubling of cumulative production.

The following labour cost and variable overhead cost behaviour by lots would occur:

Quantity Per lot	**Cumuiative**	**Average Cost per unit**	**100 labour**
100	$40		
100	200	32	(40 ×.8)
200	400	25.6	(32 ×.8)
400	800	20.48	(25.6 ×.8)

This means that the average cumulative cost of the assembly labour for the first 800 pumps is $20.48 per pump. A revised analysis which considers an 80 per cent learning cost per unit factor is shown below:

Incremental Costs to Manufacture 800 Pumps:

Purchased components	$13
Assembly labour	20.48
Variable factory overhead	20.48
Total incremental cost	$53.96
Cost to purchase	$70.00
Savings if pumps are manufactured	$16.04

Therefore, if XYZ Company is experiencing an 80 per cent learning curve, it should manufacture the pumps rather than purchase them.

WORK-ACCIDENT EXPERIENCE

Work-accident is an unfortunate but recurring event in all types of human endeavors. Public data on the subject are available in most industries. Among those industries which collect, tabulate, and publish the work-accident experience of its member firms is the American Petroleum Industry. In that industry "disabling injury" and the computation of injury experience are accomplished on the basis of USASI Standard Z16.1. One of the statistics defined by that standard is this:

The assumption taken in the foundation of the standard is that in every unit of time some constant number of exposures occurs and is some multiple of the duration. Greenberg argued that the method was misleading and that the denomination of the standard should be in units of production rather than in units of time, especially in light of evidence that the incidence of accidents was highly negatively correlated with productivity.

bHe also found that accident experience follows a learning curve pattern, showing a decreasing trend in accident sequence as productivity increases. In fact, using mining industry data, Greenberg showed again in another study that mining accidents also conformed to a learning model. Such accident-experience learning curves may be used to evaluate the effectiveness of a safety programme and to open new possibilities in the analysis and prevention of accident occurrence.

STANDARD COSTS AND EFFICIENCY VARIANCE ANALYSIS

A standard cost is a forecast of what costs should be used as a basis of cost control and as a measure of productive efficiency when ultimately compared with actual costs. In a traditional labour variance analysis, where standard costs are compared to actual costs, the standard cost is assumed to be a constant amount per unit of output.

The analysis proceeds generally by dichotomizing the difference between the actual cost and the flexible budget into wage rate and efficiency variances as follows:

WRV = H (r - r) EV = r (H - H)

where

WRV = wage rate variance,

EV = efficiency variance,

H = actual labour hours,

r = actual wage rate per hour,

r = standard wage rate per hour,

H = standard labour hours

This traditional labour variance analysis rests in the assumption that no learning phenomenon is affecting labour usage and that it is realistic to assume that standard labour is constant over the total production of the period.If learning was present, then the assumption of constant standard cost is unrealistic and the traditional labour variance analysis inapplicable.

In such a case, it would be preferable to consider one of two possible approaches:

- One approach would be to use "moving standard costs" rather than "constant standard costs." The moving standard costs would be computed on the basis of the relevant learning curve formulae.
- A second approach would be to dichotomize the

traditional labour efficiency variance into (a) labour efficiency variance due to learning, and (b) a labour efficiency variance due to factors other than the learning factors.

To illustrate the three possible approaches, the traditional and the two approaches incorporating the learning effect, let's use this example: The XYZ Company makes personal computers. Its engineering department has determined that 800 direct-labour hours are necessary to assemble the first unit of a new model and that an 80 per cent learning phenomenon is present in the assembling process. The standard direct-labour rate per hour is $20. During the month of January, 10 personal computers were assembled in 800 hours. The actual direct-labour rate per hour is $75. Discussion of the three approaches to labour variance analysis follows:

FIRST APPROACH: NO LEARNING EFFECT INCLUDED IN THE ANALYSIS

Under this approach the traditional labour variance analysis consists of computing a labour rate variance and a labour efficiency variance based on a standard labour hours per unit of 100. It will be computed as follows:

SECOND APPROACH: LEARNING EFFECT CONSIDERED WITH MOVING STANDARD COSTS

The standard labour hours per unit is adjusted to take into account the learning effect resulting in the use of a moving standard cost. In such case, the standard direct-labour hours allowed for actual production of 20 personal computers is derived using the learning curve formulae as follows:

Therefore, the analysis can now proceed as follows: As can be seen by the analysis, the labour efficiency variance is $79,800 unfavorable taking the learning effect into account rather than $4,000 favorable effect in the traditional approach.

THIRD APPROACH: TOTAL CONSIDERATION OF THE LEARNING EFFECT

In this case the traditional labour efficiency variance is

dichotomized into both a labour efficiency variance due to the learning effect and a labour efficiency variance due to factors other than the learning factors.

This approach shows the whole picture by disclosing the pure efficiency variance due to the nonlearning factors and the learning efficiency variance due to the learning effect. This approach should allow for a better analysis and effective control of labour cost.

External Reporting

External reporting may be affected by the learning phenomenon. It may be suggested that the cost savings due to the learning effect should be abstracted from the profit so actual increased productivity can be examined rather than productivity due to a repetition of tasks.

A more important problem is the distortion of profit that can occur when production costs follow the learning curve phenomenon if two conditions exist:

- The contract(s) cover two or more periods, and
- The unit price is based on a cumulative average cost permit.

To correct for the possible misstatement of profit, that a cost allocation model based on the learning phenomenon will disclose the relationships between efforts and accomplishments better than the conventional method.

To illustrate the problem of profit misstatement and how to correct it with the learning curve allocation model, let us use the data shown in

Let us also assume that 40 units are sold in 19 × 1, and 120 units are sold in 19 × 2; the unit selling price is $50 per unit in both years; the factory overhead and the direct-labour cost are each incurred at the rate of $5 per direct-labour hour; and the material cost is $1 per unit.

The income statements for both years under the conventional method of matching actual costs with revenues and the learning curve allocation model. Under the conventional method the company shows a loss of $608 the first year followed by a profit (net income) of $1,168 in the second year;

the learning curve cost allocation model shows a profit of $140 in the first year and a profit of $420 the second year. Notice that the total profit for the two years is $560 under both methods. To avoid such reporting differences which may adversely affect the market image of the firm, Morse proposed the following reporting system:

As production takes place, any excess of the projected cost of each unit over the expected average cost of all anticipated production is charged to a deferred production expense account, and inventory is charged with an amount equal to the expected average unit cost of all anticipated production.

When the projected unit cost is less than the expected average unit cost of all anticipated production, this difference is deducted from the deferred production expense account, and inventory is charged with an amount equal to the expected average unit cost of all anticipated production. As production takes place, any differences between actual and projected costs are written off as a period variance unless a change in a parameter of the model occurs.

Applying this reporting system to the previous problem yields the following journal entries:

Year 1

Deferred Production Expenses	$748	
Work in Process		748

To defer the differences between the actual costs of $2,408 and average cumu- lative costs of $1,660

Year 2

Finished Goods	$748	
Deferred Production Expenses		748

To change the differences between the actual costs of $4,232 and average cumulative costs of $4,980

Cost Reduction

Finding ways to reduce costs sometimes may be crucial to firms and is a necessity most of the time. The learning phenomenon and the learning curve offer opportunities for cost reduction programmes in general and in the preproduction planning and the product redesign areas in particular.In the preproduction planning stage, the type of learning curve to be used subsequently may be affected by the level and content of organizational planning. More precisely, the more preplanning that is done in all aspects associated with the launching of a new product, the lower the cost of the initial unit.

With the cost of the initial unit being the starting point of the learning phenomenon, the lower it is through effective preproduction planning, the greater the savings generated by the resulting learning curve.

Various studies, including an empirical one, have pinpointed the impact of preproduction planning on the time taken to produce the first unit and the dynamic rate resulting during the course of production.

Other authors have emphasized the importance of proper preproduction planning undertaken at the initial stages to lessen the scope of improvement during the course of production, which results in a flatter function, lying considerably below one which depicts a smaller amount of preproduction planning.

Bhada identifies the following factors which influence initial cost and production time, indirectly affecting the dynamic rate:

- Anticipated duration of the production run.
- Estimated rate of output.
- The type of tooling utilized.

The degree of detail presented by engineering specifications. Effort expanded on settling problems regarding manufacturing design and inspection procedures. The degree of coordination achieved between different functions within the organization. The importance given to proper working methods, planning and shop organization. The influence of experience gained on similar product and processes

The impact of preproduction planning was even demonstrated in an experiment investigating the impact of types of organization structures on complex problem solving.

Note: "Groups with higher initial performance (a values) demonstrated relatively smaller indices of performance improvement than groups that began with relatively lower initial performance."

In the same vein, Abernathy and Baloff examined the supply-demand imbalances during the preproduction stage and suggested that effective and proper planning at the production marketing phase would help prevent costly imbalances because the rate of increase in productivity was different from the rate of increase in sales.

In the redesigning state of a product, the learning curve may also be used to reduce the cost and help estimate the engineering effort required to do the job. More explicitly, it can be applied to the engineering effort in repeated design passes directed toward the reduction of total cost of the first unit. Bruns presented a two-dimensional model relating the curve of the manufacturing learning improvement to the engineering learning improvement curve.

Bruns shows that the unit cost depends on the engineering design as well as a manufacturing cost factor and uses the model to determine how many engineering design passes are needed to drive the product cost down to some predetermined target.

The model allows reconciliation of the various approaches to new-product development where, on one side, researchers and scientists are attempting to build the first unit of some useful object at any cost, and, on the other side, engineers are trying to reduce cost while meeting given requirements. Bruns concludes:

In any event, whether engineering learning improvement is applied objectively or intuitively, this procedure warns the manager that the engineering effort to achieve a goal can vary widely, and may be beyond the range of interest or capability. New materials, processes, or designs and new personnel suggest possible reduction of costs through redesign. Conversely, experienced people and a steady technology suggest that great cost progress at small expense should not be expected.

Price Estimation

The learning curve is a study tool that can help managers understand and predict trends in cost. As such it can also be used to develop price strategies aimed at controlling market share and profitability. During phase A of, the dominant producer creates a price umbrella by keeping the price constant (or showing little decline), which may attract more producers. During phase B the price declines as a result of a price war where aggressive competitors strive for dominance. Finally, during phase C the price war is over, and a more stable and competitive situation is established among the price war survivors. The weak producers may have been eliminated or have differentiated their product.

Given that the cost function (Y) follows the pattern Y = KXb, the dominant producer may adopt a parallel stable pattern for the price function: Y1 = K1Xb, where Y1 is the average price and K1 the price of the first unit. This may discourage the entry of competitors. Although initial margins are small, final margins are usually greater.

Basically prices are set using the learning curve as an anchor. They are set at low levels with slim margins but which will generate higher sales volume and profits. The preemptive pricing strategy was successfully used by the so-called trusts of the late nineteenth century. The strategy consists of deferring the rewards and using the low prices generated on the basis of the learning curve to create a shakeout in the industry. Preemptive pricing is not successful in those situations where there is a constant need for product model changes or new-product introductions. The following features were found to be important for an effective use of preemptive pricing:

- The expected product life is long.
- The product is standardized, like a commodity, with little risk that consumer tastes will suddenly turn against it.
- The expected growth of the market is rapid.
- The apparent slope of the learning curve is steeper, since the learning curve in that instance can constitute

a substantial barrier to the entry of other firms into the industry.

- The product is not patent protected.
- The company is not particularly strapped for cash.

A price umbrella at a high price followed by a sudden price shakeout. It is an aggressive strategy aimed at eventual industry shakeout and "brutal" elimination of competitors.

Although other price patterns may exist, the predictive ability of the learning curve can be generally used as a determinant in estimating the number of labour hours required for production. This facilitates the seller's pricing of the output, of course. Thus, given a knowledge of prime costs, the labour hours determined from the learning curve can be used as an allocation base for other indirect costs. Furthermore, the buyer, aware of the learning characteristics of the seller's costs, may be willing initially to pay a higher price that is to be reduced as the supplier's production increases and its costs begin declining.

Capital Budgeting

For most companies capital budgeting is a very serious and precarious proposition, and any reduction in the uncertainty of the potential cash flow is desirable. First, in a capital budgeting situation the company is likely to be at the top of its learning curve; hence, it can derive significant labour and time savings estimates from the curve. Second, the greater the proposition of labour assembly time, the more likely the curve will explain cost behaviour. Third, the more planning the company does, the more useful will be the predictive aspects of learning curves.

As an example of the application of the learning curve, let's assume the following fictional example of the XYZ Company which is considering the investment of $50,000 in equipment having a five-year expected life and no salvage value. The investment is expected to generate a cumulative expected demand of 200 units composed of 25, 40, 60, 40, and 35 units per year for the respective five years. The required minimum rate of return is 20 per cent.

The engineering estimation led to the following costs for 200 units of production: direct material, $500; direct labour ($5 per hour for an average per unit of 100 hours), $500; variable factory overhead (50% of direct labour), $250; variable selling and administration (10% of the sales price of $2,500 per unit), $250. The total fixed costs are estimated to be $5,000 per year. Based on these data the capital budgeting analysis will proceed.

It shows that a net present value in favour of production equals $6,739. The XYZ Company has, however, determined that an 80 per cent learning rate is applicable to both labour and variable overhead. It concluded that the capital budgeting analysis should instead include the correct time required as determined by the learning curve.

Using the information that the first four prototypes required 1761.2 hours, it proceeded to compute the parameters of the learning curve b and a from the average model $y = ax$ where,

y = Cumulative average time,

a = Time required for the first unit,

b = Learning exponent,

x = Cumulative production.

For an 80 per cent learning curve, b was rapidly determined to be equal to -.3219. Given that it took 1761.2 hours for the first four prototypes, the cumulative average hours per unit is y = 1761.2 hours/4 = 440.3 hours.

Using the logarithmic form of the equation $y = ax$, we can solve for a as follows:

$\log y = \log a + b \log X$

$\log 440.3 = \log a + (-.3219) \log 2$

$a = 55.04$

Using the information obtained $a = 55.04$, $b = -.3219$, the marginal formula $y = (b + 1)ax$ and the demand distribution (25, 40, 60, 40, and 35), we can obtain the respective marginal time required (4,882 hours, 4,452 hours, 5,204 hours, 3,108 hours, and 2,444 hours). All this information may then be used in the capital budgeting analysis with learning-based costs. It shows a negative present value of $161.14. Using the improved cost projections of the learning curve, the capital budgeting analysis argues against the proposed investment.

Break-Even Analysis

Break-even analysis or cost-volume-profit (CVP) analysis is an established managerial tool that attempts to formulate a firm's cost and revenue functions and the relationships between the two. Basically, it involves an examination of cost and revenue behavioural patterns and their relationships with profit. The analysis separates costs into fixed and variable components and determines the level of activity where costs and revenues are in equilibrium. The cost-volume-profit analysis is a normative model for understanding the relationships between the cost, revenue, and profit structures of a firm. It is a key factor in all decisions based on selling prices, variable costs, and fixed costs.The conventional approach to break-even analysis is used to compute the break-even volume or level of activity for which the profit generated is zero and beyond which any increase in production will lead to positive results on profit. The break-even point corresponds to the volume of activity at which total revenues equal total costs.

In other words:

$r = P_q - (F + V_q)$

where,

r = Profit before income taxes,

P = Unit selling price,

q = Sales volume in units,

F = Total fixed costs,

V = Unit variable cost.

The break-even point at which sales equal total costs and profits equal zero may be found as follows:

$P_q * - (F + V_q *) = 0$

where q^* = break-even volume. Consequently, we may write where $P - V$ = contribution margin permit. Therefore, the break-even point equals the ratio of total fixed costs (F) divided by the contribution margin per unit ($P - V$). To illustrate consider the following example. Susan Pineda plans to open a frozen yogurt business.

She determined the following revenue and expense relationships:

	Dollars	Per cent
Sales price per cup of yogurt	50	100
Variable expense per cup	30	60
Monthly Fixed Expenses		
Rent	$1,000	
Wages	1,500	
Payroll fringe costs	550	
Other fixed costs	6,450	
Electricity	500	
	$10,000	

The break-even analysis proceeds as follows:

- The unit contribution margin or excess of unit sales price over unit variable cost is $P - V = \$.50 - \$.30 = \$.20$.
- The break-even point in terms of units sold is

The above "conventional" break-even analysis assumes linearity for both the costs and the reverse functions. With regard to costs, the linearity assumption means that the unit variable cost is a constant. In other words, no learning is taking place to reduce the unit variable cost. Needless to say, this is a very limiting assumption. The unit variable cost, in general, and the unit labour cost in particular may be subject to the learning phenomenon.

A declining labour cost due to the learning phenomenon would substantially change break-even analysis and improve its use as a tool for planning and control of operations. In fact, various authors have attempted to present models for cost-volume-profit analysis which incorporate a nonlinear cost function to express the effects of employee learning. Their contributions are examined next.

Brenneck was one of the first to integrate conventional break-even analysis with the learning curve theory. He argued that as the cycle time per unit decreases because of learning, both the unit direct-labour cost and variable cost will drop. He concludes that such a decrease in cost should be incorporated in the conventional break-even analysis to improve its reliability.

McIntyre examined also the effects of the break-even equation and solution. This analysis follows.

The profit equation without learning is $r = px - cyx - f$ where r = profit that is, x units would be produced by n labour teams of one or more employees each, with each team producing x/n units. To determine the break-even point, the last equation must be set equal to zero and solved for x. Due to the exponential form of the equation and the presence of fixed cost, it is not possible to present a general solution for this breakeven quantity.

The cumulative break-even volume may be determined for specific values of the parameters, however, by using the method of successive approximation to solve the equation for M = 0. Pegels used start-up curves to determine the break-even point. Using the marginal time model, he suppresses total costs as where cx is a variable cost that is not affected by learning. He also sequences the revenue function as $R(x) = px$.The break-even point is where $TC(x) = R(x)$ which after solving for n gives the following break-even point xB: If the cost of the first unit is $AC(1)$, then the break-even formula becomes p = selling price per unit less all variable costs other than labour costs,

c = labour costs per unit of time,

f = fixed costs per period,

y = cumulative average production time per unit after x units have been produced.

The average time model, which states that cumulative average time per unit will be reduced by 1 - R every time production doubles is $Y = ax$

where,

Y = the cumulative average production time per unit after x units have been produced,

a = the time required to produce the first unit,

x = cumulative production,

b = index of learning = log R/log 2,

R = learning rate.

The profit equation which incorporates the learning phenomenon will be as follows:

$$r = px - cax{+}1 - f.$$

If there were n production processes operating simultaneously, the profit equation will be,

$$r = px - nca\ (x/n) - f$$

As an example, suppose that $AC(1)$ = \$400, p = \$300, and c = \$200. For a = 80, b = 0.32193, and a = 0.67807, one finds that, In other words, the break-even volume is approximately 75 units.

POSSIBLE LIMITATIONS

INFLUENCE OF CAUSAL FACTORS

Common to all the learning curve models is the need to estimate these two basic parameters:

- Input resources associated with the production of the first unit, and
- The learning curve characteristic or some measure of the rate reduction.

The exact determination of these two parameters is essential to the validity of the use of the learning curve. There are, however, factors which may affect the exact determination of these parameters.

Hammer, for example, alluded to the fact that the incurring of more effort in the preproduction stage would lower the initial cost while the incurring of more resources during the production stage would increase the learning rate and cost reduction as production accumulates. Conway and Schultz attempted to categorize the factors which influence cost initially and during production. The preproduction factors which will have a bearing on initial cost and influence the number of opportunities for cost reduction subsequently include the following:

- *Tooling*: Type of tooling used and degree of completion or development prior to production.
- *Equipment and Tool Selection*: Volume for which production was planned.
- *Product Design*: Extent to which manufacturability was considered and the degree of change required

subsequently. Degree to which product design and manufacturing engineering were coordinated prior to initiation of production.

- *Methods*: The degree to which work methods in detail are predesigned and the effort devoted to associated jig fixture design, flow analysis, etc.
- State of the Art—relationship between the difficulty of the task and the ability of the organization to perform it.
- *Magnitude of the Design Effort*: Time and effort devoted to the problem of preproduction manufacturing design, specification, test, inspection, etc.
- *Shop Organization*: Including branding methods, preproduction training, skill, planning organization, etc.

All these factors suggest that to be useful the determination of the first piece cost of any item should be made far in advance of production. The production factors which will influence learning subsequently include the following:

- *Tooling*: Changes during production, method of increasing capacity for increasing demand (replication or redesign of production method).
- *Methods*: Changes during production, work simplification and similar programmes, operator originated changes, method of capacity increase.
- *Design Changcs*: Degree to which manufacturing and product designs are changed to allow minor economies, specification and inspection changes as experience is gained.
- *Management*: Improved planning, scheduling and supervision to encourage progress, increase effectiveness, diminish delays and idle time.
- *Volume Changes*: Changes in rate or anticipated duration of production which affect other factors and decisions.
- *Quality Improvements*: The gradual reduction of re-work and repair operations, the reduction of scrap losses.

- *Incentive Pay Plans*: Manner in which administered, when installed.
- *Operator Learning*: Degree to which operations decrease time utilized in execution of a specific task.

All these factors affect the determination of the basic parameters of the learning curve and may cause the learning relationship computed to differ under various circumstances. The last factor, operator learning, has been considered by some writers to be the most important causal factor in those cases where the operator can contribute improvements in task method., Others maintain that in most cases the tooling, flow, and methods changes are the most significant causal factors of the learning phenomenon.

They result more from management effort than operator learning. A more reasoned position is that the learning curve depends equally on both factors. More precisely, this position is supported by McCampbell and McQueen, who maintain that the function is based on the following:

- The human element (man's ability to learn and improve and the elimination of direct thought-process activities through repetition).
- The natural process of methods improvements and his foreman.
- More efficient material handling, transportation, pallet moving, and so forth.
- Less percentage owed to scrap, rejection, and re-works.

MEASUREMENT AND AGGREGATION PROBLEMS

In trying to determine the parameters of the learning curves in industrial situations, the cost analyst should beware of various measurement problems reported in the literature and in practice.

Some of these problems follow:

- The accuracy of the industrial data may be in doubt in most firms which use individual incentives such as piece rates for wage payment and control purposes. In effect such situations may create an environment in which output is restricted, actual times are seldom accurately recorded, and considerable doubt exists as to the validity of operator times charged to direct versus indirect labour accounts.

- The determination of the production count may be difficult because such factors as varying lot sizes, varying lead times, and varying schedules distort the association between costs and production quantities.
- The learning curve is generally determined for an aggregation rather than individual operations. What items to aggregate to determine the learning curve is a difficult and serious question. The aggregation may be determined following the organization of the facility and the method of production or following the inherent characteristics of operations performed and the components of the product or operation. The problems of what to aggregate may be exacerbated by the mechanics of aggregation when product is produced at different times in different lots.

Some writers have preferred to work from disaggregated data before determining the learning curve for a product or assembly.

For example McCampbell and McQueen maintained that the learning curve model for a product would depend on each type of operation and its corresponding percentage of total unit labour:

$$C = (X_1)(Y_1) + (X_2)(Y_2) + \ldots + (X_n)(Y_n)$$

where,

C = the learning curve for an assembly, X_i =% of the labour for each operation, Yi=% curve of each operation, n = operation number.

For example, suppose:

- *Machining*: 30% of the labour with a curve of 100%
- *Punch press*: 20% with 80% curve
- *Burring, Sanding, Hand Forming*: 10% with 90% curve
- *Assembly*: 40% with 70% curve then, the curve for this product is 83%.

A fourth problem can be added:

- Whatever learning rate is found, it is important not to think of it as universal. Overwhelming evidence shows that the rate of learning differs between products, manufacturing facilities, and industries. To think otherwise is illogical and hard to verify empirically. Progress does exist for some operations but not necessarily at the same rate. No give slope is universal. Even if a given slope seems to be recurring, the learning functions are generally deter mined with tolerable amounts of error. "There is no such thing as a fundamental law of progress such as the '80% learning curve' used in the aircraft industry."

One interesting finding reported is that it is common to find different learning curve ratios for similiar products within a given production facility, and identical products produced in different production facilities.

Another extensive study of data gathered in machine shops found, however, that while each basic manufacturing operation has an individual learning function for a product, it is based on a time-proportion weighted combination of individual progress functions.

NARROW UNDERSTANDING

One of the deficiencies in the learning curve literature is the narrow understanding of the causes and existence of the learning curve. The causes and existence of the learning phenomenon have been typically associated with clearing, or adaptation on the part of direct-labour workers, especially those involved in assembly. In general the contribution of engineers and indirect labour to the learning curve phenomenon has been ignored. In short, the learning phenomenon has been limited to direct labour, manual adaptation to repetitive tasks and has eliminated the machine-paced or machine-intensive manufacture.

Some authors have considered the generality of the learning phenomenon and criticized the narrow understanding of the causes and existence of the learning curve. For example Baloff states: "However, the emphasis on direct-labour learning as the primary cause of the learning phenomenon and the implications for machine-intensive manufacture that have been drawn from it appear to have very limited applicability."

What Baloff was alluding to is the generally accepted thesis in a variety of machine-intensive industries that a distinct learning phenomenon occurs during the start-up or debugging of new products and new production processes. An example of the learning phenomenon in the debugging of automated processes was provided by Bright.

This learning or debugging is not necessarily the result of an improvement in direct labour but more likely in direct labour, indirect labour, and technical personnel. In these cases, it is more the effort of engineers and other indirect labour employees that generated the learning in the start-up or debugging.

According to Baloff, this learning includes "such cognitive activities as redesigning the product or process, altering raw-material and end-product quality specifications, evolving more effective maintenance procedures and finding the proper operating (balance) of a manufacturing process."

NATURE OF THE LEARNING CURVE MODEL

Another deficiency in the learning curve literature is the uncertainty as to the actual form or statement of the learning curve model. There is not one single model of the learning curve.

The following seven models are possible:

- The log-linear model
- Pegels's exponential function
- Levy's adaptation function
- The Stanford-B model
- DeJong's learning formula with an incompressibility factor
- The S-curve
- Glover's learning formula with a work commencement factor

Some of these models have also been described by Carlson. Given that relative superiority is attributed to each of these models and specific industrial applications have been presented, it is recommended that new users of learning curves should make some test runs in their choice of the learning curve model most appropriate to their case.

PRACTICES IN ESTIMATION OF PARAMETERS

One of the major deficiencies in the learning curve literature is the dubious practice in the estimation of the *b* parameter in the learning curve model. As one may see by a cursory review of major cost account textbooks, it is the practice to simplify the parameter estimation problem by assuming that the *b* parameter retain the same constant value from start-up to start-up, i.e., "empirical parameter value." Baloff calling for more empirical investigation to shake the tenacity of this unfortunate assumption states:

This is not meant to eschew the role of empirical investigation, however, for it is clear that the generalization of the learning curve techniques will ultimately depend on empirical demonstration of the phenomenon in a variety of contents. Empiricism can make a further contribution in scrutinizing such dubious practices as the constant *b* parameter value and "interminable progress" assumptions that have plagued past applications of the learning curve.

In fact, evidence of the instability of the b parameter has been reported by Alchian in different airframe start-ups during World War II, Asher for a number of other postwar airframe start-ups, Conway and Schultz in the electronics industry, and Hirsh in the start-ups of machine tools.

SEPARATING THE WHEAT FROM THE CHAFF

The learning curve may be used by management as an artificial device to secure contracts and justify their cost estimates. In other words management may estimate their labour requirements with a false learning curve presumably based on empirical performance. If the contract is accepted, the learning curve-based estimates are used to prove its own existence. In other words the reduced labour became cursed by budgetary action more than by improved productivity through learning.

This artificial technique may be produced by:

- Increasing the labour content of the first unit or setting it at a very high point,
- Fluctuating labour classifications by frequently shifting the designation of workers between "direct" or "support/indirect" and hence reducing the labour content on a specific unit,
- Using manufacturing methods and tooling changes to create a reduction in the labour content, and
- Using at the start of the process small manufacturing lot sizes resulting in a high labour content for the first unit. These are some of the factors which obscure the true significance of the learning curve by causing it to reflect budgetary- and management-directed influence more than the increased productivity resulting from skill acquired in reflective operations. These factors which obscure the true significance of the learning phenomenon have been mostly noted to last in the aerospace industry. That industry is conducive to the use of the learning curve as an artificial device because of specific conditions in that industry that are outlined as follows:

  Profit is a negotiated element, dependent on cost.

There is little direct incentive to reduce cost, and there is incentive to maintain a high cost level.

The basic product starts the production cycle with relatively little definition, thus requiring much rework, modification and delays and an abundance of manpower to cope with those problems.

The customer may direct changes to be made that are outside of the contractor's original contract scope, and the contractor anticipates this by carrying additional personnel.

Objective manufacturing criteria generally are not used to achieve the most efficient production.

Variable-type time allowances that are often the basis for

staffing tend to create the appearance of a "cost reduction curve."

There is customer emphasis on reduction curves which stimulates contractors to "sell" and emphasize reduction curves.

Given these conditions which may also exist in other industries, the challenge to management and to other parties is to separate the wheat from the chaff and to identify the real learning curve if there is one.

ILLUSORY SAVINGS AND VERIFICATION

Illusory savings may be the result of errors in the selection of labour hour data to be used in plotting the curve. First, automation may lead to a reduction in labour input per unit. Second, a direct-labour savings may disguise a greater use of indirect labour.

Third, a change in the "labour mix" through hiring more qualified workers may lead to savings in direct-labour hours and an increase in direct-labour cost. Finally, the savings in labour may be due to a change in volume rather than to learning.

All this creates a problem of verification. The problem of verification pertains mainly to the possibility of obtaining inaccurate data for direct labour, and to the potential inability to isolate accurately the learning factor that led to the reduction in direct labour. As a result, the learning curve in its present state has been criticized as failing to be a "scientific tool."

NEGATIVE OR DEFEATIST ATTITUDES OF EMPLOYEES

The negative or defeatist attitudes of employees may act as a barrier to the implementation or acceptance of the learning curve. Attitudes which ignore, belittle, or negate the presence of learning threaten the applicability of the learning phenomenon. For the learning phenomenon to be used effectively, positive attitudes have to be generated from the employee. Faith in the phenomenon is important. If progress is believed possible, then the learning phenomenon has a chance to occur. Open ended expectations and the absence of "ceiling psychology" are two factors most conducive to a learning effect. Some companies have been reported to have obtained more progress when the workers are not informed of the target rate. This is possible because the target set does not become a self-fulfilling prophecy. Finally, credibility in the phenomenon and its possibilities act as a major drive for its use.

As Hirschmann states: If the premise is valid that learning performance can be an underlying natural characteristic, then such performance should be found not only for more types of activities already recognized as responsive, but also for operations not previously reported or believed possible.

Petroleum refining is considered to have such operations. It is characterized by large investments in heavy equipment, and is so highly automated that learning is thought to be nonexistent or too small to be of value. What Hirschmann is alluding to is progress by serendipity whereby the assumption that continual progress can occur may also create an atmosphere conducive to a learning phenomenon.

He states again: Nevertheless, discovering such performance for operations previously considered unresponsive does provide additional tangible evidence that learning can be an underlying natural characteristic of organized activity. It does not merely extend the catalog of learning curves.

Instead, it can help to breed the correction that such performance should be found elsewhere, and thereby lead not only to scrutinizing all operations to see which additional ones are susceptible, but to assuming that all operations have learning curve potential and to devising ways of making this potential a reality.

Thus, it is prudent to reflect learning potential in plans and forecasts. White goes further by suggesting the use of learning curve theory to predict expected improvement in advance and sets these goals as an incentive to accomplishment.

ANOMALIES IN THE LEARNING CURVE SHAPE

It is common practice to assume that improvement in direct-labour activity associated with a start-up will continue throughout the production history of the product. These assumptions are at best tenuous.

For example, Asher found evidence of plateaus developing in the start-up histories of several postwar airframes produced in the United States. Similarly, Conway and Schultz found distinct steady-state conditions occurring at the end of several new product start-ups. It is generally more accepted that there are several variations to the smooth learning curve forms, mainly with respect to the start-up point.

The steepness of some curves may be due to an assumed high labour requirement. For example, if the proportion of assembly work was supposed to be lower, the downward slope of the curve would not be as steep. In addition to the steepness, there may be anomalies to the learning curve shape. Hirschmann listed the following possible anomalies to the learning curve shape.

- A leveling off or a toe up may occur due to such factors as the closing of operations at the end of a contract. The costs may increase, which is a condition known in the industry as reverse learning.
- An aberration may also occur in the middle of the curve.

Hence, if the production process is interrupted for a significant length of time, resumption of the work will reflect a sharp increase in the learning curve. The aberration may be due to inefficiencies resulting from the employees' loss of skill and from the reorganization costs. Such a situation is called a scallop. It may also result from the change in the design of a product followed by two costs:

- The cost of added design less the quoted cost of the design removed, and
- A loss of learning resulting in not being able to produce an assembly at the full quantity contracted.

Hirschmann listed a third anomaly: A leveling down or a toe down may result from major innovations or sudden improvements in the learning process. The possible anomalies in the learning curve. The leveling-off phenomenon has been observed by others and labeled as the phenomenon of plateauing. The results of the empirical analysis of different start-ups showed that the learning phenomenon occurs regularly, is generally pronounced, but is ultimately followed by plateauing or steady-state conditions. Baloff states the findings as follows:

- There is clear indication that a definite learning phenomenon occurs regularly in the several forms of manufacture investigated, and that this phenomenon is common to both new process and new product start-ups.
- The productivity consequences of the phenomenon are generally pronounced; all of the start-ups were marked by large regular increases in productivity for some months following the inception of manufacture.
- These productivity increases do not continue interminably; they are typically interrupted by the eventual development of a distinct steady-state operating condition.

In fact, Baloff observed plateauing in both machine-intensive manufacturing as well as labour-intensive manufacturing, with more likelihood of it happening in the machine-intensive cases where management is not willing to invest in capital to sustain learning.

The two phases of plateauing in the learning curve. Another interruption in the learning phenomenon can be caused by production breaks. The production break is the time lapse between the completion of a contract for the manufacture of certain units of equipment and the commencement of a follow-on order for identical units.

Anderlohr focused on production breaks between manufacturer lots and the resulting loss of learning which takes place. The following five factors associated with loss of learning are identified: production personnel learning, supervisory learning, continuity of production, improvement of special tooling, and improvement of methods. In fact, all the interruptions identified in this section lead to some form of learning loss.

For example, Hall suggested that design changes lead to two costs:

- The cost of added design less the quoted cost of the design removed.
- Loss of learning resulting in not being able to produce an assembly at the full quantity contracted.

Chapter 6

Accounting for Public Sector

Prevailing political and social attitudes point to further expansion of this segment of economic activities. Society-at-large demands that certain public and nonproprietary services be provided for the benefit of all of its citizens regardless of their ability to pay. Profit-motivated enterprises are not able to make such services available to everyone within socially acceptable norms. Moreover, upon investigation it appears that the free-enterprise system (like any other known economic system) is incapable of alleviating all perceived inequities within our society.

The result has been that society, usually via governmental and charitable institutions, has made economic commitments to not-for-profit activities as a means of correcting perceived inequities. For these and a number of more technical reasons there exists a sector of economic activity for which the profit motive is absent by design.

NATURE AND SIZE

Economists generally divide the production activities of our economy into a private and a public sector. The simplest way to define the public sector is to include within it all organizations not privately owned and operated, that is, nonproprietary organizations, as well as all not-for-profit organizations. This public sector can be subdivided by placing all governmental units (local, state, and federal) into one category and all nongovernmental not-for-profit organizations into another. However, the foregoing delineations are not clear-cut.

Despite the hybrid nature of some nonproprietary and some not-for-profit organizations, the public sector is treated. Accounting and reporting problems are quite similar between units of governments and privately organized associations having no deliberate or avowed profit motive. Hence, the general frame of reference for not-for-profit organization or agency, generally without specific regard for the public versus private ownership question

Not-for-profit organizations have the following main characteristics:

- Contributors of resources receive no direct financial interest in these resources nor proportionate benefits from the organization's operations.
- There are no individual shares of ownership. Ownership is public and cannot be sold or traded.
- Performance of services occurs on the basis of perceived social need rather than in response to strict market-related demand.
- A framework of public authorization and control is utilized. In governmental units this authorization typically covers specific financial budgets. Government constitutions grant taxing authority and usually restrict modes of expenditures. Voluntary boards of trustees often control private nonprofit organizations.
- Accountability to the public is essential, since the public supports these organizations through direct contributions and grants many special privileges, such as a tax-exempt status. Sometimes this accountability is weak (in practice at least) for privately organized not-for-profit organizations.

Growth of Public Sector Activities

Not-for-profit activities have experienced substantial growth in our society over the last forty years when measured in terms of the resources committed to them. One interesting comparison is that all government expenditures prior to 1940 do not equal the amount presently spent in one year by the federal government alone. Of our total Gross National Product, which currently exceeds 1 trillion a year, approximately one-fifth comes from federal government sources.

Table. Federal Outlays for Social Programmes

Category	Actual			Estimates		
	1960	1965	1970	1971	1972	1973
Community Development and Housing	1.0	0.3	3.0	3.4	4.0	4.8
Education and Manpower	1.1	2.3	7.3	8.7	10.1	11.3
Health	0.8	1.7	13.0	14.5	17.0	18.1
Income Security	18.2	25.7	43.8	55.7	65.2	69.7
Total Social Programmes	21.1	30.0	67.1	82.3	96.3	103.9
Total Federal Outlays for All Programmes	92.2	118.4	196.6	211.4	236.6	246.3
Per cent Social Programmes to Total Programmes	23%	25%	34%	39%	41%	42%

State and local government expenditures over the past ten years have also increased. Their growth rate has been nearly double the rate of growth of the Gross National Product. Thus governmental units of all types spend about one-fourth of the economic resources of the total economy as represented by the Gross National Product.

Beyond government-related activities, there has been a significant growth in resources committed to the remainder of the not-for-profit sector of our economy. These nongovernment, not-for-profit activities include hospitals, private colleges and universities, religious institutions, private social agencies, the Red Cross, the March of Dimes, the Scout movements, and thousands of other similar organizations. In total, the size of not-for-profit economic endeavors is huge.

We should note here that comparable public interest

resource commitments are relatively as large, and in some instances even larger, in countries outside the United States. While many other Western nations-like Canada and the Scandinavian countries-devote proportionately greater resources to federal level expenditures, the United States leads in efforts devoted to nongovernmental not-for-profit activities.

Profit and Non Profit Organizations

We must also recognize that we live in`a social environment which imposes limitations on the use of available resources. Efficient use of limited resources once fell into the category of conventional political and individual judgment. Today it is clearly a social obligation and possibly even a moral obligation. It seems reasonable, then, that every effort should be made to maximize the benefits coming from the use of available resources.

Profit-motivated and not-for-profit organizations are alike in that both must strive in principle to marshall resources as best they can. Both must ultimately justify to society the commitment of resources to their respective operations. Both have the responsibility to operate as efficiently as possible in their resource conversion processes or in their outright consumption of resources. In this important aspect of social responsibility, no differences exist between the two types of organizations.

In another important respect, profit-motivated and nonprofit organizations are fundamentally different. In a market-oriented economy, a private enterprise that continuously consumes resources unwisely does not survive. If it is unable to produce market-acceptable goods or services efficiently and thereby provide adequate returns to its employees, creditors, and investors, it will go out of existence after a period of time. An unalterable process of elimination, perhaps a Darwinian "survival of the fittest," thus operates in the private sector of our enterprise system.

The potential elimination process operates quite differently in the public sector. Perceived social needs dictate the establishment and possible later termination of not-for-profit organizations without direct or singular reliance on a market system of economic checks and balances (though economic stress may be an overriding factor in the closing of a small private not-for-profit school or college).

Some public sector organizations may even be forced to operate in an economically inefficient manner for a time because public interest considerations demand it.

In a financial control sense, profit-oriented organizations focus heavily on producing appropriate returns for creditors and investors. Hence they have accounting systems that emphasize the periodic measure-ment of results of operations.

Public sector organizations are often concerned primarily with the size of their available cash resources, since the continued existence of public sector organizations or their programmes generally depends quite heavily on cash availabilities. Therefore measurements of financial position, including cash reserves and outstanding obligations, dominate public sector accounting.

Accounting Objectives

The objectives of accounting for not-for-profit organizations can be stated as follows:

- To provide the information necessary for efficient, effective, and economical management of a nonproprietary entity and of the resources entrusted to it. This is a management control objective analogous to its counterpart for private enterprises.
- To provide information that enables managers to report to third parties and to the general public on the discharge of their responsibilities in administering the programmes of the entity and the use of the resources under their direction.
- To permit public officials to report generally on the results of organizational operations and the use of public funds.
- To confirm and report legal compliance with statutory or administrative rules and regulations that relate to the acquisition and expenditure of resources.

Accounting entities in the public sector can be categorized into five different levels of operation.

Each of these levels involves one or more of the following:

- A government-city, state, or national;
- An organizational unit within a government-a department, an agency, a bureau;
- A separately organized not-for-profit organization comparable to a governmental subunit-a college, a church, or a community health centre;
- A programme-usually a specified set of goal-oriented activities which, at times, cuts across organizational lines in large not-for-profit organizations; and
- A fund-usually a pool of resources subject to special restrictions or requirements.

Since the notion of a "fund" has a specific connotation in public sector accounting, we call attention to the definition provided by the National Committee on Governmental Accounting in its 1968 edition of *Governmental Accounting, Auditing and Financial Reporting:*

A fund is an independent fiscal and accounting entity with a self balancing set of accounts recording cash and/or other resources together with all related liabilities, obligations, reserves, and equities which are segregated for the purpose of carrying on specific activities or attaining certain objectives in accordance with special regulations, restrictions, or limitations. The nature of these entities dictates an accounting orientation that seeks to substitute *effectiveness* in meeting specified objectives for the *periodic net income* measure of private enterprise performance. A second difference relates to *compliance* with laws, special limitations and restrictions, or organizational statutes. While legality is an ever-present ancillary goal of the private enterprise accounting process, it takes on the importance of ensuring specific statutory compliance in public sector accounting.

Compliance-efficiency-effectiveness are interlocking goals when it comes to public sector accountability. *Compliance* is a measurement of congruence with statutory or quasi-legal requirements.

Example: The Bel Ami Fellowship Fund requires that grants from its resources be made only to undergraduate students at accredited colleges and universities who can establish descendancy from French ancestors. Accountability for Bel Ami funds does not concern grade point averages, financial need, or subject area of study. Compliance is established so long as awards are made only to students with French forebears.

The notions of efficiency and effectiveness. *Efficiency* is related to economic performance. It is a measure of relationships for the entity between resource inputs and outputs. Different types of efficiency measures may be specified, for example, output efficiency or input efficiency.

Example: Output efficiency relates to specified levels of resource inputs. If the seating configuration of a commercial airliner is changed from five to six persons abreast in its coach passenger section, greater output efficiency (i.e., more passenger miles per flight) is achieved.

Example: Input efficiency is measured against a desired level of output. The city of Bellevue requires 250 transit buses to run an average of fifteen hours per workday. Higher input efficiency is achieved if the average cost per mile of operating a bus can be reduced from thirty-one to twenty-nine cents. *Effectiveness* measures achievement against specified technological, social, or other performance goals. It is normally difficult to quantify effectiveness measures precisely.

Example: The buses of the city of Bellevue operate over a route network which covers the entire city. Outlying areas have less frequent bus service due to a relatively lower demand for it. But there are persons everywhere within the city limits who depend completely on public bus transportation! A fully effective system would provide the same bus service to all citizens of Bellevue. Differential service frequency reduces public bus transportation effectiveness. Note also that greater effectiveness often means a sacrifice in efficiency. Compliance, efficiency, and effectiveness all require control procedures that may be built into underlying accounting systems and processes.

TRADITIONAL ACCOUNTABILITY

The traditional mainstay of accountability in the public sector has rested with expenditure control. Expenditure control is largely a compliance-oriented activity.

Expenditure Control

Managers of not-for-profit organizations cannot spend funds comparatively as easily as managers of private enterprises.

This is not surprising, since controlling expenditures is the important constraining factor in not-for-profit organizations.

Expenditure control is typically effected in four separate, sequential steps:

- Preliminary approval by a legislative body or a board of trustees to appropriate funds to a given programme.
- Actual appropriation of funds to an approved programme.
- Obligations or encumbrances incurred against the funds appropriated.
- Disbursement of funds.

This four-step expenditure control process is especially important for governmental units. Preliminary *approval* to appropriate funds to a given programme starts the programme by providing a blueprint on how programme expenditures are to be made eventually. But approval represents *no more* than eventual permission to request funds. Many tentatively approved programmes falter every year in national, state, and local governments due to the failure of the respective legislative branches to appropriate funds for projects or programmes fully endorsed at an earlier stage.

An *appropriation* grants authority from a legislative body or a city council or a board of trustees to an agency of government or to a not-for-profit organization (for example, the local boys' club receiving an appropriation from the Central United Crusade) to either disburse funds as approved or obligate the respective government or not-for-profit organization for the future payment of money. The act of appropriation is significant for accounting because it is at this point that the accounting process in not-for-profit organizations begins.

Step 3 entails recognition of planned use of appropriated funds. If contracts are actually made but not yet fully completed, an *obligation* is recognized. Definite commitments to spend funds for specified purposes in the future result in so-called *encumbrances* (defined below) against appropriated funds.

The formal recognition of an encumbrance illustrates an act of accounting in advance of a completed transaction. Recognition of obligations to expend funds provides a necessary control against incurrence of total obligations and expenditures exceeding available appropriations.Finally, *disbursements* are cash payments either liquidating public sector obligations or making direct payments for products and services as authorized.

The distinction between cash payments and obligations or encumbrances made on behalf of the not-for-profit unit is most important. New encumbrances must cease as soon as the appropriations level is reached—irrespective of actual cash payments to date.

Moreover, since direct operating cash payments are usually needed to the very end of an individual programme, advance encumbrances must typically stop short of the appropriated funding level.

In the public sector, then, accountants must provide continuing information to programme administrators on the following:

- Total appropriations available
- Total obligations and encumbrances to date
- Estimated funds needed to complete the programme
- Cash payments made to date
- Balances (for example, unused appropriations less obligations and encumbrances needed to complete programme, and obligations and encumbrances to date less cash payments made)

Accounting Process

A highly simplified example of a small federal government agency is used to illustrate the accounting process just described. In accounting for profit-motivated enterprises, the financial position equation is usually stated as:

Assets = Liabilities + Owner's Equity, however, represents the following relationship:

Cash Fund = Obligations Payable + Agency Account

Agency (fund) Account

The agency account, or fund account, is the accounting quantity measuring the unencumbered or otherwise uncommitted amount of appropriated funds. As a bookkeeping convenience, a nominal or subaccount for encumbrances is provided as an elaboration of the agency account.

Encumbrance

An encumbrance is an internal authorization to expend agency funds in the future for a specific purpose. An encumbrance is neither an actual expenditure nor an obligation already incurred.

The actual accounting process begins by formal recognition of appropriations becoming available to allow future expenditures.

The typical process also recognizes commitments (encumbrances) as soon as they are made against available appropriations. The process does not await evidence of a completed transaction, as is usually the case for business enterprise accounting.

Financial Position and Analysis of Changes

The agency starts the current period with a cash fund balance with the U.S. Treasury of 50,000. It has obligations (accounts) payable of 20,000 and a balance in the agency account of 30,000. The latter amount represents earlier appropriations not expended. In this case, periodic appropriations do not lapse at the end of the period for which an appropriation is made.

Line 1: A current appropriation of 300,000 is made to the agency through the federal department with which it is affiliated.

Line 2: The agency director authorizes the current item-by-item budget for the next period of operation.*Line 3*. Subcontracts are let for a number of agency subprograms. If a position statement were prepared at this point, it would appear as follows:

Cash balance with U.S. Treasury	350,000	
	=======	
Obligations and contracts payable	230,000	
Encumbrances for estimated future expenditures	80,000	
Agency account (Fund balance)	40,000	350,000
	=======	=======

Line 4: Orders are placed for miscellaneous office furniture, fixtures, and supplies in the amount of 10,000. This is technically an encumbrance.

Line 5: Salaries, wages, and other office expenses amounting to 75,000 became payable. In technical jargon, this is called an "expenditure."*Line 6*. Progress payments of $180,000 are made to subcontractors. This is a disbursement.

Line 7: Payment is made of various liabilities now due, including some that were outstanding at the beginning of the period and others recorded on line 5.

Line 8: Direct expenses amounting to 14,000 are paid for items like unbudgeted travel and office expenses. A summary of the final financial position is best expressed in statement form.

Cash balance with U.S. Treasury		62,000
		======
Obligations and contracts payable	31,000	
Encumbrances carried forward	15,000	
Agency account (Fund balance)	16,000	62,000
	-----	======

From the earlier definition of an encumbrance, we note that the agency has 31,000 (15,000 + 16,000) in cash resources not yet legally payable.

The 15,000 represents authorized future expenditures, and therefore the remaining 16,000 is the uncommited, unencumbered amount of funds with which the agency will start its forthcoming budget year.

Since balances carry forward, the agency:

- Had a total of 330,000 to spend during the current year instead of the appropriated 300,000;
- Incurred cash disbursements of only $288,000, even though its operating expenses were higher (financed by an increase in the amount of obligations payable); and
- Made commitments to expend funds during the next operating year and thereby anticipated its continued existence (this can only be done on the basis of appropriate legal or administrative stipulation).

Refinements

The foregoing illustration was constructed to show that not-for-profit organizations usually expend funds for two purposes:

- To acquire directly various goods and services needed for their programmes, and
- To make payments on obligations incurred for services performed by others (i.e., local contractors). The first category represents the largest amount of non-private funds spent each year in the United States. Accounting processes surrounding it can become very complex. They may involve special recognition of inventories and long-lived depreciable assets. On the other hand, the second category may call for renegotiations with subcontractors or elaborate payment schemes tied to production performance. Furthermore, complicated expenditure allocation devices may have to be used, as is the case when Medicare or other programmes cover health maintenance furnished by physicians and private hospitals. Yet the basic accounting process is the same in all of these instances.

Control of Resources

Expenditure control, is the traditional mainstay of *compliance* accountability in the public sector. How does this traditional system of accounting achieve resource input control in not-for-profit activities?

Three major resource control techniques are used:

- Precise specifications for appropriations of funds
- Creation of special-purpose funds
- Use of various cost concepts

Expenditure

Specification. One of the more effective cost control devices in not-for-profit organizations is the exact specification of the uses of funds at the time appropriations are authorized. Almost invariably the total amount of money is specified for a given appropriation. This places an upper limit on the cost that an agency or a programme can incur within the authorized appropriation.

When cost overruns occur, the additional sums of money requested are separately identifiable and hence susceptible to management and public scrutiny and review. Public sector appropriations are typically also quite specific as to the time period for which a given appropriation is available. This control technique ensures that unauthorized expenditures will not be made from carry-forward or carry-backward appropriations (our earlier illustration notwith-standing). When used in conjunction with other control efforts, the limitation on the length of time to complete an expenditure serves a good purpose.

However, when used by itself, it may well induce expenditures not actually needed because "the appropriation will be lost if not expended by *x* date," and, moreover, "next year's budget will probably be cut because we didn't need all that was appropriated this year." Agency case histories are filled with instances when public monies were consumed almost solely to avoid *under*spending an established budget (appropriation).

Another possible appropriations specification concerns

specific identification of the purposes for which designated funds are to be used (i.e., so-called line item budgets). This technique circumscribes the ability of administrator-managers to use funds at their own discretion outside the specified purposes.

Specification of purpose is an effective control too. It is particularly helpful in audit and review functions. The auditors can match, after the fact, the purposes contemplated in the approval and appropriation processes with the purposes served by actual expenditures. If variations are identified, corrective actions can be recommended or required.

Fund Designation

Probably the oldest control technique utilized for not-for-profit organizations is the segregation of appropriations into separately established funds.

For example, a small city government may have a fire department fund, a water department fund, a traffic court fund, a street and engineering fund, a planning commission fund, a public school fund, and so on. A local YMCA organization may have a capital project fund, a special programme fund, a scholarship fund, and an office and operations fund.

Since specification of nonproprietary resources into large batteries of individual funds is still used almost universally, accounting for not-for-profit organizations is often identified by accountants as "fund accounting." Under this concept, an individual fund becomes an *accounting entity* unto itself, and financial records and controls are established with a specific fund focus. Sometimes separate funds and separate accounts for them are required by law, especially in municipalities.

In fund accounting, it is common to distinguish between a general fund and special purpose funds. The general fund normally provides the resources needed to operate the unit or agency on a day-by-day basis. Salaries of employees, building maintenance, and general office expenses are items chargeable to a general fund.

In contrast, special funds are established to yield

accountability for separately identifiable activities which make individual control procedures necessary or desirable.

The pervasiveness of fund accounting is illustrated by the fact that the semiannual Uniform Certified Public Accountants Examination usually contains at least one lengthy problem on this subject. Undergraduate accounting curricula of colleges and universities often devote at least one quarter or semester course to fund accounting.

Various Cost Concepts

Following the lead of private enterprise, accountants and administrators in the public sector have recently begun to utilize different concepts of cost behaviour for specified control purposes. The essence of cost behaviour distinctions is that different cost measurements are most useful for different managerial control decisions if specific and directly related cost measurements are established for individual circumstances.

For example, the cost of acquiring an asset can be distinguished usefully from the cost of using that asset in a not-for-profit programme. Similarly, the cost of replacing an old asset with an equivalent new asset may be more important in certain decisions than original acquisition cost of the old assets.

MATCHING EFFORTS AND ACCOMPLISHMENTS

Compliance with expenditure authorizations is a key objective of the public sector accounting function. Measures of compliance are easier to establish than measures of efficiency or measures of effectiveness, since the output of not-for-profit organizations is by and large intangible and not market oriented. Our market-oriented economic system serves, among others, the crucially important roles of allocating resources and continually threatening the survival of weak or inefficient enterprises. Thus the profit motive ensures that the entire private sector runs relatively efficiently.

For private enterprises, periodic costs (efforts) and revenues (accomplishments) are accounted for systematically, and the difference between them is reported as period net income. For larger companies, this reporting must conform absolutely to the requirements of the federal SEC. Moreover, it must be reviewed and audited at least once a year by independent outside professionals. Determination of periodic net income is presumably the most critical performance measurement for a private enterprise.

Even though in the future we are likely to see greater emphasis upon measuring and reporting a company's social, legal, and environmental performance, the latter will not replace the basic measures of economic performance. So long as private capital finances enterprise investments, economic performance will retain its prominence in the overall system.

With the absence of the profit motive in the public sector and the compounding difficulty of producing intangible and quite often elusive products, periodic matching of efforts and accomplishments in terms of concise quantitative reports has proved difficult. Thus, for many years, the public sector did little more than measure and report its dollar performance.

Dollar Performance

Traditional financial accounting systems and reports of not-for-profit organizations are oriented to identifying and summarizing how money is expended and to what extent such expenditures are consistent with authorizations or budgets. This system provides dollar accountability, but it furnishes few clues about the results that may have been achieved. The degree of efficiency in operations cannot be determined from dollar performance reports. As we have seen, dollar performance is predominantly oriented to compliance. Dollar inflows are a measure of accomplishment for private enterprises if such inflows represent revenues. However, no implication of accomplishment can be attached to the donated or appropriated dollars flowing to a not-for-profit organization. Moreover, matching of costs and revenues in the private sector produces a measure of performance (however conventionally or arbitrarily defined) which, if consistently applied, is a useful economic indicator.

Neither money inflows alone nor calculations of *net* money inflows and outflows allow evaluation of the efficiency and effectiveness of a not-for-profit organization's activity. A system of accounts and reports primarily aimed at compliance is both necessary and desirable for the public sector. However, such a system does not adequately serve today's social needs and concerns.

PPBS System

During World War II, several federal government agencies and various units of the armed services began to distinguish between monetary expenditures and operational efficiency. Moreover, the stated objectives of an organization began to be distinguished from measured accomplishments of these objectives.

These developments were the forerunners of an accounting process known as planning, programming, and budgeting system (PPBS), which is increasingly being used in not-for-profit organizations. PPBS came fully into its own when, in 1965, the late President Lyndon B. Johnson requested that all government agencies adopt this system.

PPBS is designed to create a framework within which each not-for-profit organization can consider its anticipated outputs (accomplishments) in relation to probably required inputs of resources (efforts) before it makes a commitment to the programme. Under PPBS, the supporters of an organization or programme begin their justification for financial support by identifying the goals (accomplishments) that the organization or the programme expects to achieve.

Measurement is facilitated if goals can be stated in quantitative terms, though not necessarily dollar terms. After programme goals are established, alternative courses of action are evaluated in terms of their probable achievement of the goals (i.e., probable effectiveness) and their probable costs (i.e., probable efficiency).

Decision makers then choose the plan that allows optimal goal achievements in terms of required resource inputs (i.e., optimal effectiveness-efficiency). With PPBS, some proposed programmes are never initiated because analysis shows excessive resource input requirements or low probabilities of achieving desired results. Also, PPBS allows periodic reporting just like most other formal accounting systems.

Goals in Relation to Accomplishments

The statement is made in the preceding section that identification of goals is the first significant step in a PPBS system. This statement needs elaboration.

Goal-setting procedures in not-for-profit organizations technically involve:

- Specification of objectives and
- Specification of measures of accomplishment. Operationally, these two steps constitute the goal structuring needed in not-for-profit organizations.

Example: The stated objective of Unified School District 205 is to provide kindergarten, primary, and secondary education for all residents in its district through grade level 12. From this broad objective a hierarchy of sub objectives is established, like minimizing the number of high school dropouts per year, operating a special education programme for physically or mentally handicapped students, running summer school programmes for exceptionally able students, and providing various health care and counseling services for all students in the district.

The entire hierarchy of objectives is subsequently used to measure accomplishments. College admission percentages of high school seniors wishing to enter college may be one measure of accomplishment. Lower in the hierarchy, performance on verbal and quantitative aptitude tests may measure math and language achievements of district sixth graders against national test scores.

Not only do statements of objectives influence the selection of measures of accomplishment, but the selection of measures of accomplishment may influence statements of objectives. Therefore the establishment of objectives and of criteria for the measurement of these objectives are interacting processes in the goal formation stage in PPBS.

PPBS Data Bases

As knowledge stands at present, most PPBS applications are plagued by inadequate data bases. Notwithstanding developmental efforts by the General Accounting Office (GAO), the American Accounting Association, and other concerned professional groups, relatively little is known about non-financial measures of efficiency and effectiveness, particularly where several different data bases have to be used. What information to seek and how to measure it are the two most significant barriers to making PPBS fully operational.

INDICATORS OF ACCOMPLISHMENT

Accounting for efforts expended in public sector programmes or organizations is similar to its counterpart in the private sector. Although there are certain operational differences, these are not extraordinary in nature. Accounting for costs of not-for-profit organizations can simply and directly be carried forward to any PPBS matching of efforts and accomplishments for not-for-profit activities.

The same cannot be said for the revenue or resource inflow side of the coin. Revenue measurements are not appropriate measures of accomplishment in the public sector. Even if changes in revenue flows were one of the objectives of a programme or an organization, achievement of that particular objective would still not give any indication of overall efficiency or effectiveness. Consequently, we need something other than measures of revenue or cash flows before any effort and accomplishment relationships can be established. The missing link needed for activity evaluation in the public sector has been identified as "indicators of accomplishment."

These indicators are most conveniently classified as:

- Operations indicators and
- Programme impact indicators.

Operations Indicators

These measures relate to output activities and are often

non-financial expressions of products or services produced by an agency or organization. Examples are miles of highways built in a given period, number of automobile licenses issued, number of tests administered, and number of families visited by a social worker.

In many instances, these indicators are merely statistics that measure neither efficiency nor effectiveness. Operations indicators can be classified in many ways, including, for example, measures of volume, quality, and comparison.

Example: Street lighting in Ritzville is measured in three different ways. The number of street lights maintained is a volume indicator. An illumination index in terms of kilowatts made available is an indicator of the quality of service. Kilowatt hours of electricity used per street mile during December 197X is an example of a comparative indicator. None of these measures effectiveness of street lighting as a deterrent to crime or for the prevention of automobile accidents.

Of course, operations indicators may also be expressed in financial terms. For instance, federal assistance to minority business programmes during fiscal year 1971 produced these indicators, among others:

- Government grants, loans, and guarantees by programme agencies rose from approximately $200 million in 1969 to $434 million in fiscal 1971.
- SBA direct and guaranteed loans to minority enterprises increased from $105.4 million in 1969 to an estimated $254 million in 1971.
- The dollar value of government 8(a) procurement contracts for minority owned business enterprises rose from $8.8 million in 1969 to $66 million in 1971.
- Minority firms received $77.8 million in direct Federal procurement in fiscal 1971, almost 10 times the $8.2 million of the previous year.

Operations indicators generally provide little qualitative information. They are not very useful in measuring how well public needs are being met. Often these measures are selected on the basis of simplicity and ease of calculation and understanding rather than on the basis of relevant performance measurement.

Programme Impact Indicators

Indicators of this type are often directly expressed in, or at least implied by, programme objectives. They relate directly to public or social needs or policies.

Here outputs of programmes are evaluated comprehensively vis-a-vis:

- Other programmes,
- Actual planned accomplishments, or
- Public or social needs or policies.

Example: (Efficiency vis-à-vis another programme.) The primary objective of the Space Shuttle is to reduce substantially the cost of space operations and provide a capability designed to support a wide range of scientific, defence, and commercial uses.

The National Aeronautics and Space Administration contracted with Mathematical, Inc., for an analysis of how economical the Shuttle would be compared with the present launch systems which are used only once. NASA and Mathematical officials stated that this study demonstrated the Shuttle to be economically justified.

Senator Walter F. Mondale asked the General Accounting Office (GAO) to review the cost-benefit analysis used by NASA. With the senator's agreement, GAO's report was released to the Congress in view of widespread interest in the Space Shuttle. GAO identified critical areas of uncertainty in the Mathematical study. GAO also identified the per cent of cost increase before an investment in the Space Shuttle programme would become uneconomical compared to the present launch systems.

Example: (Efficiency in meeting a social need.) The Detroit Management Information Systems Group of the international CPA firm.

Touche Ross & Co. participated in a programme concerned with measurement of one aspect of the so-called war on poverty. Welfare recipients were analyzed for certain personal characteristics, such as health, work experience, and educational background. On these indicators, deficiencies were scaled and multiplied by weights to develop an index of needs. Total needs were then aggregated to develop guides to the most effective areas for investment.

Problems with measuring programme impact indicators abound. Without technical elaboration, we can observe that some scale must be devised to measure each characteristic to be included in the analysis.

This often proves most difficult, especially if some type of index has to be constructed and a number of indices aggregated to develop a single composite measure of programme accomplishment. Despite these difficulties some public sector organizations, the Sierra Club Foundation for example, have begun public reporting of some of their programme performance in their annual reports. Other organizations, including private enterprises, seem certain to follow this lead.

SELECTED SPECIAL TOPICS

The scope of accounting for public sector organizations is as wide as the accounting scope in the private sector. Many special accounting problems arise along the line of this spectrum. Accounting for public revenues is singled out as a fairly comprehensive illustration of a special topic. As a second point of general interest, some recent standard-setting efforts are described.

Accounting for Public Revenues

Not-for-profit organizations, like all other units in our economic system, must generate resource inflows before continued resource outflows are possible. Quite naturally, the inflows and the outflows seldom match completely.

Example: If total revenue collections for the same period amounted to, let us say, $220 billion, a deficit of $26.3 billion would arise. This deficit is the difference, during 1973, between new monetary resources flowing to the federal government and its total monetary expenditures for the same period. To finance this deficit the federal government must borrow, and the national debt will increase by the difference.

Example: The Open Door Clinic is a university district medical and social aid facility. It was established with an initial grant from the federal government which was not renewed. United Crusade and state, county, and city governments were also unable to provide funds. The clinic's futurc revenue possibilities were not bright, and hence it could borrow very little money on its own account. Private contributions kept the clinic open, but on a much reduced scale of operations.

As implied in these examples, nonproprietary organizations have two major sources of funds:

- Current revenues and
- Borrowing from the public or the private sector. Public borrowing occurs largely through the sale of bonds—U.S. savings and treasury bonds at the national level and state, county, city, or school district bonds at the local level. Most governmental units have statutory power to tax citizens under their jurisdictions and consequently can offer their bonds as virtually risk-free investments. The low-risk feature accounts for the comparatively low interest rate on major government bond issues. Income tax exemption for interest from state and municipal bonds is also a factor, which is explored at greater length.

Public Revenue Origins

For not-for-profit accounting purposes, revenues are increases in expendable funds which have no corresponding liability increases and do not represent bookkeeping adjustments within the public sector.

Governmental revenues derive predominantly from tax collections. The right to levy taxes is among the most basic powers of our form of government. Other not-for-profit organizations rely heavily on voluntary contributions and transfer, payments. Both governments and other not-for-profit organizations collect revenues from both involuntary and voluntary sources. The largest single involuntary source of public revenues, namely, federal tax collections. Readers should note that, in turn, the largest single source of federal government revenue is the personal income tax.

Voluntary contributions are the major source of revenue for private nonprofit organizations. Again private individuals make the largest amounts of such contributions.

There is an impressive array of different types of sources (e.g., taxes, gifts, investment earnings, collections, contributions, etc.) from which public sector organizations derive their revenues. This is in sharp contrast to the relatively small number of types of sources (i.e., primarily consumer groups) from which revenues can be earned by private enterprises. Also it should be noted that revenue collection control is often a problem. For example, private not-for-profit organizations depend heavily on volunteers for fund raising and for some administrative activities. The use of "nonaccountable" employees often leads to loose control over the collection processes. This is an ethical rather than an accounting question but one of which we should be aware.

Public Revenue Accounting Process

Accounting for public sector revenues is similar to accounting for business revenues. In both instances, care must be taken to separate revenues from funds inflows not representing revenues. Proceeds from borrowing no more represent revenue in the public sector than in the private sector.

In several ways, however, revenue accounting for not-for-profit organizations presents problems not found elsewhere. One issue relates to accrual (recognition) of public revenues. Conventional accounting in the private sector recognizes revenue as soon as a relatively certain claim to cash is established. To satisfy the realization principle, this occurs typically after goods have been manufactured and sold or after services have been performed. In the not-for-profit setting, revenue recognition is closely related to actual cash collection. There is no criterion of "earning" public sector revenue. Hence the notion of revenue accrual is also absent in most existing practices.

Example: Wiley Township is on a July 1 to June 30 fiscal year. Real estate tax bills for 1973-74 are prepared in March 1973 and are mailed late in April 1973, with one-half of the annual tax assessment due and payable October 31 and the other half April 30, 1974. Technically, these real estate taxes accrue proportionately month by month during the entire 1973-74 fiscal year. However, for traditional municipal accounting purposes, one-half is recognized October 31 and the other half April 30 of each year.

Example: The YWCA is planning a branch in South City. It needs a new building, furniture, and fixtures, plus a director and staff for the facility. A special fund-raising effort is undertaken which yields pledges promising payment of $XX each September 15 for the next five years. Does the total pledge constitute revenue in year one? Since it is easier to pledge than to contribute money, would it be best to wait until cash is actually received before any revenue is recognized in this case? Acceptable accounting practice would be to recognize each yearly pledge on the date it becomes due and payable. Past experience may be used to establish estimated uncollectible amounts in connection with each revenue accrual. However, the accrual method of revenue recognition could be useful in the public sector. For instance, month-by-month revenue recognition could yield better financial information.

A second issue in the not-for-profit revenue accounting area centres on reporting. Conventional reports of not-for-profit organizations relate revenues to cash collections and costs to cash disbursements. But are revenues really independent variables in the operations of not-for-profit units? Or should revenues be related to the expenditures they make possible? Or should revenues be compared to the benefits that result from the expenditures? These questions remain largely unresolved. Generally, the authors favour independent revenue and cash collection reports together with separate cost-benefit reports. This solution does, however, treat revenues and costs as separate variables.

Abbreviated Accounting Process Illustration

Utilizing the worksheet format developed, it is not difficult to illustrate the accounting process relating to public revenue recognition and collection. A hypothetical case of a municipality so that taxation effects can be shown. To avoid repetition, the worksheet reflects *only* revenue transactions. Our hypothetical city started the current accounting period with a cash balance of $45,000, obligations payable of $20,000, and a General Fund balance of $25,000. The "General Fund" designation used here has the same meaning as the "Agency Account" designation used. Revenue transactions for the year are described below.

- *Line 1*: Memorandum records are made when the city council adopts a budget for the current year by authorizing expenditures of $6,400,000 and a General Fund increase of $100,000. Consequently the annual revenue needs are established at $6,500,000. These revenue needs are then compared with the estimated available revenues from all sources. After this comparison the property tax rate for the current year is set. Depending upon local statutes, a public vote may have to ratify the tax rate so established. The budget is not recorded in the worksheet.
- *Line 2*: Property tax statements, representing taxes due of $4,800,000, are mailed to all property owners in the city.
- *Line 3*: Throughout the year, city sales taxes are collected on all retail sales transacted within the city, and various fees and fines are assessed. The total amounts to $1,200,000.
- *Line 4*: Some years ago, a wealthy resident established a large endowment for use by the city. The endowment was placed in a special investment fund which yields interest income. Also, certain temporary investments were placed in the investment fund.

Together these resources yield $500,000 in interest and dividends during the year.

- *Line 5*: Property tax collections amount to 4,750,000.
- *Line 6*: At the end of the year, the assessor's office determined that 50,000 in property tax assessments could not be collected. This amount was charged off, even though additional collection efforts or public auctions of properties involved were planned.

A revenue statement for our hypothetical city for the current year would show:

Net property tax revenues collected	4,750,000
Revenue from city sales tax, fines, and fees	1,200,000
Interest and dividends revenue from special investment fund	500,000
Total addition to available cash	6,450,000

Setting of Accounting Standards in the Public Sector

Efforts to set broad accounting standards for public sector accounting are widespread and intense. These efforts are relatively less unified than the comparable private sector efforts supporting the activities of the Financial Accounting Standards Board.The United States General Accounting Office (GAO) has statutory responsibility for all accounting systems and standards used by federal government units and agencies. Hence the GAO, with assistance from advisory councils and national commissions, is a key accounting standard setter in the public sector.State auditors usually have authority to set accounting standards at the state government level. Since state and local governments interact frequently on many public service activities, state auditors also have considerable indirect influence on accounting for local and municipal government operations.

A national association of municipal treasurers and financial officers has produced an authoritative set of recommended accounting standards for municipal governmental accounting. This group regularly updates its standards. The nongovernmental portion of public sector accounting is literally inundated with accounting standards suggestions. Each branch of private nonprofit organizations appears to have a national association eager to propose accounting standards for its members.

A list of such organizations includes, among many others:

- American Hospital Association
- American National Red Cross
- Club Managers Association of America
- Evangelical and Reformed Churches
- National Association of College and University Business Offices
- National Health Council
- United Cerebral Palsy Associations
- United Community Funds and Councils of America

Fairly detailed accounting standards have been set and come into use for health and welfare organizations.

The bases of these standards are:

- The 1964 publication by the National Health Council jointly with the National Social Welfare Assembly of a book entitled Standards of Accounting and Financial Reporting for Voluntary Health and Welfare Organizations
- The 1967 AICPA audit guide entitled *Audits of Voluntary Health and Welfare Organizations*. Other comprehensive standards are available for colleges and universities, independent elementary and secondary schools, and hospitals. It appears imperative that a major harmonization effort be initiated to streamline the many accounting standards and procedures presently found in the public sector so that the financial statements of public sector organizations become more comparable and more easily understandable.

PRIVATE AND PUBLIC SECTOR ACCOUNTING COMPARED

Many accounting writers attribute a certain mystique to

public sector accounting in that they portray it as substantially different, more complicated, and differently oriented than private sector accounting. We disagree. Private and public sector accounting have more in common than is generally recognized. The existing differences are in form and procedure rather than substance. The principal differences between private and public sector accounting into five points:

- *Cash versus accrual accounting*: Private enterprises generally keep financial records on an accrual basis. Cash basis or modified cash basis accounting still prevails in much of the public sector.
- *Use of fund accounting:* Most businessmen are unfamiliar with fund accounting. This type of accounting, however, facilitates expenditure control and stewardship reporting in the public sector. The concept of separate record keeping for separate funds is not particularly difficult. Care must be taken that fund accounting based financial reports are presented in a straightforward manner, since separate reporting on a large number of separate "funds" quickly becomes confusing.
- *Treatment of long-lived assets*. In the public sector, current appropriations of funds must cover current operating expenditures as well as acquisitions of long-lived assets. The need for full current funding of even very long-term assets has generally led to non recognition of such assets as long-term items. Hence depreciable assets (and often inventories) may or may not be carried forward to future periods (i.e., recorded as assets). This mixed practice is often confusing to readers of public sector financial reports.
- *Transfer payments, appropriations, and encumbrances.* These terms are found in public sector accounting without private sector counterparts. Transfer payments are simply reallocations of existing funds from one agency or programme to another. Appropriations and encumbrances are *not* items of revenue and expense as the latter are understood in commercial usage.

- *Contributions, pledges, and non cash contributions.* Pledges to not-for-profit organizations may or may not be legally enforceable. Non cash contributions include donations of securities, works of art, equipment and supplies, and personal services. Recording of this type of "income" causes timing and measurement problems. Conventional financial accounting also has problems of this type, but their frequency and dimension differ. Thus a private enterprise may sue to collect a business receivable, whereas a church might not seek legal remedy to enforce an overdue pledge.

Chapter 7

Economic Management

INTRODUCTION

Management problems exist whenever diverse resources have to be coordinated so that specified tasks can be achieved. This process often starts with the determination whether certain resources even exist (e.g., uranium, oil, or skilled workers) or how much it would cost to acquire or possibly create them. One needs to think only of a space probe or the daily food and living requirements of the 11.5 million persons crowded into New York City to realise the enormity of certain management problems. As for economic and financial factors, accounting helps by providing decision-relevant information to the managerial decision makers.

Accounting at the enterprise or other individual organization level distinguishes between the needs of external users and the needs of internal users of accounting information. The accounting needs of private sector enterprises from those of public sector organizations. Even though the individual purposes to which accounting is put differ sometimes fundamentally one from the other, there are many commonalities within the accounting discipline. Managerial performance evaluation is a universal accounting objective, coupled in many cases with a form of wealth assessment.

Capital investment analysis goals underlie much of what is done in accounting, as do organizational planning and control requirements. And the same data-gathering and data-processing techniques can often be used throughout the accounting field! In short, the different members of the accounting family are closely related.

The economy as a whole now becomes our focus of attention. If management and investment problems exist at the enterprise level, similar problems certainly exist at the economy (or macro) level. Relative size alone hints at the importance of the management problems for the total economy. As one wag observed, "Washington, D.C., is the only place in the world where 0.1 means $100 million" (since most economic measures of the national economy are stated in billions of dollars).

MANAGER TASK

Managerial tasks for the economy as a whole comprise a wide spectrum of activities. Very important is the collection of revenues so that the federal government can function and provide the many social, political, and national security services that the public demands. Public revenue is primarily collected through *taxation*. For ease (and economy) of administration, we have a self-assessment income tax system. Accordingly, each taxpayer must keep sufficient accounting records so that he or she can determine his or her tax liability in compliance with applicable laws and regulations.

Example: Huster Bowls is a taxi driver in New York City. He earns a monthly salary of $750 by driving a Purple Cab 50 hours per week. During the year he takes three weeks' vacation. On his personal income tax return he declared a gross income of $9,000 per year plus $500 in tips. He kept no records of tips received. Upon review, an Internal Revenue agent determined that taxi tips average $.50 per hour of taxi driving in New York. With forty-nine weeks worked at 50 hours per week, Mr. Bowls was driving his cab for 2,450 hours during the year. Therefore his income from tips should have been $1,225. He is assessed income taxes on additional gross income of $725.

A second major task facing national economy managers is the preparation of a federal budget which allocates available resources to authorized public activities. The key building blocks for federal budget proposals are the so-called national income accounts. These accounts show which industries and services produced the annual Gross National Product, how much of this total of available goods and services was consumed and how much was saved (i.e., invested), and how the income of the nation was distributed between wage earners, interest and dividend recipients, social security payees, and others.

Example: Analysis of the national income accounts shows that output of goods and services is increasing at a slower rate than the demand for federal government services.

Now economy managers must decide whether to:

- Curtail federal government expenditures,
- Raise more revenue through taxation, or
- incur a budget deficit by raising the ceiling for the national debt. Each alternative can be evaluated, in part, through its probable effects on future national income.

Regulation of certain industries is a third essential component of economy wide management. The need for regulation comes about because it is in the public interest to grant business monopolies to certain segments of the economy. For instance, electric power and telephone companies are given exclusive rights to serve defined geographic areas, since it would be highly uneconomical to have several dozen power mains or telephone trunk lines buried in each street of a residential area. Public safety and convenience are additional considerations favoring the regulated monopoly approach.

Additional *regulated industries* include railways, trucking and moving companies, shipping companies, airlines, cable TV systems, warehouses, and many others. For all of them, specific accounting rules and procedures are prescribed so that the necessary regulation (mainly setting of fees and rates that may legally be charged to customers) can be put into effect on a uniform basis.

Example: Whidsee Island Telephone Company applies to the state's utility commission for a 12 per cent rate increase on its residential service. In studying the application, the commission's staff finds that certain assets of the company are not stated in accordance with prescribed uniform utility accounting rules. The ensuing adjustments reduce the company's "rate base" asset amount and thus the earnings needed to achieve the negotiated rate of return on allowable base assets. The consequence is that a rate boost of only 7.5 per cent is granted.

Our fourth area of concern relates to the management of *national policies* that affect private sector companies. For instance, it is the public will in the United States (but not in many foreign countries) that fair trade must be assured and restraint of trade through trusts and monopolies prevented. Price discrimination not supported by actual cost differences can be prosecuted in some circumstances.

Other examples of management based on the public interest include uniform cost accounting standards being imposed on all parties or companies seeking contracts or actually working under contracts with the federal government where the contract sum exceeds $ $100,000. Price and wage controls have been in effect at various times. Direct foreign investment controls were instituted in the 1960s as a result of the "dollar glut" abroad. Specific licensing is required before radio or TV stations may be operated. And, of course, the Securities and Exchange Commission (SEC) oversees the nation's securities markets and imposes rather specific requirements on the issuers of securities sold to the public.

There are, of course, many other areas in which management of some part or aspect of the total economy takes place. At home, we might think of such huge management problems as those associated with the national debt, the United States international balance of payments, Social Security transfer payments from government to individuals, or agricultural subsidies. Abroad we have the challenges of foreign economic assistance, customs and tariffs, and U.S. personnel residing in other countries. In all of these areas decision-relevant accounting information is useful in management decision making.

Total economy management is a very specialized activity-size of amounts involved and ever-changing public policy directives being two of the factors that make it so. Since special objectives underlie each component of this total management activity, each component has its own accounting requirements and therefore a different structure for its accounting function. Yet the basic nature of accounting remains unchanged. This is demonstrated in the following rather abbreviated and very general descriptions of accounting applications in each of the four management domains introduced in the foregoing paragraphs.

Taxation

Accounting for federal income taxes must conform to extensive federal laws and regulations. As an introduction to this complex and highly technical accounting application, we observe that:

- Accounting rules defined by the Internal Revenue Code are similar but not necessarily identical to conventional accounting principles,
- Managements of business enterprises have an obligation to their shareholders to pay no more taxes than necessary and
- There are timing differences between tax accounting and conventional financial accounting for some revenue and expense items.

Before we acquaint ourselves with some selected specific tax accounting procedures, we must recognize fundamentally that the purpose of tax accounting is the assessment and collection of governmental revenues in a presumably fair and economical manner according to public policy. For policy reasons, tax laws may allow special benefits to certain persons or industries, for example, blind persons and agriculture. This is in marked contrast to the performance evaluation and wealth assessment objectives that characterize general financial accounting.

Income taxes collected from individuals, corporations, estates, and trusts constitute by far the most significant sources of tax revenues. " State and local taxes are also important because they provide the resources for the continually rising financial needs of local governments. At the state level there are corporate income and franchise taxes, personal income taxes, sales taxes, excise taxes, and property taxes.

At the municipal level, one might find sales and use taxes, property taxes, business occupancy taxes, gross receipts taxes, and excise taxes.

Aspects of Income Tax Accounting

Four broad aspects of income tax accounting procedures underlie our system of income tax assessments:

- A statutorily defined tax base, that is, taxable income,
- Progressive tax rate structures,
- Distinction between ordinary income and capital gains, and
- The ability-to-pay concept. We now turn to a brief elaboration of the four taxation aspects identified.

Measurement of business performance lies at the heart of financial accounting "net income" determination. Economists work primarily with valuation in measuring "economic income." For taxation purposes, *taxable income* is simply a legally defined quantity.

As a general rule, one can state that tax procedures regard any realized economic or financial gain as income unless it is statutorily excluded from taxable income. Similarly, the only valid expenses for tax purposes are those expressly specified in the law (Internal Revenue Code and applicable regulations).

Even though several elaborate efforts are underway to bring financial accounting and taxation concepts of periodic income into closer harmony, rather significant differences between the two continue to exist. The *progressive rate structure* of our income taxation system means that different tax rates apply to different layers of taxable income.

Example: In general, the U.S. tax on corporate income is 22 per cent on income of $25,000 or less and 48 per cent on all corporate income in excess of $25,000. Hence corporate taxable income of $40,000 requires a corporate income tax payment of $12,700 (25,000 ×.22 + 15,000 ×.48). Therefore the *marginal* tax rate at the $40,000 level of corporate income is 48 per cent (i.e., the rate at which each dollar of additional income would be taxed). On the other hand, the average tax rate at the 40,000 corporate income level is 31.75 per cent (12,700 ÷ 40,000).

Tax rates are higher at higher levels of taxable income. Thus average rates are normally lower than marginal rates. If one has portions of income that are excluded by law from U.S. income taxation (e.g., interest received from investments in state and local government bonds), then the *effective* rate on one's total income is less again than the average rate for everyone else of equal total income. This latter phenomenon explains in part the relatively low actual (i.e., effective) tax rates paid by some of our high-income-bracket citizens.

Distinctions between ordinary income for tax purposes and *capital gains* are fundamental to the Anglo-Saxon concept of "separating the fruit from the tree." Ordinary income is the "fruit." It comes about from the ordinary and recurring conduct of one's business or profession. In the sense of "economic income," it is that which can be consumed during a period without impairing one's wealth. Capital gains relate to the "tree." They are identified with the sale or other disposition of capital investments (wealth). Professor Seltzer, a well-known author in the area of federal income taxation over several decades, defined *capital gains* in the following manner:

In both law and common speech, capital gains are generally regarded as the profits realized from increases in the market value of any assets that are not part of the owner's stock in trade or that he does not regularly offer for sale; and capital losses, as the losses realized from declines in the market value of such assets. In U.S. tax law some distinction between ordinary income and capital gains has been made since the Revenue Act of 1921. This distinction is important because ordinary income is taxed at a higher rate than capital gains.

Finally, the *ability-to-pay concept* is deeply entrenched in our income ta:ation system. It means, as a practical matter, that taxes are levied at a time when the taxpayer has the funds with which to pay the tax. The ability-to-pay tenet has led to withholding of income taxes from salary and wage payments and to quarterly tax prepayments by corporations. It has also produced a number of specific tax accounting procedures, such as the taxation of revenues at the time of receipt even if such revenues are still "unearned" in financial accounting terms.

Corporate Federal Income Tax

For federal income tax purposes, a domestic corporation is one organized under the laws of the United States or any of the states or territories. Any corporation that does not meet the foregoing definition, including corporations organized under the laws of any of the United States possessions, is deemed to be a foreign corporation and is taxed differently from a domestic corporation. A domestic corporation is subject to tax on income derived from all sources, whether within or outside the United States. Corporate taxation can be represented graphically by a tax formula.

Corporate Income Tax Formula

Income broadly conceived:
- Exclusions (e.g., interest from state government bonds)
= Gross income (e.g., sales less cost of goods sold, rental income, dividends and royalties received)
- Routine deductions (e.g., administrative expenses, depreciation, repairs and maintenance, taxes)
- Special deductions (e.g., 85 per cent of dividends received from domestic corpor- Ations to ameliorate double taxation)
= Corporate taxable income
X Applicable tax rates
= Gross tax
- Tax credits and prepayments (e.g., foreign tax credits)
= Net corporate tax payable

Corporate Gross Income

Gross income of a corporation, in general, includes most items considered to be income under conventional accounting principles. This extends to gains derived from most business and other economic activities in which a corporation might engage. Such items of income would include, among others, gross profit from sales of goods, commissions, royalties, interest, dividends, management and technical service fees, gain on the sale of assets used in the business, and gain on the sale of investments.

Tax on Capital Gains

The capital gains distinction referred to earlier in this section differentiates further between long-term and short-term capital gains. A long-term capital gain situation. Procedurally, the excess of the net gain from all sales or exchanges of capital assets held for more than *six months* over any *net loss* from sales or exchanges of capital assets held six months or less is termed *net long-term capital gain* and is taxed at a maximum rate of 25 per cent. This rate yields the well-known tax break on capital gains.

Example: THW Corporation sold a parcel of real estate at a gain of $84,000 and some foreign bonds at a loss of $22,000. Both items had been owned for more than six months. This results in a long-term capital gain of $62,000. The corporation also disposed of a pleasure boat acquired for its president's use five months ago. The board of directors disapproved this acquisition, and the sale of the boat was made at a loss of $32,000. Hence the *net* long-term capital gain from these transactions is $30,000. The *maximum* tax liability on this segment of the corporation's income is $7,500. If the corporation had no other income, $25,000 would be taxed at 22 per cent and $5,000 at 25 per cent for a tax liability of $6,750.

Corporate Income Tax Deductions

In arriving at taxable income, corporations are entitled to deduct all business expenses that are ordinary and necessary in the conduct of their particular trade or business.

These "routine" deductions, like items of income, are usually allowed if they conform to generally accepted accounting principles. Deductible expenses for travel, entertainment, amusement, or recreation are, in general, limited to those directly related to the active conduct of a trade or business and to items directly preceding or following a substantial and *bona fide* business discussion.

Deductions for business gifts and deductions for the cost of entertainment facilities or travel expenses are limited in various respects. Deductions may also be claimed for contributions to certain types of charitable organizations created or organized in the United States or its possessions, but such deductions are limited to 5 per cent of taxable income computed before giving effect to the charitable deduction and the so-called special deductions.

A corporation is allowed as a depreciation deduction a reasonable allowance for the exhaustion, wear and tear, and obsolescence of property used in its trade or business or held for the production of income. A deduction for depletion is permitted with respect to wasting assets such as natural resource deposits and timber.

There are two general methods of computing depletion, one based on cost and the other, termed "percentage depletion," based on certain specified percentages of the gross income from the property. The latter method, which applies to mines, oil and gas wells, and other natural deposits specifically listed in the law, has the effect in certain instances of permitting recovery through the depletion deduction of amounts in excess of cost, as the rates vary from 22 per cent of gross income for oil and gas wells to 5 per cent for gravel. Another significant deduction allowed to a corporation is the net operating loss deduction.

This deduction permits a taxpayer corporation to offset against one year's taxable income the losses of subsequent or prior years, that is, the excess of deductions over income in such years. Since all periodic income determinations, including the taxable income determination, are tentative because of uncertainties about the future, the loss offset between tax years seems quite reasonable. The net operating loss of any year may be carried back three years and forward five years and must be applied in chronological sequence, starting with the earliest year to which it may be carried.

Corporate Tax Computation

We already know that taxable income of a corporation is subject to a "normal" tax at 22 per cent and a "surtax" of 26 per cent on income in excess of $25,000. Also the tax rate on net long-term capital gains is limited to 25 per cent. Dividend deduction for dividends from another domestic corporation. †The alternative method gives effect to the rule that net long-term capital gains are taxed at a maximum rate of 25 per cent. The tax is computed by both methods, and the method yielding the lower tax is used. ††Gross tax may be further reduced by certain tax credits like foreign tax credits to arrive at net corporate tax payable.

Individual Federal Income Tax

Individuals who are citizens of the United States and foreign nationals who are residents of the United States are subject to the same tax rules and are ordinarily taxed on their worldwide income irrespective of source.

U.S. Individual Income Tax Formula

Income broadly conceived (e.g., *realized* economic gain)
- Exclusions (e.g., dividends up to $100 per taxpayer or interest from state government bonds)
= Gross income
- Deductions for Adjusted Gross Income (e.g., cost of employee travel away from home)
= Adjusted gross income
- Deductions from Adjusted Gross Income and Personal and Dependent Exemptions
= Individual taxabie income
× Applicable tax rates (various, progressive)

= Gross tax
- Tax credits and prepayments (e.g., amounts withheld from salary)
= Net individual tax payable

Individual Gross Income

Generally, individuals' income other than income from a personal business must be recognized *by individuals* in the year it is *received* rather than *when it is earned*. This includes items that are considered to be received in accordance with the concept of constructive receipt. Constructive receipt of income occurs, for instance, when interest is credited to the taxpayer's bank account or set apart for him so that he may draw upon it at any time.

A taxpayer may not postpone acceptance of income so as to delay one or more years before reporting it for tax purposes. Income can also arise by receipt of valuable property other than money.

Items includable in gross income and therefore taxable to citizens or residents of the U.S. extend to, but are not exhausted by, remuneration received for personal services, dividends, interest, rents, royalties, income from a profession or unincorporated business, prizes, awards, annuities, pensions, and gains from the sale of securities or other capital assets.

Example: During a tax year, Bob Schlau's common stocks gained market value of $3,800; he inherited $12,000 from his uncle's estate; and he won $500 on a TV show. He still held the common stock on the last day of the tax year. Only the $500 TV prize is includable in gross income; gifts, bequests, and inheritances are statutorily excluded from gross income (but may be subject to other forms of taxation).

Personal Deductions and Exemptions

Deductions for individuals fall into two different categories because of an intermediary classification between gross income and taxable income known as "adjusted gross income." Thus, some deductions are allowable from gross income in arriving at adjusted gross income, and others are allowed from adjusted gross income in arriving at "taxable income." Adjusted gross income is of special significance, since certain of the deductions allowed by law from adjusted gross income are subject to limitations expressed as a percentage of adjusted gross income.

Following is a list of the major items included in each category.

Deductions to determine adjusted gross income:

- Expenses, deductions, and losses in carrying on a trade, business, or profession, other than as an employee.
- Certain un reimbursed expenses of an employee.
- Travel expenses of an employee while away from home.
- Transportation expenses of an employee, but not expenses of commuting.
- Expenses of "outside salesmen."
- Losses from the sale or exchange of investment or income-producing property, except that a *net* loss from the sale of capital assets is only deductible to the extent of $1,000. Any unused loss, however, may be carried forward until exhausted.
- Expenses attributable to the production of rental income or royalties.
- Special deduction of 50 per cent of the excess of the net gain, if any, from sale of capital assets held over six months over the net loss, if any, from sale of capital assets held six months or less.

Deductions from adjusted gross income:

- Interest expense not connected with a trade or business or the production of rents or royalties.
- Taxes not incurred in a trade or business, other than federal taxes and state inheritance and gift taxes.
- Charitable contributions, subject to certain maximum limits.
- Medical expenses, subject to certain limits.
- Casualty losses on non business property. However,

the first $100 of each casualty loss is not deductible.

- Child care expenses within certain limits.
- Other expenses incurred for the production of income but not connected with a trade or business.
- Certain alimony and separate maintenance payments.
- Certain moving expenses incurred in assuming employment at a new principal place of work.

In lieu of the deductions listed above as allowable *from adjusted gross income,* an election may be made to claim the so-called standard deduction. The standard deduction is equal to 15 per cent of adjusted gross income, with a maximum of $2,000. The standard deduction is limited to $1,000 in the case of a married individual filing a separate return.

Alternatively, taxpayers are allowed a "minimum standard deduction" (i.e., low income allowance) of $1,300, or $650 in the case of a married person filing a separate tax return.

An individual taxpayer, in addition to those deductions discussed above, is entitled to deductions in computing taxable income for personal exemptions of $750 each with respect to himself, his spouse (if she does not file a separate return), and any other dependent.

Additional $750 exemptions are permitted to a taxpayer who is sixty-five years of age or over or blind at the close of the year, and also permitted for his spouse if she is sixty-five years of age or over or blind and does not file a separate return. To qualify, those being claimed as dependents must satisfy certain tests regarding support from and relationship to the taxpayer, along with limitations on their separately derived incomes.

Personal Tax Rates and Computation of Tax

Tax rates applicable to individuals are graduated, depending on the amount of taxable income. For 1973, the highest rate for single individuals was 70 per cent of taxable income in excess of $100,000 (there was also a 50 per cent "maximum" rate on "earned" income).

Special rate structures apply to married individuals filing

joint income tax returns, married individuals filing separate returns, and unmarried (or legally separated) individuals who qualify as heads of households.

Tax rate schedules are published by the Internal Revenue Service so that tax amounts due can be looked up easily. The standard deduction is not used, since itemizing yields a larger amount.

Tax Planning

Actual income tax procedures are often far more complex than the foregoing examples indicate. This complexity means that so-called tax loopholes are unavoidable-as soon as a known loophole is "plugged" by new legislation, the latter probably creates new loopholes elsewhere.

In addition, a historic U.S. Supreme Court ruling held that no taxpayer is responsible for paying more tax than the minimum required by law.

Combined with the complexity of tax law provisions, this ruling provides an economic incentive for planning and management of one's tax affairs.

Example:

The year 1974 was a high-income year for Walter Steuer. He expected less income in 1975. Therefore Mr. Steuer planned his tax affairs in such a way that he had available the largest possible amount of deductions for 1974 (he sold stocks on which he had suffered a loss, he had major dental work performed, etc.).

In this fashion he minimized his 1974 tax liability, which yielded benefits in terms of the time value of money and probably a lower applicable tax rate for 1974.Planning and managing transactions and events that have tax consequences is perfectly legal.

It may lead to a certain tax avoidance, which is also completely within the provisions of the law. Tax evasion, on the other hand, is the willful nonpayment of legally due taxes and therefore punishable under existing law. Tax evasion needs to be distinguished sharply from tax avoidance.

National Income Accounting

Statements (or accounts) providing indexes of the economic output of a national economy for a specified period of time are usually referred to as national income and product statements. In abbreviated form, they are known as GNP (i.e., Gross National Product) statements.

The basic objective of these statements is to present summary information about the *total* economic output of an economy. GNP statements may be expressed in current purchasing power or in some base period dollar units.

Gross National Product

The Gross National Product of a nation is the *total* market value of all final goods and services produced in the nation's economy during one year. Following the duality reflected so well in double-entry bookkeeping, GNP statements typically have one segment devoted to the total economic value of a nation's output and another segment setting forth the charges against this output, that is, the costs incurred to produce it.

These costs represent income to the various factors of production, including labour, business and social capital, and land. The duality between economic output on the one hand and its costs (incomes) on the other has led to the identification of these statements as "national income and product accounts." Since national economic product or output is simply the complement of national income, the two are equal in total by definition.

Both approaches to measuring GNP are used concurrently.

Together they constitute national income accounting; together they provide vital statistical information for the management of our total economy.

Double Counting Problem

From an accounting point of view we note that GNP is a summation of the total market value of all *final* goods and services produced in the economy during one year. Thus the GNP accounting system must take care that the prices of *intermediate* goods (i.e., goods and services for further processing, manufacturing, or resale) are not included over and over among the transactions accounted for. Why? Because the value of final goods *includes* the values of prior or component intermediate goods.

This phenomenon in greater detail. Notice how the prior price paid by each producer in the chain is subtracted from the price received as the product is transferred to the next producer-only the difference, the value added by each producer, is included in the final contribution to GNP (i.e., the price of the *final* product).

Table. Value Components of a Final Economic Product

	Sales Value	Incremental Value Added
Cattle ranch	$ 6	$ 6
Hide processor	11	5
Leather goods manufacturer	32	21
Leather goods wholesaler	36	4
Department store, briefcase department	45	9
Final cost of briefcase to consumer (total value added)		$45

In conventional accounting, we subtract total expenses from total revenues to arrive at the net income measure of performance. In national income accounting, "total value added" becomes the performance criterion which accounting procedures seek to measure.

National Income Accounting Fundamentals

Beyond the double counting problem, there are many other interesting aspects of the GNP accounting system. Some operational observations on these aspects should assist with further comparisons between GNP accounting and conventional enterprise accounting, bridging and deepening the appreciation of the complexity that characterizes GNP accounting.

National income accounting fundamentals include the following:

- The entire GNP accounting system has a production or output focus that is in contrast to the external transactions-with-third-parties focus of business enterprise accounting and the programme or fund focus in accounting for not-for-profit organizations. For instance, additions to inventories and additions to self-constructed plant and equipment are recognized as output of a firm under GNP accounting but not as revenue under conventional enterprise accounting.
- The basic GNP measurement system is current market value estimation rather than transaction cost enumeration. Convenience and practicality dictate the current market-value approach to GNP accounting. In addition to the broad application of market valuations, certain nonmarket activities are considered sufficiently important and measurable to warrant *inclusion* on the basis of value imputation. Thus economic outputs consumed directly by the producer (e.g., foods grown and consumed on farms), production services not directly compensated (e.g., services performed by owners of small businesses who do not pay themselves production salaries), and the rental value of nonfarm residential housing (e.g., all owner-occupied, single—family, suburban housing) are important examples for which imputed economic values are estimated and the estimates included in GNP totals.

On the other hand, certain types of market transactions are specifically *excluded* from GNP totals. Examples areillegal activities, like proceeds from traffic in narcotics, resales of goods produced and recognized in prior periods, like the capital gain on the sale of a factory already in operation, and transfer payments. Transfer payments are essentially legally enforced redistributions of income.

Since these payments do not constitute current productive economic activities, they are excluded from GNP estimates.

The most well-known transfer payments are governmental in origin and include Social Security benefits, veterans' benefits, disaster relief, unemployment benefits, and interest on the national public debt.

- Statistical adjustments are common in GNP accounting. The most general of these adjustments is the elimination of the effects of general price-level changes. GNP estimates are often stated in terms of current dollars as well as in terms of some base period dollars. Restatements are also needed when inventory figures conventionally prepared on the transaction cost basis by the business sector are to be included on a current market-value basis in GNP statements. This is clearly the case when business inventories are priced according to the Lifo method.
- The double-entry system used in conventional financial accounting means essentially that a single measurement is taken and that this single measurement is recorded by two formal entries in the system. GNP accounting makes typically two independent measurements for the same duality-one on output sectors and one on factor income payments. When the two measurements reconcile, in the end, the statistical reliability of the total may well be higher than that for the totals produced by the conventional financial accounting system wherein total assets are defined to equal total liabilities and owners' equities.
- GNP accounting is a system measuring economic flows rather than stocks of wealth or wealth positions. While 'conventional financial accounting distinguishes sharply between periodic income and financial position measurements, GNP accounting makes independent flow estimates each period with only minor attention to any adjustments for stocks on hand. The notion of flows of economic goods and services is the independent nucleus of the entire GNP accounting system.

The Business Sector Defined

Aside from national output and national income classifications, GNP can be allocated to still different economic activities or different economic groupings. One such grouping is a division of the economy into several so-called sectors, for example, a private business sector, a government sector, and so forth.

The private business sector provides factor incomes in the form of wages, rent, interest paid, profits, and indirect business taxes, as well as capital consumption. It therefore has a direct part in all of the national income factors specified earlier in this section. To demonstrate some large-scale relationships, Herman Bevis once aggregated published financial statements of one hundred major U.S. business corporations and produced the income statement.

If the Bevis summation were extended to the entire business sector, we would need only a few technical adjustments to arrive at a usable product or output estimate from this sector to the total economy. To give the reader an appreciation of what is included in business sector GNP accounts, the following U.S. Department of Commerce definition is of interest:

The business sector is defined broadly to include all organizations which produce goods and services for sale at a price intended at least to approximate costs of production. In the main, it covers all private enterprises organized for profit, both corporate and non-corporate, including farm operators, independent professional practitioners, and lessors of real property. Mutual financial institutions, cooperatives, and nonprofit organizations serving business are also included, as well as government enterprises. Owner-occupied houses and buildings used by nonprofit institutions serving individuals are considered to be business establishments selling their current services to their owners.

Relationship to Federal Budget

The direct impact of national income (macro) accounting on the management of the economy is put succinctly in the following quotation from the 1972 edition of the National Industrial Conference Board's *The Federal Budget—Its Impact on the Economy:* Economic growth, cyclical fluctuations, and current economic activity are usually reviewed in terms of GNP and its components. Because GNP accounting is one of the most highly developed statistical systems and encompasses on an internally consistent basis all sectors of economic activity, it presents by far the most useful framework for comparing various government activities and relating them to other sectors in the economy. Moreover, the use of federal budget data as they are classified in the GNP accounts makes it possible to review each major government function in terms of a twofold division:

- Purchases of goods and services and
- Transfer payments. While the government spends money in both cases, the immediate economic effects differ significantly. In the former case the government's own decision determines directly what and how much is produced and used, whereas in the latter case this decision is made—within certain limitations—by the recipients of the funds rather than the government "donor."

Management of the economy as a whole is thus achieved largely through the federal budget, which directly controls all federal government activities and indirectly influences many parts of the private sector. Through appropriate accounting analysis of the federal budget, we can compare and contrast the economic output and potential of each sector within the economy. We can judge the effects of U.S. investments abroad and investments by citizens of other countries in the United States. We can judge effects of inflation and unemployment. GNP accounting statements lead to conclusions about the necessity of foreign investment control or domestic price or wage control. After policies are initiated, accounting information helps to evaluate them and plan future actions.

During that period, total federal expenditures almost tripled. Yet expenditures for "international affairs" relating to national security have remained almost the same over this period, as have expenditures relating to the conduct and regulation of commerce or veterans' programmes. On the other hand, total health and welfare expenditures have risen faster than total expenditures, as have outlays for education and space programmes.

It might be noted parenthetically that more than 70 per cent of the item "General Government" expenditures consists of interest on the public debt. While the amount of this debt has increased only moderately since the end of World War II, interest rates have advanced appreciably, especially over the last decade. Phenomena like interest rate changes complicate the lives of managers in all sectors but are especially consequential when amounts as large as the public debt are involved. In his 1975 State-of-the-Union message to the U. S. Congress, President Ford estimated that the size of the U. S. public debt will exceed $500 billion by June 30, 1976.

GNP Statement Analysis

GNP statements, like all other financial information summaries, increase in usefulness if significant content relationships can be singled out and highlighted. For example, ratio and trend analyses provide added usefulness. These techniques apply to GNP statements the same as to conventional private enterprise financial statements.

Partial statement decomposition is another financial analysis technique. It is broadly applied to GNP statements and is thus worthy of brief attention. Essentially, the GNP figure is used as a base for deriving the amounts of national income, personal income, and disposable personal income, respectively.

Relationship of Major GNP Subsidiary Measures

Gross national product:
– Capital Consumption and Indirect Business Taxes
= National income
– Undistributed Corporate Profits, Corporate Income Taxes, and Social Security Contributions

+ Transfer Payments to Persons, and Consumer and Government Interest Paid
= Personal income
– Personal Taxes
= Disposable personal income

ACCOUNTING FOR COMPANIES

In the United States the regulation of certain industries through public commissions started long before generally accepted accounting principles (GAAP) were reasonably well defined.

This type of regulation usually included the prescription of so-called uniform accounting practices. The uniform practices evolved have become deeply entrenched and cannot easily be changed. Both the regulators and the regulated companies and industries have based their managerial decisions on them for decades and generally resist exchanging the familiar for the unfamiliar.

Moreover, the cost of change is fairly high. If all U.S. railroads would suddenly have to change from the Interstate Commerce Commission (ICC) prescribed accounting rules to full application of GAAP, the costs of converting existing accounting systems, bookkeeping forms, computer programmes, and the like would be comparable to a complete conversion from Fahrenheit to Centigrade temperature measurements for all home thermometers, clinical applications, weather reports, and so forth!

Another characteristic of accounting practices prescribed by regulatory agencies is the specific intent of many of the prescribed methods.

State insurance commissions establish the accounting rules that insurance companies must follow. These rules reflect a preoccupation with the sustained solvency of insurance companies—that is, their ability to pay all legitimate claims arising under policies they have entered into.

The insurance commissions have stated that such a viewpoint is fully in the public interest and the interests of individual policyholders, since it encourages the companies to maintain their ability to pay claims. Prescribed bank accounting practices have a similar solvency orientation (with the intent of protecting depositors).

When it comes to railroads, utility companies, airlines, and trucking and marine shipping firms, rate setting and rate regulation (i.e., service rates charged to customers) are the principal objectives of the uniform accounting rules enforced by the responsible regulatory agencies. Because of industry economic differences and different regulatory goals as expressed in underlying public laws, prescribed accounting practices differ from regulated industry to regulated industry.

In those areas where prescribed regulatory accounting practices differ from GAAP, and there are many such areas, major financial reporting problems result. Stockholders and the public receiving financial reports of regulated companies may be misled because they do not realise the effects of the different accounting practices applied. Comparability with other companies and industries suffers, and even economic competitiveness or access to capital may be affected. Furthermore, it is not self-evident that the "rules of the game" might be different.

For example, the SEC does not exercise control over securities offerings or general accounting practices of railroads, since the latter are under the control of the ICC. The SEC has control when railroads are included in the statements of holding companies filed with the SEC, but such technical niceties do not remedy the broader difficulty.

The New York Stock Exchange does not require listed companies that are railroads to have independent audits of their financial statements.

Also, for railroads that do have audits, the NYSE accepts qualified audit reports with respect to variances from GAAP caused by regulatory prescriptions.

Therefore, the NYSE has policies for railroads not applied to any other industry.

Recognizing existing financial reporting complications, the ICC permitted a major accommodation with its January 25, 1962, order. A portion of that order reads:

Sec. 25.1 Financial Statements Released by Carriers. Carriers [interstate transportation companies] desiring to do so may prepare and publish financial statements in reports to stockholders and others, except in reports to this Commission, based on generally accepted accounting principles for which there is authoritative support, provided that any variance from this Commission's prescribed accounting rules contained in such statements is clearly disclosed in footnotes to the statements.

Since accounting for companies in regulated industries varies from case to case, we must necessarily limit our discussion to a few examples.

The two arbitrarily chosen illustrative cases are the railroad and insurance industries. Both reflect significant variations from GAAP. Brief attention to these cases, however, does not yield an exhaustive treatment of the accounting scene under public regulation.

Accounting by Railroads

Earlier in this section we mentioned that rate setting and rate regulation are the principal objectives of accounting for regulated industries such as the railroad industry. Specifically, the rates allowed are calculated so that the company involved is able to earn a negotiated rate of return on an administratively determined capital asset investment base. In other words, revenue from rate charges is so set that the resulting estimated net income equals a predetermined return on the base assets. Rate hearings before regulatory commissions are complex, lengthy, and costly procedures.

Two of the more critical problems with prescribed railroad accounting practices are non-recognition of deferred incomes taxes and so-called retirement accounting for most track property (gradings, rails, ties, ballast). If early in the lives of depreciable assets higher depreciation allowances are charged for tax purposes than for financial reporting purposes, current income tax obligations are reduced. If no compensating tax deferral is undertaken, net business income after taxes is temporarily overstated. In turn, this suggests a rate of return on investments above the level actually achieved (at least as measured by conventional accounting practices). This may tend to cause over investments and possibly railroad excess capacity. Worst of all, it may affect rate structuring in disharmony with economic facts. So long as railroads are regulated by the ICC, the latter bears the responsibility for the prescribed major variance from GAAP. Retirement accounting is a practice entirely peculiar to regulatory prescriptions for railroads.

Example: The Mountain Pacific Railway (MPR) extends its track properties to a newly established industrial park in the city of Prentice. Land for this extension was partly donated by the park developers and partly acquired from various owners along the proposed track route. Accounting for the land acquisitions is in accord with conventional methods and procedures.

In constructing the new track, however, MPR must record all initial costs of grading and installing rails and ballast as a non-depreciable asset. It cannot allow for depreciation on these items. When repairs to the track become necessary in due course, all repair costs are currently charged to expense. Also charged to expense are subsequent replacements of everything relating to the track property—rails, ties, signal machinery and so forth. Hence the term "retirement" accounting! The costs of track properties have no periodic income determination effect until the time of retirement!

If subsequently MPR decided to install bypasses and other betterments on the Prentice industrial park track, material costs (but not labour and other costs) would again be recorded as non-depreciable assets.

By treating railroad track structures as non-depreciable, a presumption of perpetual economic value is made on the part of the ICC. This is contrary to present-day fact. There is also a consistency flaw in that other property investments by railroads, most importantly rolling stock, are depreciated regularly over the periods of their respective economic lives. Here a major discrepancy is fostered. Finally, retirement accounting leaves the door open for some management manipulation. Anyone who has ever lived in New York City and ridden on the Long Island Railroad will have had a first-hand experience with badly kept track structures. Management is probably reluctant to charge current operations today with track costs which should have been charged years ago as track depreciation.

If a track gets bad enough it may have to be abandoned. In turn, if the abandonment is large in amount, it may qualify for extraordinary loss status in reporting period results. Hence management may well be motivated in given cases to manage ICC accounting prescriptions first and actual railroad operations second.

Accounting by Insurance Companies

Insurance companies are regulated by numerous laws enacted by the individual states. These laws prescribe in detail how accounts are to be kept and financial statements prepared. Fortunately, the accounting prescriptions are fairly uniform from state to state due to the influence exercised by the National Association of Insurance Commissioners (NAIC). Nevertheless, regulatory emphasis on insurance company solvency has resulted in *insurance statements* rather than wealth assessments and performance evaluators.

In many important respects there are broad variances between financial statements prepared on the basis of GAAP and those prepared on the basis of regulatory insurance accounting rules. The following selected illustrations demonstrate the nature of accounting as prescribed for insurance companies.

- *Nonadmitted assets*. Items failing into this category are required to be omitted from statements of financial position. They include equipment, furniture and fixtures, receivables from agents, three- month past due premiums, loans on company stock, and mortgage loans other than first liens.
- *Prepayments*. Commissions, taxes on premiums, and all other acquisition costs incurred in selling insurance and issuing insurance policies are not recognized as prepaid expenses. They are charged

to current expenses as incurred.

- *Interperiod income tax allocation*. Deferred income taxes are not recognized. This is especially important, since portions of insurance company earnings can be placed into so-called policy-holders' surplus without prior taxation.
- *Unauthorized reinsurance*. If fire or casualty risks are reinsured with other companies not authorized to do business in a particular state, reserves are required without reference to the financial soundness of the reinsurer. Such reserves may be excessive.
- *Gains and losses on investments*. Insurance Company portfolios customarily show common and preferred stock investments at market values. In fact, the NAIC publishes a list of market values each year for use in valuing stocks for purposes of annual financial statements. But unrealized appreciation or depreciation of investments is transferred directly to owners' equity, which misstates the respective periodic income figures in relation to corresponding financial position balances. Upon realization of such appreciation or depreciation, respective amounts are recognized as part of current operating income.
- *Life insurance company investments*. In the case of life insurance companies, all realized gains or losses on investments as well as losses on mortgage loans flow directly to retained earnings, that is, owners' equity. This procedure avoids income statement disclosure and misstates reported period net income of insurance companies relative to other types of business enterprises.

The foregoing points suffice to illustrate that regulated insurance company accounting yields financial statements substantially at variance with conventionally prepared financial statements.

OTHER REGULATORY ACCOUNTING

Accounting practices prescribed by public utility

commissions must be used by public utility companies in all matters of utility rate making. The process of utility rate making is much like the one described above for railroads. Since every citizen consumes some electric, gas, or telephone usage nearly every day, utility rates have major economic importance. Regulatory accounting for public utilities is cumbersome in its detail and classifications but is not at fundamental variance with GAAP.

Prescribed bank accounting, on the other hand, is in many ways at variance with GAAP. It is quite similar to insurance company accounting, especially with respect to points 1 and 2 above.

Another bank accounting peculiarity is that stock savings and loan associations are permitted to create huge allowances for uncollectible loans, out of which certain distributions to stockholders may be made after full corporate income taxes have been paid on amounts to be so distributed. Also, certain before-tax allocations to general reserves are required. In both cases a serious income tax allocation problem results.

Financial statements based on accounting practices prescribed by regulatory authorities may or may not be comparable with GAAP-based statements. Sometimes reasons for existing variances are inertia or legislative inflexibility. Other times they reflect a direct public interest and prevailing industry conditions.

The management of the economy simply requires that certain industrial and service activities be publicly regulated. Therefore, a caveat for readers of financial statements of regulated companies: Be fully aware of underlying accounting practices in interpreting such statements!

NATIONAL POLICIES

Persons with responsibility for the management of the economy as a whole or sectors or sub-sectors of it must discharge their managerial obligations in accordance with the public interest as expressed in various public laws and in expressly formulated national policies. Accounting procedures and reports are a major implementation tool in this regard.

Antitrust Legislation

It is a national policy of the United States to prevent undue concentration among large business enterprises so as to ensure fair competition. Federal antitrust legislation was enacted to provide a legal basis of enforcement and achieve the goals of this national policy.

Antitrust legislation was successfully used to split up the former petroleum industry empire of the Standard Oil Company during the 1930s. In more recent years it has prevented undue concentration in the manufacture of household bleaching agents, forced the duPont Company to distribute to its shareholders a large holding of General Motors Corporation shares, and prevailed upon ITT to sell to the public a major block of shares of its Avis automobile rental subsidiary.

The number of antitrust cases successfully brought and concluded by the U.S. Justice Department are legion. Moreover, highly dominant business enterprises like IBM and AT&T are finding themselves in the constant shadow of potential antitrust prosecution. What does accounting have to do with the enforcement of antitrust legislation? Quite simply, enforcement would be impossible without factual and relevant accounting information.

Example: Company B, a large commercial airframe manufacturer, has tendered offers to combine its enterprise with MD Company, another large airframe manufacturer. Financial reports of both companies are analyzed and their respective cost structures studied. These accounting information-based evaluations demonstrate that the companies would jointly control 75 per cent of the domestic commercial airframe market, both companies individually have already achieved optimal economies of scale, so that significant cost savings cannot be realized from the proposed merger, and several suppliers of aircraft motors and equipment would be placed in a very dependent economic position vis-à-vis the resulting combined enterprise. As a consequence, the U.S. Justice Department seeks a court order to stop Company B from making the tender offer.

Securities Legislation

Operations of financial markets in the United States are governed by the various United States Securities Acts and their amendments. The national policy underlying this legislation is full disclosure of relevant financial facts prior to public sale of securities and a fair and well-functioning national securities market. Again accounting procedures play a major role in the achievement of the objectives of this national policy.

The SEC requires formal registration including audited financial statements from each company planning to sell a securities issue to the public. Until such a prospectus is accepted by the SEC, the respective securities may not be offered for sale. Subsequently, periodic filings of audited and un-audited financial statements must be made by issuers of securities and by securities market intermediaries like brokers and dealers. While SEC registrations and filings contain information of a non-accounting nature, their main thrusts are accounting oriented.

Example: DEF Corporation is a fast-growing conglomerate which has experienced liquidity problems in recent years. Many of its operating assets are leased from a large number of lessors. Since DEF common stock is traded on the NYSE, the corporation has an annual financial statements filing requirement (Form 10-K) with the SEC. When the 1973 filing from DEF Corporation was reviewed by the SEC's Chief Accountant's Office, it was noted that certain leasing disclosures required by the SEC Accounting Series Release (ASR) No. 147 had been omitted.

A so-called deficiency letter was sent to DEF Corporation requesting compliance with the ASR in question. This produced an intensive review of all DEF leasing facts by the CPA firm that had attested to the SEC filing with an unqualified auditor's report. Finally a conference was arranged between representatives of DEF Corporation, its CPA firm, and the SEC. Certain additional leasing disclosures were agreed to after which the filing was accepted by the SEC.

With respect to SEC influence upon the financial accounting policymaking process we observe a rather significant administrative policy formulated by the SEC itself (in contrast to a national policy evolved through federal lawmaking). This SEC policy is that the SEC looks to the private sector for leadership in establishing and improving accounting principles and standards. The SEC made a formal statement to this effect in its ASR No. 150 (1973). It means that the SEC presumes financial statements to be misleading if such statements are prepared in accordance with accounting practices for which there is no substantial authoritative support in the private sector. The same ASR (No. 150) formally endorses the Financial Accounting Standards Board (FASB) and recognizes FASB-promulgated accounting principles and standards as substantially authoritative.

National policies are not always formulated directly and overtly. This is the case in the area of government contracting. Several legislative activities in recent years support the conclusion that a national policy is slowly emerging to the effect of insisting that government-purchased goods and services be produced as effectively and efficiently and be priced as competitively as they would be in the private sector of the economy.

The importance of this policy is demonstrated by the data on federal government expenditures. Huge amounts of economic resources flow into government contracting each year. A large number of private enterprises engage in performing these contracts either directly or as subcontractors.

While GAAP has circumscribed many aspects of financial reporting since 1938, cost and management accounting practices have been left completely to the discretion of individual firms. This meant, among other things, that government agencies were often charged in widely different ways for the costs (plus a percentage profit) of government-purchased goods and services. Special problems arose with military procurement due to the complete absence of private markets for most military hardware. Competitive market prices do not exist for these goods. Faulty contract cost estimates and subsequent cost "overruns" made much newspaper history during the late 1960s.

Out of this background came the establishment of the *Cost Accounting Standards Board* (CASB). By federal law, this board is responsible for uniform regulation of pricing, administration, and settlement of federal government contracts where the contract sum exceeds $100,000. The CASB is discharging its obligation by establishing Cost Accounting Standards. After final publication in the *Federal Register* and a short waiting period, CASB Standards become federal law. Since many firms work simultaneously in the private sector and in government contracting, they will probably employ the CASB Standards throughout their respective cost accounting systems. This is another instance where accounting is called upon to perform a much-needed public service.

Chapter 8

Risk Management

Volatility, in general, is associated with instability. This, in itself, is a testament to our seemingly growing incapacity to control our created economic and financial systems. We first declared gold and silver to be deemed money.

Currencies, which were convertible into gold and silver, eventually gave way to another man-made system of infrequently adjusted fixed rates of exchange among the leading currencies where one currency, the U.S. dollar, was convertible into gold.

Then this system gave way to another predominantly "dirty" managed system of floating exchange rates, where a currency is convertible only into another currency.

Many of the world currencies have limited convertibility to other currencies. Companies doing business in these nations have to adapt their financial affairs to fit the situation. That is to say, the conduct of business is guided, among other things, with an eye on how much currency is being accumulated.

Even for convertible currencies associated with industrialized nations, the conduct of business is influenced by which currencies are being accumulated and which are being liquidated.

Changes in currency exchange rates since the early 1970s have been significant. Therefore, these changes have significantly impacted the reported profitability of subsidiaries and affiliates when their financial reports were translated to the standard currency of the parent company.

CONTROLLABLE AND UNCONTROLLABLE LOSSES

Running a business has its inherent risks. Many of these risks cannot be managed—that is, they are beyond the control of management. These include the risk of a general downturn in business activity that reduces the volume of sales and the risk of competitors slashing prices to aggressively expand their market share.

A company must face the risk of competitors transforming the nature of the market by introducing an improved, or a new, version of a product that makes a company's product dated or obsolete. There is the risk of adverse government legislation, regulatory requirements, barriers to trade, and product liability suits. The list goes on, but added to this list is volatility in currency exchange rates. A receivable due in ninety days may not have the anticipated value in the domestic currency of a company that was envisioned when the transaction was consummated.

The risk of a currency exchange loss is a risk that has been dealt with by financial managers since the early 1970s. One might consider this potential loss of value in a financial transaction as uncontrollable in the sense that management cannot influence future currency exchange rates. Indeed, this is not so. Unlike a downward step in general business activity, an industry-wide price war, or a new product introduced by a competitor, there are ways for a company to protect itself against potential adverse changes in currency exchange rates. The availability of financial instruments to deal with this risk makes it controllable and gives meaning to the phrase "risk management."

PRICE VOLATILITY

Increased volatility transcends currency exchange rates. Prices of certain commodities that once were stable are now volatile. For example, the price of gold was constant from 1934, when President Franklin Roosevelt set the price of gold at $35 per ounce, until President Nixon shut the gold window in 1971. Although gold is not a commodity that affects the operations of most companies, its shift from a stable-priced commodity to one subject to wide swings in prices is instructive as to the nature of the problem of price volatility facing modern managers.

The purchasing managers of gold-consuming companies experienced a nearly forty-year history of paying $35 per ounce. During this time, the demands on the financial acumen of the purchasers to minimize the acquisition cost of gold were not overwhelming.

Little thought had to be given to inventory valuations and the potential of an inventory loss. Since 1971, the purchasing managers have had to endure the transition from purchasing gold at a fixed price to a price that is influenced by the supply and demand balance of gold and market perceptions of changes in that relationship. The percentage change, a measure of volatility, is the annual price swing divided by the mid-price for gold for the indicated year.

Daily quotes can be higher or lower than indicated. In 1980, spot gold spiked at over $800 per ounce for a short period of time. This is hidden in calculating monthly averages. Monthly or annual averages tend to mask the true nature of the volatility that is present in the daily, or spot, market. Purchasing managers focus on the current, or daily, market and must react to volatility on a daily, not on a monthly or annual, basis.

Volatility is better expressed as a percentage change from a base value than as an absolute difference between high and low quotes. The 1983 swing in prices of $102 per ounce appears to have greater volatility, or change, than the 1975 swing in prices of $37. Yet the volatility, as measured by the degree of change from the mid-value, is the same for both years. The $102 swing in prices in 1983, when compared to the mid-price of $439, is a measure of volatility of 23 per cent. This is the same measure of volatility in 1975 when the $37 swing is compared to the mid-price of $162.

VOLATILITY IMPACTBS PROFITABILITY

Nevertheless, the volatility of gold prices is going to

affect the profitability of a company that consumes gold in its operations in two ways. Gold purchased in 1980 at an average price of $600 per ounce generated either operating losses or inventory write-downs when gold subsequently fell to $400 per ounce.

Therefore, the task of management takes on a new dimension of meaning compared to what it was when the price of gold was fixed by government fiat. Poorly timed purchases of gold as a raw material with respect to the selling of the gold product can lead to substantial operating or inventory valuation losses, a risk not present when the price of gold was stable.

Loss from operations caused by a severe downturn in general business activity might be considered by managers to be beyond their control. An inventory loss may or may not fall into this category. Inventory is necessary for the smooth operations of a company and inventory requires management attention in terms of its quantity and safekeeping.

So while a manager is focusing his or her attention on what he or she considers to be more important matters concerning marketing, production and financing, a loss may suddenly emanate from the warehouse. In his or her mind, this should not occur because one would not expect that something safely stored in a well-operated warehouse could generate a loss. Yet it can, if the price of whatever is stored in the warehouse declines substantially. Obviously, this uncontrollable loss becomes a controllable loss when managers accept the responsibility to minimize potential inventory losses and have some means of preventing the loss from occurring.

For most inventories, management's tools may be limited to managing the quantity of inventory and, perhaps, terms of sales. But for other types of inventories, including inventories of currencies, there are means of insuring against such a loss. For generic forms of inventories such as metals, foodstuffs, energy, and currencies, there are a variety of risk management products available to reduce or contain the magnitude of a potential loss in the carrying value of an inventory.

VOLATILITY IMPACTS INVESTMENT DECISIONS

The discussion so far has been primarily from the buyer's perspective, where volatility introduces the potential for operating and inventory valuation losses. The other perspective is that of the seller, in this case, a gold mining company.

Another complication arising from volatile gold prices is loss of confidence in the financial analysis associated with the decision-making process leading to a capital investment. When prices are constant, the projected revenue of a financial analysis of making a major capital investment in mining capacity can be viewed with a fair degree of confidence. As long as costs are reasonably accurate, and most companies have a fairly good handle on costs, a financial analysis with constancy of prices is reasonably reliable as long as the volume of output is realizable.

Instability in prices affects the confidence that management has in the validity of investment decision models. In 1940, one would confidently project a continued price of $35 per ounce in the decision-making process on making an investment in a gold mine.

What price would one assume in 1980 to hold for the next ten to twenty years in order to justify the capital investment in expanding mining capacity? Five hundred dollars per ounce might have been considered reasonable at that time, but one would lack confidence in that price holding for the next decade or so because of past price volatility. In subsequent years, an average projected value of $500 per ounce turned out to be wrong.

A capital project whose financing costs depended on an average price of $500 per ounce would certainly have impacted negatively on a company's earnings, and conceivably could have led to its bankruptcy. Therefore, volatility detracts from the confidence management can place in the underlying financial analysis of the investment decision process.

VOLATILITY COMMON IN TODAY'S WORLD

Increasing volatility is not restricted to currency exchange rates or gold. The cost of energy, as reflected in the cost for oil, was essentially constant at close to $2 per barrel from the 1930s until 1972. Interest rates were also stable up to this time. Yet by reviewing this table, one can see that there are times of general calm, and other times of tumult, in price volatility. The degree of volatility from year to year is itself volatile and unpredictable.

This is an important point that adds to the challenge of risk management—hedging generally should be put in place before tumult in prices strikes the market. However, hedging during times of relative calm is sure to raise some questions as to its cost and need.

In viewing the table, islands of stability in a sea of volatility can be seen for interest rates from 1975 to 1978 and from 1985 to 1988. The price of oil was relatively stable from 1974 to 1978 and from 1982 to 1985. Other periods exhibited enormous volatility.

It was no fun being a corporate borrower from 1977 to 1981 or purchasing oil from 1973 to 1974, or from 1978 to 1979. But there is always the other side of the coin. Those with savings seeking interest income would not consider 1982 to 1985 memorable times nor do oil producers have fond memories of 1985 to 1986, or 1987 to 1988. Viewing price changes from the two perspectives of buyers and sellers creates a potential market for risk management products. The seller is interested in fixing the sales price so that he or she does not have to worry about falling prices eroding profit. A buyer is interested in fixing cost so that he or she does not have to worry about rising costs eroding profit.

What appears to be an adverse change in price for one party is considered by the other to be an opportunity. This makes it possible for those involved as middlemen or market makers in risk management products to put a deal together, because each party has a different view of the consequences of the same price change.

The airlines have historically flown on thin profit margins because of competitive pressures within this industry. Airline executives learned about the impact of price volatility on profits the hard way. Both the cost of money and jet fuel are important in an airline's operations. With thin profit margins, 25 per cent jumps in interest rates (10 per cent to 12.5 per cent) or jet fuel costs (60 to 75 cents per gallon) are sufficient to obliterate profit margins. During the 1970s, both jet fuel prices and short-term interest rates spiked at three times, or 300 per cent, their levels at the start of the 1970s.

The normal "knee-jerk" response to higher prices is to jack up the airfares. Airline executives learned that such enormous increases in the costs of money and fuel could not be entirely passed on to the consumer in the form of hikes in airline fares. Although the business traveller may be relatively indifferent to the cost of airfare, the vacationing public is not. The vacationing public makes up a sizable portion of airline traffic and is, in general, sensitive to the price of a ticket. As airlines raised ticket prices to compensate for these unheard of swings in the cost of money and fuel, the vacationing public stopped buying airline tickets.

The vacation in Europe gave way to a vacation on the Jersey shore. The reduced number of passengers made it impossible for the airlines to recoup the incremental costs. The volatility in the cost of money and fuel on air fares and the ensuing loss of passenger volume was more than sufficient to destroy the profitability of the industry and to drive certain airlines into bankruptcy. Airlines that did protect themselves partially from these changes in costs through shrewd management of the risks that they faced found themselves at a competitive advantage. They number among the survivors.

Yet during those times of relative stability in prices for gold, interest, and currency exchange rates prior to the 1970s, managers of certain industries had to deal in a world of price instability. Lumber, copper, and foodstuffs were, and still are, exposed to the vagaries of sharp price swings. Managers of firms that bought or sold these commodities were keen to protect themselves from adverse price changes through risk management. Financial instruments have been around for over a century to address this need. These financial instruments were expanded in scope, and modified as necessary, as price volatility spread to precious metals, energy, and interest and currency exchange rates.

A discussion on risk management can be easily adapted from one commodity to another. Risk management techniques can be applied to tangibles (grain, lumber, oil, and metals) and to intangibles (interest rates, stock prices, and currency exchange rates). A proposed risk management product can be tailored to anything that exhibits sufficient price volatility to create a need for individuals as normal buyers or sellers of the tangible or intangible item to seek protection from such price swings.

In addition, a proposed risk management product should be attractive enough for speculators to assume risk in their quest for personal gain. A proposed risk management product requires an acceptable means of settlement and a large number of actively trading participants. Their trading activity in hedging or speculating provides the revenue to cover the cost of operations and the requisite liquidity for the buying and selling of the risk management product.

Both hedgers and speculators are required for the successful laying off of risk among the participants. The presence of speculators adds depth to the market, by their volume of buying and selling. They are said to bring information to the market by taking positions based on their analysis of available data, which, in turn, influences prices. They often are the mainstay of balancing orders when the "legitimate" hedgers are primarily on one side of the market. For instance, when gold was $800 per ounce, mining companies may have been eager to fix their future production at a price around $800.

Consumers of gold may not have been so eager to fix their costs at $800. There is now a mismatch between the number of buyers and sellers. The transference of risk, which is the purpose of risk management products, cannot be accomplished because the market has become one-sided. However, the presence of speculators provides the mining companies with the opportunity to enter into financial transactions that would stabilize their future revenue by transferring the opportunity of further gain in prices to the speculators.

In this example, gold mining companies who entered into futures contracts to fix the price of future production at $800 per ounce turned out to have made the right decision. Consumers of gold and speculators who represented the other side of the transaction lived to regret their decision. Risk management products are a means by which the risk of a rise or fall in a price, or the opportunity associated therewith, is passed from one party to another. Risk management products do not obviate the risk; no more than fire insurance stops fires.

CURRENCY RISK MANAGEMENT

Currency risk management has to do with taking action to avert the risk of loss because of the nature of the currency held by a company and because of the nature of future commercial transactions that lead to an exposure to a currency.

Currency risk management is more complex than risk management of a commodity such as copper. A global company must think about its exposure in a hundred currencies, whereas a company dealing in copper has one commodity to worry about. Management views of a currency as favorable or unfavorable depend on whether it is strengthening or weakening in relation to other currencies and on whether a company is long (held in reserves) or short (owed to others). A copper mining company with inventory to be sold and a copper using company with copper in a warehouse to be consumed do not as readily shift between a long or short position as does a global company with a hundred affiliates dealing in a hundred currencies.

A copper-consuming company can easily quantify its exposure. Copper on hand, plus anticipated receipts and commitments less planned shipments, pretty much measures the exposure.

Besides dealing in many currencies, a global company has two types of currency exposures: transactions and translations. Although transaction exposure is more easily understood, as payables and receivables in various currencies, translation exposure involves other aspects of the balance sheet. Moreover, the nature of the consolidation process affects the magnitude of translation risk.

Management usually tries to simplify the confusion over currencies by referencing all currencies to one currency—the currency of the nation of domicile. An American-based company's management thinks of all currencies in terms of a dollar equivalent. British, German, and Japanese managers view currencies in their pound, deutschemark, or yen equivalents. There is also a tendency to reduce excess holdings in various currencies to the currency of the company's nation of domicile.

Although understandable, it is possible that holding cash reserves in the nation of domicile may not be the optimal course of action. If the pound or dollar is weakening with respect to the deutschemark and yen, is it wise to convert all deutschemark and yen holdings to pounds or dollars as quickly as possible just because management happens to be British or American? One aspect of the transition from a multinational company to a truly global company may be in the way the company thinks of currencies. A global company may not think in terms of a single dominating currency, but in terms of several major currencies with changing attitudes on which to hold. Perhaps its financial records and earnings reports may not be in a single currency.

But for now, it is easier to discuss currency risk management in terms of a single currency in relation to others. The discussion that follows is based on a U.S. domiciled company, but the principles are similar to those of companies domiciled in other nations.

TRANSACTION EXPOSURE

A common practice for affiliates operating in various countries is to receive payment for goods sold in the currency of its nation of domicile. Suppose that a company consists of three affiliates operating in the United States, Germany, and France. These affiliates buy and sell among themselves and normally, but not always, expect payment in their currency of domicile. Normally, when the American affiliat (A) purchases goods from the German affiliate (G), it generates a deutsche-mark (DM) payable. When it purchases goods from the French affiliate (F), the American affiliate generates a French franc (FF) payable. Similarly when the German or the French affiliates purchase goods from the American affiliate, the American affiliate has dollar receivables.

Although this is common practice, it is possible for an affiliate to buy goods from another affiliate and pay for it in its own currency, and to sell goods to another affiliate and receive payment in the affiliate's currency of domicile. It is also possible that a third currency not related to either of the affiliates may be used as a means of settlement. Suppose, at a point in time, the inter company receivables and payables.

Managers of a U.S. domiciled company would view these currency transactions in terms of dollar equivalents. Translating these payables and receivables in terms of a deutschemark being worth about $0.60 and a French franc about These receivables and payables can be combined as in A to obtain the net exposure to each currency.

Receivables and payables in the same currency are natural hedges. Thousands of individual receivables and payables can be combined to obtain the actual exposure of a company to a particular currency. In this example, the actual exposure of the company consisting of three affiliates in terms of inter company buying and selling is a long position of $54 worth of deutschemarks (90 DM), a short position of $300 of French francs (1,500 FF), and a long position of $40 (U.S.). Once the natural hedges within, and without, a company have been combined, management is in a position to evaluate its actual exposure to various currencies and to decide on a course of action to reduce potential currency exchange losses. Some commercial banks offer a "netting" or payment-clearing service to companies with global operations. All the affiliates of a company enter their inter company receivables and payables, in terms of the actual currencies to be received or paid, through a telecommunications system into a common computer data bank.

On a periodic basis, and under management control, all inter company receivables and payables are netted and an affiliate receives, or owes, one payment. As an example, a Belgian affiliate may have dealings with a hundred different affiliates in as many nations. Generally speaking, most payables are in the currency of the nation of domicile of the affiliate and most receivables are in Belgian francs, but this may not be true for all transactions.

At specified periods such as a month, and assuming that there are more in receivables than in payables in these inter company transactions, the Belgian affiliate receives one payment in Belgian francs. All associated inter company receivables and payables contained within the computer data base, which could number in the tens, the hundreds, or even the thousands, are thereby liquidated with the issuance of a single payment. If the Belgian affiliate has more payables than receivables, then it makes one payment in Belgian francs, and again all associated receivables and payables are liquidated. The bank makes all spot conversions of currencies necessary for the affiliates to receive or pay in their respective currencies of domicile.

Management can incorporate projected payables and receivables into the system in addition to actual payables and receivables in order to improve its measurement of exposure to various currencies from inter company transfers. The netting service provides management with a full range of reports such as currency exposure, cash balance, transaction, consolidation, and working capital reports. These reports are used for control purposes, for cash management, and for measuring a company's current and projected exposure to various currencies from inter company transfers. A full measurement of exposure also requires projected payables and receivables to other companies outside the netting system.

It is also conceivable that several global companies could join together in such a system, further reducing the administrative processing costs of making individual payments to affiliates in the same global company and to affiliates in other global companies. Conceptually, this is not unlike credit cards where individuals make one monthly payment, which covers a multitude of individual purchases from many merchants, and where merchants receive one monthly payment from the credit card company, which represents the purchases of many individuals.

TRANSLATION EXPOSURE

Currency translation exposure applies to balance sheets and income statements denominated in a different currency than the company's nation of domicile. Translation exposure is determined by applying the appropriate exchange rate to the various items of the balance sheet and income statements. The rules regarding which exchange rate is to be applied to individual line items of a balance sheet and income statement differ with the consolidation method. Therefore, the amount and treatment of translation gains or losses vary with the method of consolidation.

As an example of the possibility of obtaining different measures of exposure to translation gains or losses, suppose that a company has an affiliate in country X and management is fearful of a 20 per cent devaluation of the local currency (LC). For a U.S. company, however, there are two possible methods of consolidation. One is the current rate method (Financial Accounting Standards Board [FASB] 52) and the other is the temporal method (FASB 8).

If, on the other hand, management had determined that the functional currency was the U.S. dollar, the temporal method of translation would be applicable as prescribed by FASB 8. The temporal method must also be selected as the method of consolidation if the affiliate is operating in a hyperinflationary economy, which is defined as one where the currency has a three-year cumulative inflation exceeding 100 per cent. Cash and accounts receivable total 1.9 billion LC and liabilities total 3.2 billion LC, resulting in a negative exposure, or short position, of 1.3 billion LC. Under FASB 8, inventories and fixed assets are recorded at historical values and are not exposed to changes in currency exchange rates. This short position, or negative exposure, of 1.3 billion LC will result in a translation gain of $26 million (1.3 billion LC x $0.02 LC/dollar change in the currency exchange rate). This gain is reflected in the income statement, not directly in the equity portion of the balance sheet.

Under FASB 8, the inventory is still recorded at the historic rate of $0.10. This means that in subsequent periods of operation, sales will be translated at 1 LC equal to $0.08, but cost of sales, as goods are withdrawn from the "old" inventory, will be translated at a rate of 1 LC being equal to $0. 10 until the "old" inventory is depleted. New additions to the inventory will be translated at 1 LC equal to $0.08. The existence of the "old" inventory has a negative impact on future translated profit until it is depleted. In addition, depreciation expense on existing fixed assets at the time of the devaluation is translated at the rate of $0.10 to the LC after the devaluation, further depressing translated profitability.

Both the exposure to translation gain or loss and the accounting treatment of gain or loss differ widely between FASB 8 and FASB 52. The course of action pursued by management in its anticipation of a devaluation of the LC is, in this example, dramatically different as a consequence of the method of consolidation. In one case, there is a risk to translation loss that impacts the equity portion of the balance sheet. In the other, there is a translation gain with negative ramifications on future income.

FURTHER COMPLICATIONS

All assets and liabilities in the previous discussion are denominated in LC. The reason for this is that management is referring to the income statement and balance sheet as presented by the affiliate to the parent. The affiliate has translated all currencies contained in its financial statements to LC before presenting them to the parent organization. However, in today's global business environment, an affiliate usually deals in many currencies. Suppose that the affiliate in country X sells to local, Japanese, Thai, and U.S. markets and that the temporal method of consolidation (FASB 8) applies. Accordingly, cash, receivables, and liabilities are exposed to the risk of a revaluation or devaluation.

There is no net exposure to the U.S. dollar because assets and liabilities already denominated in U.S. dollars do not require further attention. Certain non-balancesheet adjustments have to be made for management to realise the actual exposure to various currencies. One adjustment is the omission of cash on hand, because cash on hand is usually the minimum necessary to operate the business on a day-to-day basis. That being the case, management does not have to take action to protect these minimal, and necessary, holdings. Other adjustments involve the effect of known future transactions, which are not yet reflected on the balance sheet, such as future sales contracts, firm commitments, and operating lease payments.

If it happens that the long exposure in one currency equals the short exposure in another, the two cannot be offset against each other. They both must be dealt with separately because it is unlikely that any two currencies will move in tandem. Exposures are expressed in dollars because it is assumed that the company is U.S. domiciled. Managers of a corporation can more readily grasp the magnitude of the exposures if they are expressed in the common currency of the company.

The analysis of exposure performed by British management would be in pounds and the risk of translation exposure would take into consideration the U.K. method of consolidation. This would hold for all nations of domicile.Including non-balance-sheet items such as future sales, purchase commitments, and leases changes the exposure to various currencies. In this example, the long position in

Japanese yen has increased, the long position in Thai baht has decreased, and the short position in LC has increased.

The data base is now complete for management to take an overview of the situation and consider what actions, if any, are necessary to protect the company with regard to its exposure to various currencies.Measuring the exposure to transaction and translation risk requires a centralized information system in order for management to determine its exposure to various currencies. Without this information, managers involved in risk management are not able to act effectively.

This information must be presented on a timely basis because it is possible for a company's exposure to a particular currency to swing from a long to short, or from a short to long, position in a brief period of time. Usually, monthly reports from all affiliates are consolidated and analyzed on a global basis for management to have a continual measure of the actual exposure of a company to all currencies.Affiliates may report their exposure to various currencies by telecommunications means using a specified electronic spreadsheet format.

Once the parent has the spreadsheet reports from the affiliates, they can then be combined into one master spreadsheet that calculates the company's global exposure to all currencies. Besides timeliness of data and ease of display for measurement of exposure, such an information system places the management of the parent in a position to exercise control over the financial decisions being made by the affiliates to prevent them from taking actions that would make managing exposure to transaction and translation risk more difficult.

MANAGEMENT EXPOSURE

Management may feel comfortable being exposed to certain currencies that it feels will maintain or increase in value with respect to the currency of domicile of the company. For those currencies where management fears a loss of purchasing power, various methods can be employed to reduce the exposure to these currencies, which are briefly described below.

- Local cash balances should be kept to a minimum level consistent with cash needs necessary for the operation of the business. Excess cash and profits should be remitted as quickly as possible from the subsidiary or affiliate to the parent by increasing the frequency or size of dividends, royalties, and licencing and management fees, remaining cognizant, of course, of tax considerations and local currency exchange controls.
- If management believes that a devaluation is imminent, one possible course of action may be to raise selling prices. In a competitive pricing environment, this will depress the sales volume, reduce receivables, and increase inventory. This, of course, is against the natural inclination of local management because raising prices to this extent also depresses profits. But this course of action is not intended to depress profits, but to reduce the potential of loss from an imminent devaluation.

  Investment in inventory, as a non-monetary asset, is a means of protection against the financial loss of a devaluation associated with cash balances and receivables. Transforming cash and receivables into tangible assets reduces the extent of write-downs of liquid assets. If FASB 8 applies, inventories are not written down because they are carried at historic cost. In addition, tangible assets tend to preserve their value as a currency loses purchasing power because they can be sold for a higher price after the devaluation. Once the impact of the devaluation on the local economy is over, selling prices can be reduced to competitive levels to enhance sales and reduce inventory. Of course, these price hikes have to take into account any local price control regulations that may be in effect.
- Speeding up collection of receivables, and for that

matter, slowing down payment of payables, would result in higher cash balances, which might then be invested, along with any other excess cash, in increased inventory or other tangible assets. However, as everyone's receivable is someone else's payable, the net result of this course of action might be a nationwide stalemate on paying bills until after the devaluation. Excess cash holdings can also be invested in a strong currency foreign asset, such as an investment in a related affiliate or in a new subsidiary. Local government regulations on currency exchange may constrain or eliminate this latter option.

- Sometimes companies engage in "back-to-back" loans as a means of trying to reduce the impact of a devaluation, or a series of anticipated devaluations. Suppose that parent A has affiliate A operating in a nation where the local currency cannot be exchanged for a more desirable currency. One way to reduce the exposure to the local currency is to engage in back-to-back loans by lending surplus local currency to an affiliate (affiliate B) of a non-related company (parent B) that needs the local currency for its own purposes. Simultaneously, parent B makes a hard currency loan to parent A. In a typical arrangement, both of these loans are paid off at a stipulated future date in their respective currencies. This exchange of cash for a receivable in a local currency at least has the benefit of making hard currency available to parent A at a negotiated interest rate that is usually advantageous to parent A. This gives parent A some slight benefit in its holdings of a local currency. The problem of what to do with excess holdings of the local currency has been deferred, but not solved.
- Leads or lags are timing differences in the payment or settlement of payables and receivables. This technique has two purposes. One is the funding of affiliates. Suppose that a Korean company sells

$100,000 worth of goods to a Spanish company monthly. If these goods are sold on 60-day terms, the Spanish company owes the Korean company $200,000 on a permanent basis. If the Spanish company requires more funds, this can be accomplished by changing the terms to 120 days, that is, increasing the lag. This will increase the amount payable to the Korean company to $400,000 on a permanent basis. If the Korean company requires funds, then the Spanish company can pay currently, or, perhaps, in advance, which is known as a lead.

The other purpose of leads and lags is to shift the currency exposure between two nations. Suppose that management believes that the Spanish peseta will devalue in the near future. The Spanish affiliate could be instructed to speed up inter company payments; that is increase the lead, and obtain whatever financing is required from local lenders to make this possible.

This reduces the exposure of the company in pesetas, before the devaluation occurs, by reducing its cash reserves of pesetas and increasing its payables in pesetas in the form of bank loans.

The caveat here is that if all companies are making bank loans for the purpose of converting the proceeds to a different currency, then interest rates for these loans can become quite high, negating some of the benefit of reducing the exposure to currency exchange losses. Moreover, if everyone is joining in the rush to get out of pesetas, the devaluation becomes a self-fulfilling prophecy.

RISK MANAGEMENT PRODUCTS

The techniques just described can seldom accomplish all of management's objectives. To add to management's arsenal of tools to manage the risk associated with adverse changes in currency exchange rates, interest rates, and commodity prices, a host of risk management products have been devised by financial engineers. J. D. Finnerty, a professorat Fordham University, in an article titled "Financial Engineering in

Corporate Finance: An Overview," appearing in the Winter 1988 issue of *Financial Management*, defined "financial engineering" as follows:

Financial engineering involves the design, the development, and the implementation of innovative financial instruments and processes, and the formulation of creative solutions to problems in finance.

Financial engineers work closely with a client firm to first identify and measure the potential exposure to risk and then create a solution to obtain a desired outcome. Some financial engineers specialize in the quantitative analysis of determining the exposure to risk. Others are responsible for coming up with what may be an innovative and creative solution. Still others are involved with the practical aspects of implementing the solution. Financial engineering usually requires the services of accountants, lawyers, tax specialists, analysts, modeling professionals, programmers, and information specialists.

Financial engineering is a sign of the times—as volatility of prices and interest and currency exchange rates increases, so does the risk of potential loss faced by corporations, and, therefore, the need for outside expertise to manage the risk of potential loss. The efficacy of financial engineering depends on modern methods of communication and the interfacing of communications and computers for the dissemination of information on various financial and commodity markets. Modern technology in the networking of computers allows multiple users to tap the same data base and use the same spreadsheet financial models for rapid analysis in preparing timely and effective recommendations to clients, both internal and external.

One interesting example of the technological impact of computers and telecommunications on financial markets is "programme trading." Stock market index futures are used by portfolio managers as insurance, or protection, against a falling market. Suppose that a mutual fund manager is worried about a falloff in the stock market. By shorting the index futures, any falloff in the stock market, which creates portfolio losses, is compensated by profits made in the index futures. Programme trading is the exploitation of discrepancies between the price of stock market index futures and the underlying market value of the stocks represented by these futures. Speed of execution of orders, computerized matching of buy and sell orders, buying and selling of "baskets" of securities, and rapid analysis of the complex mathematics associated with identifying pricing discrepancies are necessary technological preconditions for the existence of programme trading.

Stock market index futures can be viewed as a financial tool, devised by financial engineers for stock portfolio managers to protect themselves against volatility in stock prices. But financial engineers are also hard at work devising innovative and creative ways for individuals and firms to increase their yield on investments.

By examining the spread between index futures and the underlying value of the basket of securities, financial engineers can provide the necessary information and the means to buy one and short the other, locking in a superior return over investing in other securities such as Treasury bills. This particular financial tool, created by financial engineers to protect portfolio managers against adverse changes in stock prices, is also exploited by financial engineers to enhance the return on investment for investors.

The irony of the situation is that the exploitation of a financial instrument to enhance yield may also be responsible for increasing the volatility of stock prices. If this is the case, then the medicine is both treating and contributing to the disease.

The ability to gather information promptly and accurately, and disseminate the information immediately throughout the world can be considered a risk management tool. This, too, may be responsible for increased volatility. A manager of a chocolate factory who first learned about a cocoa crop failure in West Africa in the nineteenth century from a captain of a sailing vessel probably had sufficient time to act on this information to protect his company's interest in cocoa beans before his competitors learned about it. His individual buying of cocoa beans would probably not affect the market to any great degree. The slow dissemination of the information about the crop failure allows for an orderly adjustment of prices.

Nathan Rothschild supposedly learned of the defeat of Napoleon at Waterloo by homing pigeon. This allowed him to buy depressed stocks in London before anyone else knew of the allied victory and sell them when everyone else knew. Leaving aside the moral implications of having sole access to vital information, the buying and selling by Rothschild probably reduced the volatility in the London stock market because his buying occurred when everyone was selling and his selling occurred when everyone was buying. In today's world, all those who deal in cocoa beans and stocks and everything else are tapped into the same source of news. No one has a timing advantage, which means that all act in unison, and by so doing, increase the volatility of prices.

CURRENCY EXCHANGE AND INTEREST RATES

There is a connection between futures in currency exchange rates and interest rates. This connection ties these two markets, which allows financial engineers to devise ways of hedging in interest rates by means of hedges in currencies and vice versa. Suppose that an American has $1,000,000 to invest and six-month (180-day) U.S. Treasury bills offer an annual yield of 4.0 per cent.

If the investor completes this transaction, he would have approximately $1,020,000 at the end of the 180-day period. Suppose, however, that the investor notes that a French government security is yielding 4.5 per cent in 180 days. If he converts his dollars to francs, he will earn more interest, but will be faced with a currency exchange risk at the maturity of the French security.

Suppose that the current spot rate for francs is 5.527 francs to the dollar and the 180-day forward contract is 5.538 francs to the dollar. The investor could convert his dollars to francs, receiving 5,527,000 francs, which when invested in the French 180-day note, yields 5,651,358 francs (5,527,000 × 4.5 per cent × 180/360). Simultaneously with the conversion of dollars into francs, the investor also sells a 5,651,358 forward contract at the 180-day forward rate of 5.538 francs to the dollar. Upon receipt of the 5,651,358 francs in 180 days with the maturing of the French debt security, the investor fulfills his obligation under the forward contract by converting 5,651,358 francs to $1,020,469. This is in excess of the $1,020,000 he would have received had he invested in the U.S. Treasury 180-day bill.

The forward or futures rate for a currency is set not by the market impact of investors attempting to maximize their return as much as by arbitragers seeking a riskless return. An arbitrager enters into a riskless covered interest arbitrage by borrowing funds in one country, converting to another currency, investing the funds in another country, and selling a forward contract to cover the conversion back into the original currency to repay the loan. An arbitrager would continue entering into such transactions until the difference between the currency exchange spot and forward rates narrows sufficiently to remove the riskless profit

of entering into such transactions. This is accomplished by the continual buying of spot contracts and selling of forward contracts, which causes the price of the former to rise and the price of the latter to fall until the riskless profit differential disappears. The role of investors in maximizing returns on their assets and arbitragers in seeking riskless profit opportunities establishes a link between interest rates and the spread between spot and forward currency exchange rates. This makes it possible for financial engineers to devise ingenuous solutions to interest rate exposure by entering into a currency exchange contract or to manage a currency exchange risk through an interest rate contract.

It also makes it possible for financial engineers to reduce interest costs by having a company borrow from financial institutions in other countries without exposing the company to a currency exchange loss. For instance, a Canadian company was able to borrow in yen from a Japanese financial institution at a favorable interest rate, which exposed the company to the possibility of an adverse change in the Japanese yen/Canadian dollar exchange rate. Financial engineers addressed that risk by having the company enter into a long-term currency exchange contract. The net effect of these two transactions was a lower effective interest rate to the company by borrowing in Japan and hedging the currency exchange risk rather than by borrowing directly in the Canadian capital market.

FUTURES AND FORWARDS

The terms "futures" and "forwards" are oftentimes used interchangeably for contracts between two parties that require a specific action to be taken at some later date. As these contracts generally take the form of a delivery of an underlying asset such as a certain amount of currency or a quantity of a physical asset, they are sometimes referred to as contracts for deferred delivery. There are, however, important differences between futures and forwards.

A futures contract is traded on public exchanges with highly standardized terms other than the price of the contract, which is set by the market. A forward contract is traded in "over-thecounter" dealer markets where all terms, including price, must be negotiated between the buyer and seller. Over the counter means that a formal exchange or clearing house is not involved in a forward contract—deals are done on an individual basis with a dealer playing the role of a middleman or broker.

A clearing house or association stands between the parties of a futures contract, which removes the necessity of identifying the parties involved in the futures contract. This is similar to the trading of stock on a stock exchange—it is done between brokerage houses with the brokerage houses responsible for making the final settlement between the ultimate buyer and seller of the shares of stock. In a forward contract, each party is directly responsible for the fulfillment of the agreed terms and, therefore, their identity is a critical factor in the negotiation process leading up to the mutual agreement of contractual terms and conditions.

Futures markets, like the stock markets, are government regulated, whereas forward markets are not. The financial integrity of the futures market is ensured by each party to a futures contract maintaining the required margin, which can be likened to a performance bond. No such mechanism exists in the forward market. This is another reason why the identity of the parties, and their reputation, is a critical part of a forward contract.

In addition, the active market in futures contracts makes it easy to terminate a transaction by buying back the futures or entering into another that offsets the original transaction. In a forward contract where terms and conditions are uniquely defined for each contract, such ease of termination is not only difficult but may be impossible. There is liquidity in the continual buying and selling of futures in the futures market, whereas there is virtually no liquidity in the forwards market.

On the surface, one would wonder why anyone would enter into a forward contract rather than a futures contract. The primary reason is that the futures contract, being a highly standardized contract, may not fit the particular needs of an individual or company. Suppose that an importer must pay 20 million Japanese yen in forty-nine days. A futures contract is in units of 12.5 million yen to be settled thirty, sixty, and ninety days in the future. The futures contract dces not meet the importer's specific needs. Rather than over or under hedge either in the amount of yen and the duration of time, by taking a position in futures on the futures exchange, the importer might negotiate a deal that meets his or her precise requirements with a forward contract arranged in the over-thecounter market.

SWAPS

Swaps are financial products originated by financial engineers in response to the growing instability in prices and in interest and currency exchange rates during the 1980s.

Started in 1979, swaps became a popular financial instrument in 1981 because of the publicity associated with a currency swap arranged by Salomon Brothers between the World Bank and IBM. Currency swaps rapidly spread to swaps in interest rates and commodities. Swaps are built around the same basic structure as forwards and have been described as a series of forward contracts. Two parties, called counterparties, agree to one or more exchange(s) of specified quantities of underlying tangibles or intangibles, sometimes called notionals if there is a cash rather than a physical exchange of the underlying asset. Cash payments are the usual means of settlements between the counterparties of a swap.

A swap is usually arranged by a financial intermediary that negotiates a final deal between two counterparties entering into a swap. The intermediary, known as a swap dealer or market maker, receives his or her remuneration in the bidasked spread between the two counterparties. Three illustrations are provided to explain the principal "plain vanilla" swaps.

Interest Rate Swap

Counterparty A is a company that requires $10 million to construct a factory. The creditworthiness of the company is not sufficient for an issue of fixed rate interest debt, but a bank is willing to lend the company $10 million on a floating rate basis. Counterparty A worries about the floating rate interest rate increasing over the next ten years and wants to hedge, or protect itself, against this risk. Counterparty A is willing to sacrifice the opportunity of having to pay less in interest expense if floating rates fall in order to safeguard itself from the risk of having to pay higher than the fixed rate that can be arranged through a swap.

Counterparty B is a company, or a financial institution, whose creditworthiness is sufficient for it to issue fixed interest rate debt. Suppose that counterparty B borrows on the basis of its own creditworthiness $10 million at a fixed interest rate of 10 per cent. It could lend the money to counterparty A, but then counterparty B assumes the credit risk of counterparty A repaying the loan. Instead of lending the money to counterparty A, counterparty B deposits the funds in a floating rate account. Suppose that the floating rate is currently 8 per cent. Counterparty B transfers the interest income of 8 per cent on its $10 million deposit to the swap dealer in return for a fixed rate of 10.3 per cent.

Counterparty B neither makes nor loses money on the floating rate deposit and makes a 0.3 per cent spread on its capacity to issue fixed rate debt. Counterparty B has no credit risk in borrowing the $10 million in that the proceeds of the loan have been placed in a floating rate deposit that is sufficient to pay off the principal of the fixed rate debt.

The swap dealer passes the floating rate interest payment received from counterparty B to counterparty A. In return, counterparty A pays the swap dealer 10.4 per cent fixed rate of interest. The difference between receiving 10.4 per cent interest from counterparty A and paying 10.3 per cent interest to counterparty B is the swap dealer's remuneration. Counterparty A takes the floating rate interest of 8 per cent and pays the floating rate interest plus any applicable spread to its lending institution. If the interest rate on counterparty A's loan is the floating rate plus a spread of 0.75 per cent, then counterparty A is actually paying 8.75 per cent on its loan. Therefore, the net cost of interest to counterparty A is the 0.75 per cent differential to be paid on the floating rate loan plus the fixed 10.4 per cent to the swap dealer.

There is no point in counterparty A paying 10.4 per cent to the swap dealer and receiving the floating rate of 8 per cent from the swap dealer. It is easier to net the difference and pay that to the swap dealer. Under the circumstances, counterparty A pays the difference between 10.4 per cent and 8 per cent to the swap dealer, or 2.4 per cent applied against the notional amount of the interest rate swap, in this case, $10 million. Counterparty A pays less if the floating interest rate rises. If the floating rate goes above the fixed rate, counterparty A will receive money from the swap dealer. This extra money will be used to pay the higher interest charge associated with counterparty A's floating rate loan.

Therefore, counterparty A has accomplished his purpose of swapping a floating rate for a fixed rate loan. His cost of interest is the fixed rate of 10.4% plus the spread of 0.75% on the floating rate loan. He is no longer at risk in having floating rates rise to a level that may imperil his financial survivability. For this, he has foregone any opportunity to benefit from floating interest rates being less than the arranged fixed rate.

A single payment is also made between counterparty B, representing the difference between the 10.3 per cent to be received from the swap dealer and the floating rate to be paid to the swap dealer. The swap dealer simply passes the payment between the two counterparties extracting his piece of the action. The swap dealer is making 0.1 per cent interest spread between counterparty B receiving 10.3 per cent and counterparty A paying 10.4 per cent on the notional amount of the principal. He has accomplished his objective in arranging the swap.

Counterparty B has borrowed funds at 10 per cent and has lent them out at 10.3 per cent with the difference being remuneration for entering into the transaction. This fulfills counterparty B's objective in entering into the swap. However, in entering this swap, counterparty B has given up any benefit from rising interest rates. He has deposited the funds from a fixed rate loan in a floating rate account and turns the interest earnings over to the swap dealer. If the floating rate were to go to 20 per cent on funds borrowed at 10 per cent, counterparty B would have been better off not entering into the swap.

Counterparty B can undo the transaction by purchasing an interest rate futures, but from the point of view of the swap, he has given up the benefit of rising floating interest rates. Therefore, he might have been reluctant to enter into the swap if he had strong feelings that floating interest rates would rise. However, by counterparty B depositing the funds from the fixed rate loan in a floating rate account, whether floating rates rise or fall, counterparty B has locked in his return. This is the spread between the fixed rate paid by the swap dealer and the fixed rate being paid on the incurred debt.

It is possible that counterparty B does not borrow the funds at a fixed rate of interest. Counterparty B may be a financial institution that feels that interest rates are going to fall and may delay arranging its fixed debt financing. It is possible that it does not intend to arrange any borrowings, but to cover itself through the purchase of interest rate futures should interest rates begin to rise. If counterparty B perceives this to be a desired course of action, then the swap dealer would definitely find it easier to put the swap together if both counterparties have opposite viewpoints on the future direction of floating interest rates.

The swap can be considered as a series of forward contracts in which the termination of each individual contract occurs at the time of payment of the interest rate differential, say, every six months. Collectively, in this example, the swap represents a series of twenty forward contracts that cover ten years of interest payments. Credit risk is not transferred in a swap. Both counterparties A and B have arranged their floating and fixed rate loans based on their individual

creditworthiness. Each is responsible for the repayment of the underlying principal of the loan. If, by change, counterparty B did not arrange a fixed rate loan, then its creditworthiness must be sufficient to cover the differential in interest rates should its assessment on the future direction of rates be proven wrong. Even here, there are means for counterparty B to minimize, or avoid, losses.

The only connection between the two counterparties is the net payment representing the difference between the floating and fixed rates of interest. The bankruptcy of one of the counterparties affects only the interest rate differential payment between the two counterparties. In addition to the potential bankruptcy of a counterparty, swap dealers such as Drexel, Burnham, Lambert of junk bond fame, have gone bankrupt. The U.S. Bankruptcy Code has been amended to ensure that netting provisions of swaps be honored by the bankruptcy courts in the event of the bankruptcy of counterparties and swap dealers. Interest rate swaps have become so common that the plain vanilla variety are frequently arranged directly between banks without the services of a swap dealer.

Currency Swap

A currency swap can be arranged when one of the counterparties has more advantageous access to a financial market. Suppose that an American company desires to finance a factory to be built in Germany in deutschemarks at a fixed rate of interest. Further suppose that a German company has access to lower. fixed rate interest financing in Germany than the American company.

To complete the picture, suppose that the German company desires to borrow in U.S. dollars for its business purposes, at a floating rate of interest and the American company is in a position to borrow in the United States for less than a German-based company can do on its own. This situation of each party having access to lower cost loans than the other party permits the origination of a swap, where the German company borrows deutschemarks from a German financial institution at a lesser interest rate than what would be charged to the American company. The American company borrows a like amount of dollars for a lesser interest charge than what the German company could have negotiated.

A swap dealer then arranges a currency swap whereby the two companies can take advantage of borrowing at lesser cost in different markets. Each swaps the principal amounts of the loans, which are the same, and each makes interest payments to the swap dealer as agreed, with the American company making deutschemark payments that are sufficient for the German company to pay off its loan and the German company making dollar payments sufficient for the American company to pay off its loan. The swap dealer takes a little out of the middle.

A plain vanilla currency swap does not involve an exchange of a credit risk. Both companies borrow on the basis of their own creditworthiness. Each merely exchanges, or swaps, the payment of debt and interest such that the American company ends up paying a fixed rate German denominated debt, which it desired, and the German company ends up paying the type of dollar denominated debt, which it desired. Three exchanges are necessary. The first is the exchange of the principal of the loan, then the interest payments, and, at the end of the swap period, the final repayment of principal of the respective loans. Although currency swaps are usually floating/fixed rates of interest—that is, one counterparty paying a floating rate of interest and the other a fixed rate of interest—currency swaps can also be floating/floating and fixed/fixed.

This plain vanilla currency swap is also called an exchange of borrowings because that is exactly what it is. Its origin lies in each company's advantage in borrowing in its respective domestic market. However, the plain vanilla can easily become a more sophisticated variant because the exchange of borrowings may not exactly fit the desires of the two counterparties. An interest rate swap may have to be arranged along with the currency swap to change a floating rate loan to a desired fixed rate loan. The tenor, or the length of the repayment period, or the amount of the loan, may not entirely match the desires of each counterparty.

The swap dealer may turn to a financial engineer to introduce a new level of complexity to transform an undesirable cash flow stream into one that is desired by the two counterparties to the currency swap. It is possible for the repayment of principal to be amortized with the regular payments of interest similar to a level payment type of financing common for home mortgages. By combining swaps with other swaps or with other financial instruments, all sorts of variants can be created, limited only to the imagination of the financial engineers and the needs of client firms.

Commodity Swap

Counterparty A is an oil producer who has financed his wells with loans. If oil falls below a certain price, he will not be able to generate the earnings necessary to pay the financing charges associated with drilling and developing the oil wells. This may force the oil producer into bankruptcy.

Counterparty B is a refinery operator who sold a portion of his output at a fixed price and wants to stabilize the price of oil required to be purchased in the future in order to preserve the profit margin of these fixed priced contracts. Counterparty B worries about an increase in the price of oil that would destroy the economic worth of his fixed price contracts.

A swap dealer, being in touch with both individuals, can arrange a plain vanilla swap. The oil producer sells his actual output, called "actuals," into the spot oil market and receives the spot price, which may be higher or lower than the agreed fixed price of the swap. If higher, he must pay the difference between what he receives and the agreed fixed price to the swap dealer. If lower, the producer will receive the difference from the swap dealer. On the other side of the swap dealer's ledger is counterparty B, the refiner. Counterparty B buys his oil needs, or actuals, from the spot market and pays the spot price. If the spot price is higher than the agreed swap price, counterparty B receives what the

producer has paid to the swap dealer. If the spot price for oil is lower than the swap price, then the refiner pays the difference to the swap dealer, which is passed on to the refiner. In order to avoid disagreements between the two counterparties as to what is the spot market price, the counterparties agree to base the spot price, not on actual purchases and sales, but on a spot price from a published source, such as the monthly average spot price for oil quoted in the financial press.

No matter in what direction the net payment is flowing, the swap dealer takes out a margin for his or her trouble, before passing the money to the other party. The swap dealer assumes no risk, which is why both the oil producer and the refinery operator must refer to the same published source for spot market quotes, such as a monthly average, to remove day-to-day price fluctuations, and other causes of price differences from becoming part of the calculation of what is to be paid between the two counterparties.

Otherwise, the swap dealer would become embroiled in disputes over price differentials between what an oil producer receives when he sells and what a refinery operator pays when he buys. Although the producer is selling his output to the spot market and the refiner is buying his input from the spot market, the net effect is that they are essentially buying and selling from each other at the swap price. The swap can go on for as long as the two counterparties desire, again illustrating the point that a swap can be considered a series of forward contracts.

The question may arise as to why the producer and the refiner did not enter into a contract with one another directly, as is practiced by banks for plain vanilla interest rate swaps. First of all, the buyer and seller may not have known of each other's presence or need—this is the classic role of the middleman. It is easier for a bank to canvass the market for interest rate swaps if there are relatively few banks providing the fixed rate portion of an interest rate swap. In the oil business, where there are hundreds of producers and refiners, a middleman or swap dealer, may be needed for the sorting out process of identifying and bringing together the two counterparties.

Another reason for having a swap dealer involved in a transaction is that frequently the needs of the producer and refiner do not exactly match. The producer may want to fix the price of oil for a quantity and for a duration of time that does not exactly fit the refiner's needs.

A deal cannot be directly negotiated between the two counterparties. However, a swap dealer can set up a swap that does match each of the two counterparties' needs. To do so, he or she may have to arrange another swap to take care of the differences in quantity and timing, or hedge the position for his or her own account.

Swap Variants

Swaps have grown from nothing in 1979 to a level of about several trillion in notional outstandings in the early 1990s. Notional outstandings do not necessarily mean actual deposits of funds in banks or assets in warehouses. Notionals are reference points from which the amount of payment between counterparties is calculated. In the previous case of a plain vanilla interest rate swap, the notional amount of the swap of $10 million was the reference point from which the interest rate differential payments between the counterparties were calculated. Plain vanilla swaps have given way to all sorts of variants that have been created to meet the specific needs of the counterparties to a swap. Variants to the plain vanilla swaps are as plentiful as mutations in a jar of fruit flies; a sampling follows.

An accreting swap is one where the notional principal increases, and an amortization swap is one where the notional principal decreases, over the life of the swap. An annuity swap transforms an irregular cash flow payment stream to a regular one. An asset swap is based on assets rather than liabilities. A basis swap deals with a mismatch between assets and liabilities. A blended interest rate swap combines two swaps to produce a more attractive overall rate. A callable and puttable swap gives one or the other counterparty the right to terminate the swap after a specified time. A capped swap is a swap with a cap, or a maximum limit, on the floating payment side of a swap. A cross currency swap is an exchange of cash flows of one currency for another that reverses at some point during the swap period. A debt-equity swap isn't even a swap, but a substitution of equity in local companies in lieu of interest or principal payments of a heavily indebted nation.

A deferred swap is one where the payments are deferred for a specified period, whereas a delayed LIBOR reset swap is one where the floating payment is based on a future rather than the present London Interbank rate. A differential swap is the swapping of floating interest rate payments referenced to different currencies.

A discount swap has a large balloon payment at the end of the swap period to take into account the discount on the regular payments as opposed to a highcoupon swap where the fixed payments are above the market rate with some sort of compensating adjustment at the end of the swap period. A dual currency swap contains rights to repay principal and interest in a choice of currencies at preset exchange rates. An escalating rate swap permits the fixed rate side of a swap to escalate with time. An extendable swap contains the right for the payer to extend the swap. A forward swap is one that is arranged at some point before the start date. A naked swap is one without a corresponding asset or liability, an interesting concept. A reversible swap gives one side the option to alter the payment basis after a certain period as compared to a reverse floating swap where the floating rate payments are inversely proportional to interest rates.

The roller coaster swap alternates the counterparties between paying fixed and floating rates. The seasonal swap is one where the notional amount varies with the time of the year to fit the needs of companies that borrow on a seasonal basis. A spreadlock swap has one payment stream referenced to a fixed spread over a benchmark rate. The tax-exempt swap has its fixed rate interest tied to tax-exempt bonds. The warrant-driven swap is a swap with a warrant allowing an issuer of a bond to extend a swap if it exercises a similar warrant on a bond. The yield curve swap is one where the two interest rates reflect different points on a mutually agreed yield curve. The zero-coupon swap is one where one or both counterparties make one payment at maturity.

Finally, there is the swaption. A swaption is an option on a swap. The swap is set up in all respects except for the starting date. One of the counterparties to the swap pays a swaption premium for the right to start the swap at any point during the swaption period, say, in six months. If he or she does not exercise the swaption, the swap terminates without execution at the end of the swaption period. Swaptions have their family of variants.

Swap dealers are not in business to accept risk, but to transfer the nature of risk between the two counterparties. Swap dealers work off their "swap book" to tailor a swap to meet the needs of the two counterparties. In so doing, they may introduce an element of risk into their swap books. Swap dealers then enter into other swaps or hedges to remove the element of risk that may be present in their swap books. Swap dealers usually wish to neutralize any risk in their swap books to protect their remuneration, which is in the bid-ask spread between the two counterparties of a swap. However, if the swap dealers are confident about the emergence or continuation of a price trend, they may accept a degree of risk in their swap books to profit thereby.

PUTS AND CALLS

Futures and forwards are contractually binding agreements. Swaps, as a continuing series of forwards, are also contractually binding. These contractually binding agreements mean that each party must transfer a specified underlying asset, or a cash equivalent thereof, at known points in time. Puts and calls are options where the purchaser of a put or call has the right, but not the obligation, to buy or sell an underlying asset.

A buyer of a call has the right, but not the obligation, to purchase something at a stipulated price, whereas the buyer of a put has the right, but not the obligation, to sell something at a stipulated price. However, the seller of a call or a put does have an obligation to sell the underlying asset at the stipulated price when the call is exercised or to buy the underlying asset at the stipulated price when the put is exercised. An American option can be exercised from the time it is written until the time it expires. A European option differs in that its exercise period is limited to a short period of time before its expiration date.

Staying with American options, pricing of options depends on several factors. One is the exercise price in relation to the underlying value of the asset. If the exercise price is $20 and the underlying value of the asset is $22, then the option has an intrinsic value of $2 and is described as being "in the money." If the underlying value is $20, the same as the exercise price, the option is described as being "at the money." If the underlying value is $18, the call option has no intrinsic value, but still has extrinsic value. Extrinsic value depends on the difference between the market and exercise prices, the remaining time to expiration, and the volatility of the price of the underlying asset.

The smaller the difference between market and exercise prices, the longer the time to expiration, and the greater the volatility of the price of the underlying asset, the greater the extrinsic value of the option even though it may have no intrinsic, or inherent, value. Another factor in the pricing of options is interest rates, because a grantor, or a writer, of an option is seeking income by writing calls. Generally speaking, an option writer grants options on an owned asset. As an alternative, he or she can sell the owned asset and invest the proceeds in a secure interest bearing financial instrument. Because the grantor has the choice to sell the asset and invest in interest-bearing financial instruments or underwrite options, option writing premium income must be attractively priced in relation to interest-bearing securities.

All of these factors are built into the first complete option pricing model developed by two professors, Fisher Black and Myron Scholes, in 1973. Options are generally priced based on models derived or adapted from the original BlackScholes model. The model is a mathematical expression containing the difference between the current price of the underlying asset and the strike price, a measure of past volatility in the price of the underlying asset, time to expiration and the interest rate on a secure deposit.

The purpose of the model is to determine a theoretical price for an option. Dealers sometimes use the Black-Scholes model to examine prices being quoted by grantors or writers of options, by reversing the model to obtain the implied volatility in the quote. Some dealers use the implied volatility to differentiate quotes on different options for the same asset. By being able to identify options with differently implied volatilities for the same underlying asset, dealers can use this information for putting deals together or in hedging their own portfolios.

Moreover, implied volatility can be charted and analyzed as to what feelings participants in the option markets have toward volatility. A period of falling implied volatility can be interpreted to mean that participants in the market feel that prices are approaching an island of stability in a sea of volatility. Rising implied volatility means that participants see storm clouds on the horizon. This information is of value for market makers in options.

OPTIONS IN RISK MANAGEMENT

From the perspective of a company attempting to manage the risk of price volatility, options can be used to change the cost profile of an asset in a way that serves the interest of the company. Suppose that a company buys an asset that management feels can vary in price from $15 to $25 per unit and the current price is $20.

The company does not want to find itself in a position of paying much over $20 per unit for the asset. It buys a call option for $1 per unit with an exercise price of $20. For that portion of its needs covered by the call option, the company has changed the cost profile.

A company wanting to contain its costs to $21 per unit for the asset has done so by purchasing the option. The profit from the call option compensates for the extra cost of purchasing the asset. This protects the company whenever the price of the asset moves above $20. If the asset does not move above $20 per unit, the company has added $1 to unit to its acquisition cost. This can be likened to the premium cost of an insurance policy to protect against paying a higher than desired price for the asset. A company must weigh the cost of protection against the benefit of having the protection.

Suppose that a company has acquired a large supply of inventory at $20 and wishes to insure itself against a loss in value. The company buys a put option with an exercise price of $20 for $1. If the market value of the asset declines, the intrinsic value of the put will increase.

The company, in wanting to protect itself against loss, has maintained the value of the inventory at $19 per unit regardless how low the market value of the asset may sink. The profit from the put option compensates for the loss in inventory value. The cost of this protection is $1 per unit, which one can view as an insurance premium if the value of the asset remains above $20 per unit.

The portion of the inventory that is protected by the put is said to be hedged against a price decline.

Suppose that the price of the commodity is $20 and the company buys a put and a call, called a straddle, for $1 per option.

If the price of the asset falls below $18, the profit from the put can be used to hedge against a write-down of the inventory. If the price rises, the profit from the call can be used to hedge against paying above $22 per unit. If the price of the asset hovers between $18 and $22, the company would have been better off not purchasing the straddle. Straddles are useful when management expects increased volatility in the price of the asset but is unsure of the direction of change in price. The straddle offers double protection in limiting the maximum amount to be paid for the asset and in limiting the maximum amount of loss of holding the asset in inventory. In offering more protection, the insurance premium also costs more.

Suppose that the company decides to buy a call option with an exercise price of $20 for $1 and sells a call option with an exercise price of $22 for $0.50. The net cost of buying and selling the options is $0.50. What would be profit profile of this course of action?

The idea of selling the second call is to reduce the cost of the hedge by the amount of premium earned on the selling of the call. A company would employ such a strategy of buying and selling a call option at different strike, or exercise, prices if it was worried about a rise in price in the commodity, but was convinced that such a rise would not go over $23. If management were proven wrong and the price did exceed $23, it could buy its way out by purchasing another call option to compensate for the "loss" associated with the call that was sold. Once a company begins to protect itself against price rises or declines through some sort of hedging technique, there is a tendency to keep purchasing and selling options to "undo" those past hedging positions that are costing the company money. In time, a relatively simple hedging position can become quite complex.

If the two call options in the previous example expire at the same time, it is called a vertical bull spread. If the call with the lower strike price is sold and the one with the higher strike price is bought, there would be premium income and the strategy would be called a vertical bear spread. If the expiration dates are not the same, but the exercise price is the same for the two options, these strategies are called a horizontal bull or bear spread depending on the expiration dates of the purchased and sold options. If there is a mix of expiration dates and strike prices, the strategy is known as a diagonal spread.

To show that there is virtually no limit to the imagination, a butterfly spread would involve four options. All have the same expiration date. Two options with the same strike price are sold, whereas one with a higher strike price is purchased along with one with a lower strike price. If the buying and selling of the options are reversed, this is called a reverse butterfly or a sandwich spread.

What risk does management fear the most? The financial engineers can dream up a solution. There are barrier options (four major types including knock-in and knock-out options), basket options, binary and digital options, call and put spreads, chooser options, compound options, condors, cylinders, difference options, embedded options, forward start options, hi-low options, lookback or path-dependent options, straddles and strangles, table tops, and tunnels, which are similar to cylinders.

Someone in the company better have a firm understanding of where the company stands when the price of the underlying asset changes. Although there is no commitment undertaken by the company when options are purchased, there is certainly a commitment associated with sold options as there are with swaps, futures, and forwards. Therefore, there should also be someone in a company with a firm handle on what commitments have been undertaken by a company in its hedging programme. This someone should not be the person directing the company's risk management programme.

RISK MANAGEMENT FOR OPTION MARKET MAKERS

The role of market makers in options is to have a balanced position in options with little exposed risk. They are not in the options market to assume a risk. Their role is to be intermediaries in the exchange of risk between two parties. In this role, they may have to assume some risk in order to complete a deal. Then they take action to neutralize, or hedge, the risk assumed in putting the deal together. A hedged portfolio of options may no longer be fully hedged because the price of the underlying asset changes. Price changes in the underlying asset can transform out-of-the-money options to in-the-money ones and vice versa.

As a matter of interest, option market makers themselves have a risk management challenge in maintaining a neutral position and living off commissions and bid-ask spreads between buyers and sellers of options. To do this, they depend on a world of Greek letters. Delta is the price sensitivity of an option to price changes of the underlying asset. When an option is deeply out of the money, a move in the price of the underlying asset has little or no effect on its price (delta = 0). For an option deep in the money, there is an exact one-for-one relationship between its price and the price of the underlying asset. On a per unit basis, as the price goes up by one, the value of a call would also increase by one (delta = 1).

For puts that are in the money, an increase in the underlying value of the asset reduces their value by one (delta = –1). The delta associated with a short call in the money would be –1 and the delta associated with a short put in the money would be +1. For options where the market price is approaching the exercise price, there is an intermediate, not a one-for-one, relationship between changes in underlying value and in the value of the option. Therefore, delta values vary between 0 and 1 for long calls and short puts, and between 0 and -1 for short calls and long puts.

The net risk of a dealer's exposure to options on the same underlying tangible or intangible asset can be quantified by totaling the deltas of all the options. A "delta neutral" portfolio of options would be one where the sum of all deltas is near zero. However, there are complications associated with maintaining a delta neutral portfolio of options because, as just discussed, the delta of an option varies with the underlying price of the asset. The rate of change of delta with respect to changes in the price of the underlying value is measured by gamma.

Theta measures the erosion of an options premium as the expiration date nears. Theta can be positive or negative depending on whether there is a long and short position. Rho measures the sensitivity of the option's price to changes in interest rates, whereas kappa, or vega (not a Greek letter, but an old Chevy car model) measures the change in an option's price with respect to changes to the volatility of the price of the underlying asset.

Needless to say, delta, gamma, theta, kappa or vega, and rho measures of a portfolio of options are not calculated by hand. In addition, there are other Greek letters in a dealer's lexicon—beta trading is used by option traders to take advantage of similar financial instruments having diverging volatility, whereas omega is the risk associated with a buyer or seller of an option where the accounting of the option will be in a different currency than the option.

OPTIONS IN FUTURES

In addition, financial engineers have originated futures options. Calls and puts can be exercised calling for the delivery or sale of the underlying asset. Futures options are puts and calls on futures.

A review of the U.S. financial press shows that one can buy and sell puts and calls on futures of U.S. Treasury notes and bonds, various currencies with both American and European variants including a cross trade between German marks and Japanese yen, various agricultural products, metals, various stock indices, and crude oil and oil products. Settlement of futures options is in cash, not a delivery or acceptance of an underlying asset. A futures option out of the money at the time of expiration is worthless.

EXCHANGE FOR PHYSICALS

There should be a strong linkage between an expiring futures contract and the cash price of the physical asset for futures to be effective as a hedging tool. Very few expiring futures end up with an exchange of physical assets. Usually, a long position is liquidated by selling the futures and a short position is liquidated by buying futures. But the possibility of a long position ending up with the physical possession of the underlying asset ensures that expiring prices and cash prices are very close to one another. For instance, an expiring copper future could end up with a change in ownership as 25,000 pounds of copper. The copper futures market has an associated warehouse holding a sufficient quantity of copper of the specified purity to provide for a change of ownership between the owner of an expiring futures contract and its seller.

Oil is a much less "homogenous" market than copper. The cash market in crude oil is based on commonly traded types of oil such as Saudi Arabian Light, North Sea, and West Texas Intermediate. The futures in crude oil traded on the New York Mercantile Exchange calls for delivery "at any pipeline or storage facility with pipeline access to Arco, Cushing Storage, or Texaco Trading & Transportation Inc...." In the world of oil, this is a rather limited transformation of "paper" barrels to "wet" barrels. To take into account the wide variety of grades of oil and time and place of delivery, the financial engineers devised exchange for physicals (EFPs). EFPs extend the circumstances surrounding delivery of futures by permitting buyers and sellers of futures to agree to the exact buyer and seller, the nature of the crude oil, and place, volume, time, and other details of delivery. Payment is made by exchanging long and short positions in expiring futures.

BACKWARDATION AND CONTANGO

The relationship between the futures and the cash markets determines whether a market is in backwardation or contango. When a futures contract is selling for less than the current cash price, the market is said to be in backwardation.

Using oil as an example, a backwardation market permits an oil company to sell a part of its inventory that is to be refined in the future in the cash market and buy a, say, two-month future. In two month's time, the "paper" barrel is transformed to a "wet" barrel through an EFP, if necessary, to process the oil.

This would only occur if the discount for the futures compared to the cash price is sufficient to make this a profitable transaction.

In calculating this profitability, one must bear in mind that an oil company can invest the cash proceeds of selling oil in inventory in an interest-bearing security.

There are also transfer, shipping, and other costs involved with the delivery of the futures, or the EFP, that have to be taken into account.

A contango market is one where there is a premium on the futures in relation to the cash price. If the premium on the futures contract is large enough, and if there is sufficient storage capacity at the oil company refinery, it may be to the oil company's advantage to buy extra oil in the cash market and short a futures contract.

On the maturing of the futures contract, the oil company delivers the oil rather than making a cash settlement. The spread between the cash and futures market has to be sufficient to cover the storage costs and the interest costs of investing in what amounts to extra inventory.

CAPS, FLOORS, AND COLLARS

Calls and puts have a finite life usually measured in months. Rarely do their expiration times exceed one year. Another example of financial engineering creativity are multi period options.

These were created to address the need for providing a maximum rate of interest on a loan, called an interest rate cap. Loans usually run for more than a year and, therefore, calls and puts with an expiration time of one year or less do not provide a solution for a company that desires to hedge against rising interest rates on a multiyear floating rate loan.

The writer of an interest rate cap agrees to pay the holder of the cap the difference between a reference rate above the ceiling rate, applied against a notional principal, every six months during the two to five year tenor, or length of time, of the cap, or any other agreeable tenor. The reference rate is a published rate such as the London Interbank or U.S. Treasury bill rates.

The ceiling rate is the maximum rate the holder of the cap will pay on a loan covered by the notional principal of the cap.

For this protection, the cap holder pays an upfront fee. The effective interest rate has the appearance of a multi period call. The amortization of the upfront premium over the life of the cap is analogous to the premium paid for a series of single period calls.

If interest rates do not rise to the ceiling rate, the holder of the cap is simply paying a higher effective interest rate. This is analogous to the previous example of illustrating how a call limits the maximum amount to be paid for some underlying asset.

If the price does not rise to this limit, the premium for the call increases the effective acquisition cost for the underlying asset.

Explation

If interest rates rise above the ceiling rate, the profit from the cap offsets the higher cost of interest effectively capping interest at the ceiiing rate.

Obviously, the closer the ceiling rate is to current interest rates, the higher its cost. This holds true for call—the closer the exercise price is to the current price of the asset, the higher the premium.

A buyer of a call, or a cap, must decide on the amount of premium and the protection afforded by that premium in covering his or her perceived risks.

Interest rate caps are sometimes combined with interest

rate swaps or with currency swaps to produce an interest or a currency rate capped swap. Caps can be assignable with the owner's permission, much as a call can be sold when its protection is no longer needed.

An interest rate floor is similar to a cap except that the purchaser of a floor receives payment when the reference rate drops below the contract rate. The classic use of a floor is an insurance company borrowing fixed rate money to be loaned out at a floating rate. In so doing, the insurance company is betting on an upswing in interest rates. If interest rates fall, the insurance company may not earn enough to service its policy holders. An insurance company can protect against this risk by purchasing an interest rate floor, which guarantees a minimum interest rate should the floating rate fall below the contract, or floor, rate.

Caps and floors do not involve the exchange of a credit risk. They are cash settlements at prescribed times whereby a purchaser of a cap does not pay more than the ceiling rate and the purchaser of a floor does not earn less than the floor rate. Because the principal covered by a cap or floor is not exchanged, the cash payments are based on a notional amount of a loan.

Explation

If a cap is 10 per cent and the referenced floating rate is 12 per cent, and the notional amount is $10 million (MM) and settlements are made every six months, then the purchaser of the cap will receive the difference (2 per cent × $10 MM × six months/twelve months) or $100,000 from the market maker.

He then applies this against his floating rate loan, reducing its net interest cost from 12 per cent to 10 per cent. If the floor is 8 per cent and the referenced floating rate falls to 6 per cent, then the seller of the floor has to pay the market maker $100,000. This raises his effective interest cost from 6 per cent to 8 per cent, thus fixing his minimum interest rate at 8 per cent.

A financial engineer can create collars from caps and

floors. A collar is the purchase of a cap coupled with the sale of a floor. The proceeds from the sale of the floor reduce the cost of the cap. What this effectively does is lock the interest rate between the floor and ceiling rates.

If a company has a floating rate loan on a certain amount of principal, a collar on the same notional amount of the loan fixes both the maximum and minimum interest rates. If floating interest rates exceed the ceiling rate, the company will receive a cash payment that compensates it for the incremental interest expense that is above the ceiling rate, thus capping the interest rate on the loan at the ceiling rate. If floating rates fall below the floor rate, the company will not benefit from the lower interest costs because it is obligated to pay the difference between the floating rate and the floor rate, applied against the notional amount of the collar, to the market maker.

If interest rates stay between the floor and ceiling rates, the lender has increased his effective interest rate in the amortization of the cost of acquisition of the collar.

The concept of the interest rate collar as a multi period option to set a ceiling and a floor rate for interest rates can be applied to currencies and commodities.

A currency collar is a series of multi period cash settlements, where the holder of the collar limits his exchange rate within a prescribed band.

This is accomplished by a cash settlement representing the differences in actual currency exchange transactions and the contractual upper and lower exchange rate limits-the ceiling and floor rates of conversion.

For a premium, a company can collar, so to speak, the currency exchange rates on, say, Swiss franc to dollar conversion within a prescribed upper and lower rate of exchange based on a stipulated notional amount of currency. This is a powerful financial tool in managing the long-term exposure to a currency risk.

The collar is applied to commodities. For the payment of a premium, the holder of a collar, sometimes referred to as a range forward, can limit his purchases of a commodity, such as oil, to a prescribed band. Using a publicly available source of pricing for oil as a means of measuring spot purchases, a holder of a range forward receives money from the market maker when spot purchase prices exceed the upper limit or ceiling price. When spot purchase prices fall below the lower limit or floor price, the holder of the range forward must pay the difference to the market maker.

When prices are between the floor and ceiling prices, the effective cost of oil is the spot price plus the premium paid for the collar, or range forward.

The buyer of a collar or a range forward is obtaining protection against paying more than the ceiling price, but, in so doing, gives up the opportunity of buying for less than the floor price. He has, in effect, avoided a risk that he cannot endure by giving up an opportunity that he could enjoy.

RISK MANAGEMENT ACCOUNTING ISSUES

FASB 52 sets forth a series of conditions for accounting for currency exchange futures as hedges, avoiding having to "mark to market" the value of a futures on the last day of each accounting period.

Mark-to-market gains and losses flow through the income statement, which adds to the volatility of earnings. Managers take a dim view of the mark-to-market accounting treatment of futures because of its unpredictable impact on earnings. Earnings, in the mind of many managers, should reflect the result of operations and not be distorted by the "snapshot" valuation of futures contracts.

FASB 52 also accords the same accounting treatment to currency exchange forward contracts as to currency exchange futures contracts.

In 1984, FASB 80, "Accounting for Futures Contracts," was issued to deal with futures contracts for other than currency such as stock index, commodities, and interest rates. FASB 80 defers the loss or gain of a futures contract if the company owns, or is liable for, the delivery of the underlying asset.

Description

The gain or loss of a futures contract can also be deferred if there is a legally enforceable obligation to make or accept delivery of the underlying asset. And the third criterion for deferring a gain or loss is entering into a futures or forward contract on the basis of an anticipated transaction. This transaction need not be legally enforceable.

In other words, if in management's judgment, there is sufficient probability of some transaction occurring to warrant entering into a futures or forward contract, and even if there is nothing legally binding to enforce the consummation of the contract, the gains and losses of the associated futures or forward contract can be deferred.

Under FASB 52, deferral of gains and losses can occur only if the currency exchange forward or futures contract reduces the risk of loss of a specified transaction. FASB 80 has a much broader interpretation of the conditions permitting deferral of gains and losses associated with other forms of futures and forward contracts.

In particular, hedging based on anticipated transactions, in addition to exposure to risk of existing conditions and firm commitments, is permitted deferral of gains and losses. Mark to market, or the immediate recognition of gains and losses associated with non-currency-exchange futures and forward contracts, is required only when the futures and forward contract cannot be related to any underlying or anticipated exposure to risk.

In essence, FASB 52, which applies only to currency exchange futures and forward contracts, and FASB 80, which applies to all other futures and forward contracts, are inconsistent in the accounting treatment of futures and forward contracts. This, not surprisingly, has sparked a continuing controversy among accounting professionals.

Explation

Neither FASB 52 nor FASB 80 addresses options. In 1984, the American Institute of Certified Public Accountants (AICPA) began to study this issue, which led to the publication of the "Options Issues Paper" in 1986. The paper tends to apply the principles underlying FASB 80, rather than FASB 52, to options.

That is, using options to hedge against anticipated happenings should be treated similar to the treatment of futures and forward contracts in FASB 80. The "Options Issues Paper" has neither been endorsed by the Securities and Exchange Commission nor has there been follow-up in the form of a published FASB statement.

Therefore, the issue of accounting for options is essentially yet to be fully resolved. Hedge accounting frequently has the effect of shifting reported gains or losses from one period to another. Given that the rules of accounting for hedges involving options are still evolving, management must be accordingly cautious on their approach to accounting for hedges.

In 1990, FASB 105, "Disclosure of Information about Financial Instruments with Off-Balance-Sheet Risk and Financial Instruments with Concentrations of Credit Risk," came into effect. Futures, options, and financial swaps fall within the definition of a financial instrument as set forth by FASB 105.

The purpose of FASB 105 is not to specify accounting principles applicable to these financial instruments. Its purpose is footnote disclosure of the off-balance sheet risk associated with certain financial instruments and also concentrations of credit risk.

Off-balance-sheet risk is the risk of an accounting loss that exceeds the amount recognized as an asset or liability on the balance sheet.

Prior to FASB 105, a company could have entered into a speculative futures contract that might have resulted in a potential loss far exceeding the amount of investment that would be recorded on the balance sheet.

No further special accounting or disclosure was required. Normal accounting treatment would handle any gain or loss attributed to the futures contract.

With the adoption of FASB 105, footnote disclosure is

now required if a company takes a speculative position in a financial instrument that can result in a loss exceeding the acquisition or carrying cost of the financial instrument.

FASB 105 describes the nature of the footnote disclosure and also requires disclosure of credit risk where financial instruments are concentrated by geographic regions, industries, or customer groups that have common exposure to adverse economic developments.

Index